#305258

TALL SHEEP

TALL SHEEP

Harry Goulding,
Monument Valley Trader

By Samuel Moon

UNIVERSITY OF OKLAHOMA PRESS : NORMAN AND LONDON

Moon, Samuel.
    Tall sheep : Harry Goulding : Monument Valley trader / Samuel
Moon.
        p.   cm.
    Includes bibliographical references and index.
    ISBN 0-8061-2415-6 (alk. paper)
    1. Goulding, Harry, 1897–1981. 2. Monument Valley (Ariz. and
Utah)—Biography. 3. Navajo Indians.   I. Title.
F817.M6G686   1992
979.2'59—dc20   91-50866
    [B]   CIP

Text and jacket design by Cleo Patterson.

My work on this book is dedicated to Harry Goulding,
who did not live to hold the book in his hand

CONTENTS

ILLUSTRATIONS

MAPS

PREFACE

The sources of the book are 117 hours of interviews, 46 with Harry, 39 with Navajos, and 32 with other Anglos, recorded between September 1973 and December 1979, the largest number of them during the summers of 1974 and 1975. There are excerpts from two interviews in Doris A. Paul's book, *The Navajo Code Talkers.*[1] The interviews with Lamar Bedoni, Mildred Heflin, Edward D. Smith, and Nedra Tódích'íi'nii come from *Southeastern Utah Project,* Utah State Historical Society and California State University, Fullerton (CSUF), Oral History Program. I am especially in debt to Gary L. Shumway, Southeastern Utah Project director, and Shirley E. Stephenson, CSUF Oral History Program archivist, for making this collection available to me, and to Professor Shumway for many thoughtful suggestions and acts of kindness.

For the interviews with Navajos who could not speak English, my interpreters in the field were Tom Holiday, and later, his nephew, Greg Holiday. Occasionally, when Greg was not available, young English-speaking Navajos would interpret for older members of their family. All of these Navajo-language interviews were later carefully translated and transcribed by Mary Toledo of Blanding, Utah, through an arrangement made by Professor Shumway with the Utah Navajo Development Council. In return, my entire collection of interviews will become a part of the Southeastern Utah Collection.

I have edited these materials as narrative, eliminating the question-and-answer format and the hesitancies, false starts, and irrelevancies that inevitably creep into conversation. However, I have tried to keep the varied and colorful flavor of the speech of the individual speakers, feeling that it contributes to a sense of their character, which is interesting in its own right and is an inseparable part of what they are saying.

The spelling of Navajo words is the standard spelling, taken from Young and Morgan's *The Navajo Language.*[2] Navajo is a quantitative and tonal language. That is, it makes a difference in meaning if a vowel is pronounced with a long or short duration, or with a high or normal tone. Vowels with a long quantity are written double *(saad, dooda),* vowels with a high tone are written with an accent mark *(shá, bínaaí).* A reverse cedilla nasalizes a vowel *(sǫ, sęęs).* An apostrophe represents a glottal stop *('át'é, 'a'áán).* A sound we do not have in English is represented by *"ł,"* rather like a voiceless *"l,"* where the tongue is held in an *"l"* position and breath is expelled without using the voice box *(łóó', tł'ah)*. Some Navajo names have come over into English and are spelled as English words, for example, "Cly" or "Yazzie."

My admiration for the Gouldings and my gratitude for their unending hospitality knows no bounds. My visits with them at Page, Arizona, and with Mike's brother Maurice will always be a source of pleasure in my memory. In 1963, the Gouldings retired and gave their property to Knox College in exchange for a life income. Harry died in 1981 at the age of eighty-four, Maurice in 1987 at seventy-three.

I am also deeply grateful to my wife, Doris, for her faithful transcription of sometimes extremely difficult material, where field conditions were not always ideal, to say the least, and where literal accuracy of speech patterns was essential. My colleague, Rodney Davis, has been especially helpful to me in his suggestions and as a sympathetic listener. I am profoundly in debt to two readers for the University of Oklahoma Press who went over my manuscript in scrupulous detail from the vantage point of their intimate knowledge of the area. Knox College generously provided financial assistance for my interviewing trips to Monument Valley. Jeff Douglas of the Knox College Library staff has been of inestimable service in locating difficult sources for me. Many typists worked on the manuscript at various stages of its development, particularly Martha Francois and Carolyn Suydam, who became engrossed in the story themselves, and whose enthusiasm for it encouraged me to persist.

SAMUEL MOON

Galesburg, Illinois

Introduction

Harry Goulding had a trading post in Monument Valley from the 1920s to the 1960s. During all those years, he carried on an unending love affair with the Valley and its Navajo people. With the land it was love at first sight; with the Navajos his love grew as they came to know and accept him and show themselves to him. He gave his life to Monument Valley and the Navajos of the Valley through good times and bad, and as such things happen, they gave themselves back to him. His words, as you will read them here, are those of a passionate, unquestioning partisan, speaking for the people and the land he loves. This book is the story of the life the Gouldings made with the Navajos, as they and the people who knew them tell it in their own words, until the time of their retirement in the early 1960s.[1]

Harry Goulding was born in Durango, Colorado, in 1897. He grew up in the Four Corners area, where his father, two uncles, and three aunts pioneered one of the first sheep ranches in the San Juan Basin. They had come from England, first operated some placer mines near Naturita, Colorado, and then went into sheep ranching. During Harry's childhood, the Goulding family owned up to twenty thousand head of sheep on range scattered from Aztec, New Mexico, to the Hermosa River country between Durango and Silverton, Colorado, with headquarters near Aztec. He finished the tenth or eleventh grade of schooling, but he preferred being out on the range. He grew up working with Mexican, Navajo, and Ute sheepherders, carrying provisions and moving camps.

After serving in the army in France from 1917 to 1919, he met his wife, Leone Knee, in 1921. She was born in Stockton, Kansas, in 1905. Her father worked on the railroad and was a wheat rancher there, moved to another ranch near Deer Trail, Colorado, out of Denver, in 1910, and to Chama, New Mexico, where he became a fireman on the narrow-gauge railroads, in 1917. After three years, they moved to Aztec, where, a year later, she and Harry fell in love. They were married in 1923.

Harry first saw Monument Valley on a vacation trip he took in 1921 and knew at once that he wanted to return. At that time it was inhabited by Paiutes and a few Navajo families, but in 1925, most of the Paiutes moved out, and Harry and his new wife moved in and became traders to the Navajos.

Harry had always had trouble spelling Leone's name, and when they arrived in Monument Valley, he renamed her "Mike" because, as he said, he knew how to spell that. "Tall Sheep" is the name the Navajos gave to him: Dibé Nééz in Navajo. He was a tall man, they said, and he had long ("tall") flocks of sheep when strung out on the trail. New names and a new beginning for them both.

When I first approached Harry with the idea of doing a book, he agreed on the condition that it be at least half about the Navajos. It has not been difficult to keep that agreement; the Gouldings' life is so intertwined with the lives of their Navajo neighbors that it could not be otherwise. Thus, we are given glimpses into the customs and beliefs of the Navajos of Monument Valley. The Goulding years also coincide with a critical period in the history of the Navajo people, and their life inevitably participates in that history as it unfolds in their remote corner of the Navajo reservation. The book takes us into large events as they play out in local circumstances—the very specific, lived experiences of particular people enmeshed in a web of forces reaching far beyond their local horizons.

The period from the 1920s to the 1960s, from before the Depression until after World War II, brought deep challenges and revolutionary change to the Navajos. It was the third of the great revolutions in their history. The first, perhaps better described as a long and gradual evolution, occurred over the years following their arrival in the Southwest from what is now northwestern Canada and Alaska, no later than the fifteenth century. They arrived as small, primitive bands of hunters and gatherers. In the Southwest they acquired corn agriculture, the art of weaving, and much of their mythology from the Pueblo Indians, and by the eighteenth century, horses and sheep from the Spanish settlers, and with these acquisitions they slowly transformed their lives into a flourishing pastoral society.

The second revolution was imposed upon them by their defeat at the hands of Kit Carson during the Civil War, their enforced Long Walk to a concentration camp at Fort Sumner, and then back to their home country and reservation status. They were no longer free to choose their lives for themselves. The women, who had been the shepherds and weavers and the centers of family life in this matrilocal society, were able to continue much as before; but the men, although retaining their position as hunters and farmers, builders, traders, and religious and political leaders, had lost an important part of their male cultural role: that of warriors engaged in raiding neighboring tribes and settlers, and in defense against counterraids.

The third of these great revolutions, with which our story is concerned, begins with the forced curtailment of their pastoral way of life in the 1930s by overgrazing, the dust bowl drought, and the stock reduction program of

John Collier, and continues with the expansion of their horizons during World War II and their increasing adoption and adaptation of white American ways and institutions during the postwar years. Our story ends with Harry Goulding's retirement as a trader in 1963, although the postwar thrust in Navajo development continues to the present day.

While the story of the Navajos during these decades is one of great suffering, it is also a story of endurance and growth and accumulating strength, for the Navajos are a people whose special genius has been from the beginning to create a strong center while learning from their surroundings, to integrate new experience into a strongly held tradition, and to maintain a cultural integrity in spite of cataclysmic change. The Gouldings, as sympathetic participants in their lives, provide a vantage point from which to view the events of these decades. Thus, our focus is on the conservative, traditional Navajos of the remote northwestern part of the Navajo reservation, and the profound impact of the twentieth century upon their life. This account ends before the changes in consciousness of contemporary Native Americans, which generally began in the 1970s and are centered in the growing movement for Indian rights.

With all its stark beauty, Monument Valley was a primitive, an almost empty country when the Gouldings arrived there. The classic period of the Navajo trading post would soon be drawing to a close. The Gouldings, like other traders isolated by great distances and difficult travel, developed a life of interdependence with the Navajos, interpreting the regulations of a strange and remote federal government, nursing the sick, burying the dead. The Gouldings never took a profit away from the reservation; they traded with the Navajos, one of them told me, the way the Navajos traded with each other.

The twentieth-century revolution in the Navajo way of life began when John Collier, Roosevelt's commissioner of Indian affairs, saw that the Navajo range was alarmingly overgrazed and knew that their livestock must be drastically reduced in numbers. He instituted a crash program of stock reduction, which left the Navajos shocked, outraged, and emotionally devastated and led to a radical curtailment of the Navajos' pastoral way of life.

Stock reduction was accompanied by other New Deal programs in restoring the range and developing agriculture, which provided some work for the Navajos. They were paid by check—and this, together with some railroad work, marked the beginning of a cash economy and the beginning of the end of the barter and pawn system and of their strict ties to the local trader, upon whom they had depended for credit. The Collier program also encouraged a unified tribal government with democratically elected tribal council members and the building of day schools and medical clinics on the reservation.

In 1939, in the midst of this turmoil, Harry persuaded John Ford to come to Monument Valley for the shooting of *Stagecoach,* the first of Ford's great westerns. Ford returned in 1946 and added seven more films to the list by 1964. Goulding's was headquarters and Harry the guide for all these films.

World War II inaugurated the second wave of change begun in the Collier years. Navajo men responded to the call to arms, although illiteracy kept their numbers in military service down to 3,600. In addition, there was more off-reservation work on the railroads, in defense plants, and as migratory farm workers. Fully 10,000 Navajos were employed in war work. Uranium was discovered on the reservation, and some of the earliest mines were in Monument Valley, before Hiroshima, when the bomb was still a secret to the world. It of course made a difference to the economy of the Valley, but the big uranium boom did not come until after the war, when it contributed wages to many Navajo miners and a substantial income to the tribe in royalties.

All of this war work brought a greater exposure to the white world, but the real impact of the world at large occurred when the Navajo veterans returned. The effect of the experience that the veterans brought back and disseminated among their people was to make the Navajos ready for reform. The postwar decades, extending beyond the limits of our story to the present day, show a continuing growth and strengthening of the Navajo people.

Their first priority now became education, and there has been a steady increase in the number of schools on the reservation and in the number of Navajos attending school. In 1969, they opened the Navajo Community College, their first venture into higher education, which offers study of traditional life as well as the subjects of the conventional American curriculum. By the 1970s, almost every hogan had children who could speak English. In addition, they had developed a written form of their own language and in 1964 were publishing the *Navajo Times,* which, although an English-language newspaper, does include some material written in Navajo.

Tribal council government survived the pains of the Collier years and strengthened as the Navajos acquired more and more experience in dealing with federal government agencies and private outside business interests, and with internal matters of education, a Navajo police force, grazing permits, the building of roads, tourism, a Navajo park service, and the merchandising of crafts.

After the war, the uranium boom gave them experience in dealing with the mining companies, and when a rich new oil discovery was made in 1956, they were in a position to deal with it in a wise and responsible fashion. The development of uranium and oil, and to some extent coal, led to the improvement of the system of roads on the reservation, which in its turn encouraged tourism and the establishment of the Navajo Tribal Park in Monument Valley. There seemed by now to be a synergy of forces at work, each accomplishment prompting and supporting another in a growing web of successes.

In 1950, Harry Goulding gave a free lease to the Seventh-day Adventists to open a clinic and in 1960 a mission hospital on his land in Monument Valley. He played an important role in the development of roads on the reservation and in establishing the tribal park in the Valley. In all these things, he was able to see the shape of things to come, and he had a special talent for bringing the right people together at the right time.

This is not to say that the Navajos have no problems. The statistics on education, income, and standard of living are still shocking, but in relative terms they have radically improved. The Navajos are a strong people who are living through a revolution conservatively, adjusting the new to their tradition and their tradition to the new, taking things as they come, slowly and deliberately.

This book is not only about a period in the history of the Navajos; it is also about people in their simple humanity. One of the values of oral history is that it humanizes its subject. In the words on the page, if they are well caught, is the living voice of the speaker, and in the voice entire ranges of personality and character.

There is Harry himself, the epitome of the westerner, who did not feel right out of his boots and jeans and wide-brimmed hat; who never asked what a man did for a living and never explained himself, but took a stranger at face value, and expected the same treatment in return.

At times, he enjoyed playing the westerner, laying it on for city folks like the office staff at United Artists in Hollywood. He was uncomfortable in a white-tablecloth restaurant, but on his own ground he was perfectly at ease with Barry Goldwater or a sourdough prospector; with Hosteen Cly, a Navajo family patriarch; or Shine Smith, a renegade missionary cut loose from church connections. He took an unbounded delight in people, whatever their station in life.

He was a man of his time, with a vocabulary that includes words like "squaw" and "buck" and "Navvie," but he did not condescend to the Navajos. Indeed, some of the old men he met in Monument Valley became powerful father figures for him, and he quietly accepted many Navajo ways as his own.

Gradually over the years, attracted by the Navajos and the Monument Valley landscape, visitors began to come to the Valley, and the Gouldings were their hosts. In the thirties they built a couple of rock cabins for guests, and after the war one of the first motels. Harry showed these visitors the country and the people. Perhaps, in his passionately partisan way, he exaggerated the virtues of the Navajos. He was an uneducated man and had some colorfully mistaken views of the Anasazi cliff dwellers, which he stubbornly refused to alter. But he was a superb storyteller, with the storyteller's gift for putting his values and point into a well-shaped anecdote.

There is Mike, his modest, steady, loving wife, who never blinked at the pioneering hardships of early days in the Valley, but was always there, pitching in with the sheep, trading, running a spotless kitchen, cooking for the early visitors, keeping everything going. There is Maurice, Mike's younger brother (whose name, western style, is pronounced "Morris"), the essence of the trickster god, Coyote, but who like Coyote was loyal to the Navajo people, and who idolized Harry.

There is Bert Davis, the illiterate trapper, who stayed with the Gouldings in the early days, and who comes to us only through Harry's words, bringing with him the ripe odor of his coyote bait. There are Navajos like Fred Yazzie, proud of his heritage and tenacious in his claim to the Gouldings' land; Ted Cly, tour guide for the Gouldings and believer in witchcraft; Luke Yazzie, quiet and dignified, but remembering in detail how he brought in the first uranium ore sample from Monument Mine No. 2 and did not get the royalty he thought he was entitled to. There is Frank Douglas, the black cook of many years at Goulding's. Their voices are the life itself of that place in those times.

It is to these people, their voices and their stories, that we turn now, to their memories of life in Monument Valley during the momentous years beginning in the era of the classic trading post and ending with the nascent and emerging self-consciousness and self-sufficiency of the Navajo people following World War II.

Part One. The Twenties

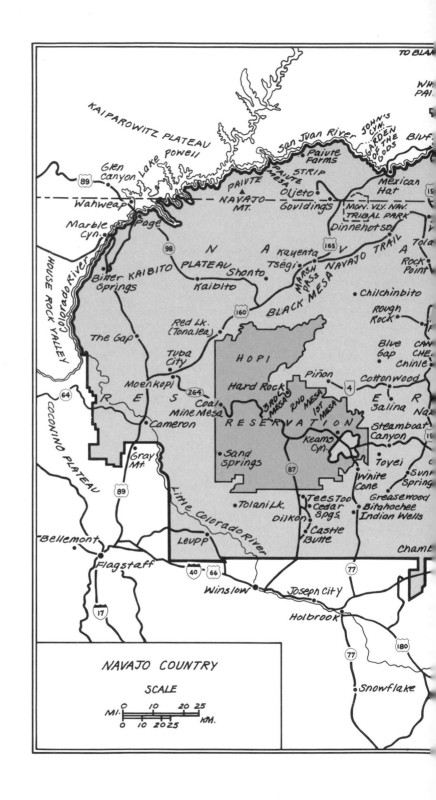

NAVAJO COUNTRY

SCALE

MI. 0 10 20 25
0 10 20 25 KM.

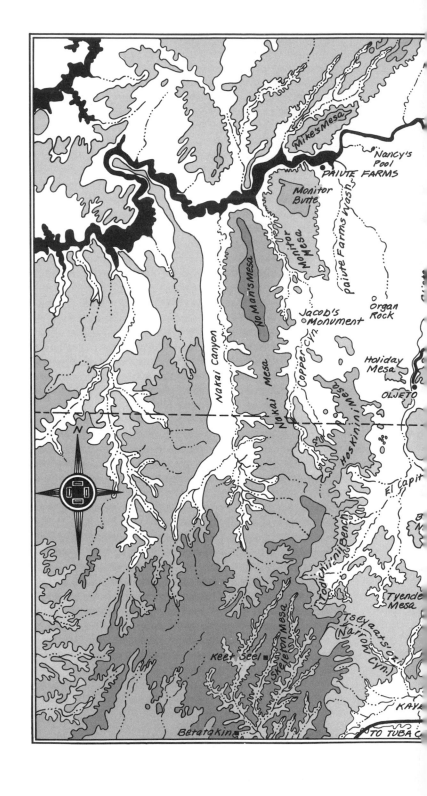

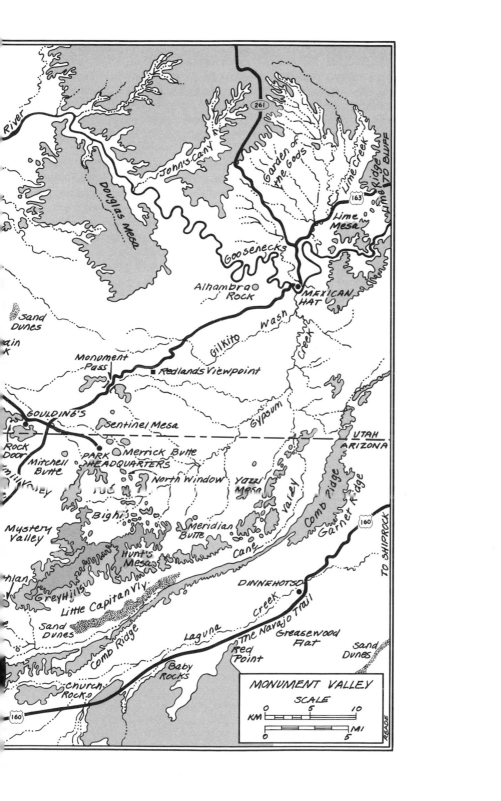

River

Douglas Mesa

John's Cany

261

Garden of the Gods

Lime Creek

Lime Ridge · LIME TO BLUFF

163

Lime Mesa

Goosenecks

Alhambra Rock

MEXICAN HAT

Sand Dunes

ain K

Gilkito Wash

Creek

Monument Pass

Redlands Viewpoint

Gypsum

GOULDING'S

Sentinel Mesa

UTAH
ARIZONA

Rock Door

Mitchell Butte

PARK HEADQUARTERS

Merrick Butte

Valley

North Window

Yazzi Mesa

Valley

Comb Ridge

Garner Ridge

160

Mystery Valley

Bighi's

Meridian Butte

Cany

TO SHIPROCK

hlan

Grey Hills

Hunt's Mesa

Little Capitan Vly.

DINNEHOTSO

Creek

The Navajo Trail

Sand Dunes

Comb Ridge

Laguna

Red Point

Greasewood Flat

Sand Dunes

church Rock

Baby Rocks

160

MONUMENT VALLEY

SCALE

KM 0   5   10

MI 0   5

READE

1 ▬ FINDING THE VALLEY

HARRY GOULDING: When Mike and I drove down to Monument Valley in the fall of '25, there was a place where we could land on snow. Up near Mitchell Butte there's a wash comes down, and there was a couple of trees growing; one is still there. There was a nice bend in there and a little shelter from the wind. We just camped under those trees close to that wash. We wintered on snow the first year, melted snow for water. There was a little spring on up above where old *Bidághaa' Łibá* got his water; Old Grey Whiskers, he'd have let us use his water, but we didn't need it.

We just stayed there that winter. Then we prospected around a little bit, and there was a spring back up that canyon where the hospital is now, not in the main canyon, but right in against them cliffs there's a little canyon off to the left. There was a spring in there, but in the summer it'd dry out. I figured I could develop it and make enough water to take care of us, and even water our sheep, so we stayed over where we were until we got this spring developed to where we could get clean water. When we got done, we moved over there with our tent and store tent and all, and old José was with us and put his tent up. It was right down at the mouth of the canyon where the old corral is now.

MIKE GOULDING (Harry's wife): When we finally got to the Valley, I just thought it was a beautiful place. I felt very much at home; no shocks, I felt like I'd been there before, I didn't feel strange at all. Started thinking about what we had to do and just got into it.

The tent was probably about ten by twelve. Harry had it boarded up, it was a wall tent, and it had a floor after a while. It had a floor and boards up about three feet and then your tent. You could stand up easily in it. On the first trip, that was just strictly camp gear; but after we got settled, later, we had a table of sorts, and four benches to sit on, because we fed José, and sometimes we'd have the Navajo boy there and we'd feed him. We had a bed, and I had a trunk. Then we got a nice big old white Monarch range. We put it outside and put a Navajo shade over it. Otherwise, you'd just roast in that tent, you know. Of course in the winter, why that was our heat, we brought it in to keep warm. So then I had a good oven and a good stove. We had a phonograph later that we brought down, and our Jimmy Rogers songs, and had a bit of music. Old time Jimmy Rogers, oh Harry just thought he was the greatest. I'd give anything if I had those old records. I think we brought the stove and phonograph down probably in '26. And I had two beautiful kerosene lamps, one in each tent. I've still got them both.

The store tent was just the same as the house tent only bigger. We had a counter and shelves and a stove. Harry had made a trip in before we came down and brought the store tent and flour and coffee and stuff like that. You catch on pretty quick to the things you've got to have in the store to trade. It was just mostly foods and a few clothes until we built the trading post. And you keep on adding as you learn the things they need.

Seems like the time went so fast. Everything was new, and you were busy too. I did some embroidering and I liked to crochet. If I was watching the store, I could crochet, things like that. I tried to get the most out of every day, because I figured I wasn't going to do it again the next day. You're not going to pass it again.

HARRY GOULDING: Where I first got the smell of Monument Valley was when I was buying stock. I was going over into Utah and buying the feeder end off of the Mormon folks' lambs over there and shipping them. Oh, three or four years I'd been buying in there every fall or spring for wool. I'd come into Monticello and them places. At Blanding I talked to Mr. Lyman,[1] and he told me then about the Paiute wars, but he didn't say anything about Monument Valley. Sometimes I'd come down McElmo Canyon and down in. I got down as far as Bluff one time. They knew where the Valley was, and I'd see a country off down there and talk a little bit about it. They just said, "Oh, it's a big country." But there's places you can go just below Blanding where those monuments show up pretty plain. You can't dwarf them things. But I never seen enough of it to put it together as anything as big as it is, and when John Stevens and I went down there I never dreamt that there was going to be anything like what I found.

John Stevens had a big stock set-up just out of Pagosa Springs in Colorado. I got awfully well acquainted with John Stevens. He loved to see what was on the other side of the mountain, just like I do. One day he said, "Harry, why the dickens don't we get together some day and make a trip?" It was in the fall of 1921. We wanted to go somewhere neither one of us had been. I says, "By golly, John, I'd like to see what's going on in this Navajo reservation. Take off and go across over to about Winslow," we figured on putting in about twenty days on the thing, "and then come back around down below there, Holbrook, and back across that way."

So we came right down past the Four Corners stake. We wanted to take that in. From there on you'd get little swales. We'd come up over a swale, and then another, and then another. It was getting kind of late and, well, this one swale was a little higher than the others we'd been coming to, but we says, "We can go on and cross just that one more, get it behind us."

So we went on, and it wasn't a swale, it was a cliff that we could look over. And here, out on the valley floor, were these big long sunset shadows from those monuments pointing at us. Well, we both just stopped right there and set on our horses, it seemed like fifteen minutes or more, and never said a word. Then we happened to look at each other at the same time, and we both said the same thing: "Let's camp!" We'd passed a pothole down below there that had water in it. "Let's camp!" So we set her down right there.

We were on the edge of Comb Ridge and we'd look off that ridge into Monument Valley. We stayed there for about four days. We went in and found some big Anasazi ruins, Poncho House, in that Chinle Wash country down in there.

Then we went down into the Valley. We didn't get past it. We never went any farther. We just spent all of our time down in there. We ran out of grub. First we traded our spurs for goat meat, that old Arbuckle's coffee, flour and salt, baking powder. It was Paiutes in there, and they traded then at, Oljeto was there, and going up toward Shiprock there was a trading post over in there. The Wetherills were at Kayenta, but Oljeto was a little closer to the Paiutes to trade. Finally we came to our saddlebags and our chaps, and then our bridles. After we traded them, we used a rope for a halter. We even traded our lariat rope. We had to use a piece of our pack rope, put it around the nose of the horse, tie it and then put it around his neck; you can make a kind of a halter out of it. We stayed there in the Valley about ten days longer than we should have.

■ The San Juan River separates the Mormon country from the Paiute Strip, which is the area between the San Juan River and the Arizona-Utah border, extending from Monument Valley westward to the Colorado River. The Paiute Strip is rugged, inhospitable country. It had been occupied by the Anasazi cliff dwellers until the end of the thirteenth century, when they abandoned the region, apparently as the result of an extended drought, although the reason for their leaving is still unclear. They moved to join the Hopi villages and other Puebloan communities at Zuni and along the Rio Grande.[2] Since that time until very recently it has remained a border land, crossed and recrossed by neighboring tribes, unoccupied by Anglos except for two or three traders.

The Navajos and Apaches, Athapascan tribes, had migrated southward from Canada or Alaska and were latecomers to the Southwest. The earliest archaeological evidence of their arrival in the region dates from A.D. 1390 to 1500.[3] The center of Navajo country was to the east of the Paiute Strip, in what is now northwestern New Mexico, but there are signs of early Navajo habitation well to the north of Monument Valley. Archaeological evidence and contemporary maps show occupancy of the area south of the Colorado River in Utah through the seventeenth and eighteenth centuries. By the early years of the nineteenth century, oral documentation from the Navajos themselves continues to place them in the same area and also south of the

San Juan in the Paiute Strip. There were many fording places across the river, and the Navajos seem to have ranged freely north and south from the Paiute Strip to the Bear's Ears and even to the Henry Mountains.[4]

At the time of Harry's visit, however, the Navajo reservation ended at the Arizona-Utah border, and the Paiute Strip was inhabited mostly by Paiutes. They also occupied some land in Allen's Canyon, just west of Blanding.

HARRY GOULDING: When we came out, we decided that we'd go around on the other side of the San Juan River, on the Bluff side. We crossed the river on that bridge at Mexican Hat and went on up to Bluff, and when we got up there, they were having a meeting. The Mormons and the Colorado cowboys, stock people, were going in and cleaning the Indians out, the Paiutes, because the Paiutes were killing their stock and sometimes stealing one once in a while. That was going on north of the river.

They had called all the Paiutes in to this meeting. The Mormon folks would like to talk to them, and the head of the soldiers had come down and maybe could help them out some way or other. The meeting was going to be the next day.

I asked John, I says, "Would you mind camping here? Let's pitch camp, and then we can go and listen in on this conflab." I was getting interested in that country down there. John loved it, he enjoyed it to no end, but he couldn't quite see going back there to stay like I was thinking.

■   The Mormons were having troubles with the Paiutes, who lived on poor land, resented the Mormons' crowding presence, and were raiding their cattle and sheep camps. The immediate problem began in the spring of 1921, when Bishop's Boy and Dutchups, two young Paiutes from Allen's Canyon, had stolen a calf and were pursued by a posse of eight. One of the Paiutes was wounded and the other escaped by swimming the river. They were subsequently jailed, and then escaped from jail. In June, Governor Mabey[5] met with the Paiutes of Allen's Canyon, including their two leading spokesmen, Poke and Posey, at which time the Paiutes promised to end their raiding.[6]

The meeting in Bluff that Harry and John Stevens attended in September was called by Elfego Baca, representing Secretary of the Interior Albert B. Fall, to investigate the conditions that had given rise to the past spring's disturbance. According to the Moab newspaper, Baca said that he would "recommend to the department that the government purchase all patented land from settlers in and around Bluff and lay out a reservation running up and down the San Juan River from that town," and that the government train the Paiutes in agriculture. In return, the Paiutes would evacuate Allen's Canyon. No doubt the Paiutes south of the San Juan would be free to join them. "The proposed plan to colonize the Paiutes near Bluff, holding them on a prescribed territory, is expected to meet with the approval of the white settlers in the southern county," the newspaper reported.[7]

HARRY GOULDING: And so the soldier talked to the Paiutes. There were some Navajos around listening in, naturally, but they were just visiting with the Paiutes there. The Paiutes told the soldier that they couldn't believe him. If you know an Indian, you can tell a little bit about what's going on. You could see that he wasn't getting anywhere with the old Paiutes, they were just listening. An Indian is a good listener. So they were listening, but I could see that what the soldier was saying wasn't amounting to anything at all.

Then an old Mormon got up, and he told them that they would give them land up around Blanding. There was some ranchland where they could raise stuff. There was water. It'd be a better place for them to live. Their children could go to school with the Mormon children, and they'd do everything they could for them.[8] After two or three of these old fellas got up, and they each made a talk and invited them to do this, there was a little change come. A little wee change in an Indian means an awful lot, and I thought to myself, the old Indians are listening to that. Some of it is sliding off of them. They're wrapping some of it up.

I decided I'd like to keep an eye on what happened next; it seemed to me that them Paiutes might be getting ready to move out of the Valley, and that might make room for me. I sure liked that country.

We went on back home after the thing was over, and it wasn't long after that I met Mike. There never was another girl like Mike, or will be. We began to seeing each other, and we had wonderful times together. Then her father died and she moved to California, and well, I couldn't stand that, so pretty soon we got married.

MIKE GOULDING: The first time I'd ever seen Harry and I guess the first time he'd ever seen me was in the old American Hotel. I had been sick with typhoid fever from October until almost Christmas, and I wasn't supposed to have any food that would irritate my intestines, because they were in a very delicate condition, and mother was very careful with me. But this Sunday my girlfriend and her husband-to-be and a boyfriend that I was going with, we went down to the American Hotel for dinner. I was going to get something I wanted to eat that mother didn't know about. It didn't happen to hurt me. And when we got through with dinner, we went into the ... it was more like a living room than a lobby. There was an old piano in there and we were playing and singing, and Harry was sitting over there in a chair. He and the old fella that ran the hotel were good friends, so he'd come there for his dinner, and afterwards he was just sitting there having a good time. He looked like a rancher. He had his old jumper, his levis and boots, and a western hat. I just liked the looks of him.

There were no introductions or anything, but I found out afterwards who he was. I was impressed, naturally, and I guess I favorably impressed him, because we finally got to going together.

We went to Silverton because my mother had hay fever so bad and my father was stationed up there working on the railroad. We'd set up camp and stay there in a pretty spot. My friend from Durango came up and camped with us, and Harry would come up. We'd go fishing and had all sorts of good times, the whole family, all of us. We went out to one of the lakes, Molas usually, not very far from Silverton, and it was good fishing then. We'd all go out together, picnic and fry fish, and what have you. Harry was a good fisherman, he and his brother Charlie used to always have fish in camp, and a little deer meat.

Harry and I had some chances to get off by ourselves once in a while. It was a wonderful summer. Had a *good* time. My father kept close track of my boyfriends, and so did my brother, Chet. Not like this one, and like that one all right. But everybody liked Harry. He had his own charm.

MAURICE KNEE (Mike's younger brother):   Harry was the first guy that ever did make overtures to Mike that my Dad would have anything to do with. He liked him. Harry, he caught the train, he rode in the engine with Dad. And I remember, he had a little deal he carried in his pocket, full of dimes—a little metal container he could flip a dime out. That's how he kept my brother Paul and me away when they wanted to be alone. He'd flip a dime apiece here and here, and down we'd go for an eskimo pie. We had a whale of a summer.

MIKE GOULDING: Then, of course, we had the tragedy in our family, we lost our father. He was a railroader. It was a confusion of orders. He was on what they called the Eastern, a passenger train coming from Alamosa to Durango, and they always had to have help to get up over that Cumbres Pass. And what is it they call those engines when they go down? Anyway, it was just an engine and a coal car coming down to meet them and help them up over the hill. They hadn't read their orders right. They were supposed to be on this siding, but they came by the siding, they kept on coming. It was a head-on. He was killed, and his engineer. And Harry was so kind when we needed a lift, you know, to go to Durango when they were bringing my father's body in.

So then Mother's brothers came to her aid and got her to move to California where they could help her, and the kids were educated there. Harry and I, we kept writing, carried it on, and we finally set a date. We corresponded for, I guess I was out there two months or more, I can't remember, but he wrote lots of letters, a letter every day. He decided, I guess, that he didn't want me to stay in California, that was the gist of it, I'd better come back. We were married February the 19th, 1923. I'd just had my eighteenth birthday. Harry was twenty-six.

Harry was buying and selling sheep, hides and wool and everything pertaining. We lived at Aztec the rest of '23 and '24. Aunt Molly would come and go, and Uncle Abe was always there. And then we moved down to Monument Valley.

HARRY GOULDING: The folks come over from England. Uncle Abe came first. He got out here into the Southwest and he wrote back to them what a lovely place it was, up around Naturita, Colorado, up there in the mining country. There was three brothers, Uncle Jack and Uncle Abe and my dad, and then three aunts, three sisters, come over. They homesteaded that bottomland along the river at Naturita, and they were there for quite a number of years in the horse business and working placer claims up and down the San Miguel River there.

Then they sold everything out, the placer claims and the horses and their land, and they went to sheep ranching. They homesteaded land along the Animas River up in Colorado and near Aztec, New Mexico, for winter range. That was our big headquarters. The winter range was scattered out, some out in the Farmington Glade country; then just north of Durango about nine miles they had quite an area of range, and some of it clean over across near the Navajo reservation. Pine Ridge, near Durango, was the summer headquarters. Their summer range was in the Hermosa River country, up in the high mountains. Some of it went quite a ways above timberline, and there on down. They had the choice of the country. They brought the first sheep into that San Juan Basin country, all that Big Basin country in there, the first sheep among them cattle people.

They were all single when they got over in there, but Dad got married and then us kids was born. My mother left when I was three years old. I don't remember a thing about it, but I know that she must have been in the wrong, whatever it was. Nobody talked about it much, and I never inquired about it, but I know that Dad wouldn't do anything that would cause her to run off.

Aunt Molly really raised us. Then Art Greene's mother died, she was one of my father's sisters, and that left him out of a mother, so Aunt Molly took care of him too. I remember that she had pretty near perfect control over us, and a lot of times when Art and I thought we'd get away with something, Aunt Molly some way would know and would tell us about it when we wasn't going to say nothing. She was clever, awful clever, in those respects, but she was nice to us kids, never any whippings or anything of that kind, just some lectures once in a while, but never any abuse at all.

Uncle Abe never married, and he loved children, he had a way with children, he could handle us better than anybody else. He drew our attention and our feelings. We all liked Uncle Abe. If we'd do anything bad, why he'd line us up and he'd get a newspaper, fold her all up, and then just as we went by him why he'd whack us with it. That was a terrible beating we got, with a newspaper, but he could lay it on and make it feel to us like it was something to have to go by him and get that whomp. I think it was because we thought so much of him, and for him to have to do that I think affected us some. I'd go around walking, sticking my belly out, trying to look like Uncle Abe.

The folks had a pretty big outfit, they was running twenty thousand head. I stayed out in camp. It was kind of a pleasure to be out with the stock. You're moving with the seasons, and then you'd come back and forth to the headquarters ranch occasionally during the summer. My job was carrying provisions to the camps and moving camps. We'd leave a camp in one place about, oh, maybe ten days, and then we'd move to another camp, and then come on around and use that camp again when the vegetation had grown enough.

Dad had Mexicans and Navajos and Utes all working for him. It wasn't done apurpose, it was just that Dad would find a good man, and he didn't care who he was or what his nationality was, he'd hire him. And it was a good idea because they would get into a competitive mind always. We consulted them and visited, give them a little more interest in the thing, and they would get together and decide where to put the next camp.

Those old herders, they were awful nice to us kids. We'd generally go to old José's camp to eat, because he'd go all out extra for us kids to make us a nice meal. He was the one herder that we preferred over everyone else— although some of them old Mexicans were awful nice people. But old Joe, he was more like part of the family, he'd been with Dad so long, and he loved to have us come to his stage camp. And then Mike and me, we brought him with us when we came in here to the Valley.

José was an Indian who was taken captive by the Mexicans when he was just a little boy, before the Civil War. The Luceros stole him from his Indian family, and then they sold him to the Montoyas, sold him as a slave. Then the government finally said, "No more of that stuff. Turn them people loose." So old Joe went to work for Dad, years and years and years. His name was José Lucero Montoya y Gouldies. He couldn't say Goulding, it was Gouldies. He didn't know any Indian. He didn't know any language at all when he was captured, so he learned Mexican.

■ The slave trade began in the Southwest with the Conquistadores of the sixteenth century, when the Spaniards raided the Indians for slaves, and the tribes of the region also raided each other for slaves whom they traded among themselves and to the Spaniards for horses. Some argued that the purpose of slavery was to "Christianize" the captives. There are sickening stories of atrocities on all sides, and the slave-taking continued until the Civil War brought it to an end. Frank McNitt prints a list of 148 Indian slaves freed in July 1865 in two counties of the Colorado Territory, 113 of whom were Navajos.[9]

HARRY GOULDING: José worked for Dad until after Dad died and then he worked for me as long as I had the stock. When I sold my stock and the two camps there, generally when you sell a bunch of sheep, the camp equipment and everything goes with them, but José said, "Don't sell my house, my home." So he brought it down and put it on our headquarters farm, and he lived there right with us. He done his own cooking, he wouldn't eat with us. We'd get him to come in once in a while and have a Sunday meal or something like that, but he had his little stove and his camp boxes and everything. It was just a regular sheep camp. Old Joe: he was a great old fella, he was nice to go with.

Every year I'd come back to the Valley. After that meeting the Mormons had with the Paiutes at Bluff, I wanted to see what was going on, whether there would be more trouble, or whether the Mormons would keep their word about relocating the Paiutes, because I was thinking about moving in if they moved out. I'd always take a load of merchandise that the trading post'd need, and that'd help pay the way down. There was no fighting going on then, and by golly, I'd go back another year.

Finally I went down there one fall and here they was, the Paiutes, leaving, all strung out in a long line. This was in the fall of 1923. There must have been a hundred head of them. About twelve families stayed behind and didn't go out with this group, but there were at least ninety people leaving. There was quite a string of horsebackers, and then they had some wagons, and the Paiutes had that old way of going, a travois. The oldtimers used to drag sticks behind their horses and lay the pile on them. You could bring a lot more with a horse or mule dragging that stuff than you could pile on top of his back. And then there were some people back behind, and a lot of horses in there. They had all their stock with them, cattle and sheep.

I got over close enough to where I could get a nice view of them. It was about sunset and that late sun was starting to work on those monuments. I didn't even no more but know what a camera was then, but I wish I'd had a camera with me that day! They was all in a line winding on out through that rough country. If you've seen one of them old-fashioned wagon trains. . . . It was more like a stock train than a wagon train. I'll never forget it. The whole Monument Pass was on fire, beautiful.

I went back up to Bluff to see if I could find out what was happening. I stayed overnight with the boys there at the oil well. They were drilling right in the Paiute Strip here, sort of southwest of Mexican Hat. I stayed overnight with them, and the next day when I went out, the Paiutes were up past Bluff. It was about noon and they were having something to eat. I found out at Bluff that they had had the Posey War that spring. A couple of Paiutes had raided a sheepherder's camp and stolen everything they could find, and one thing led to another. They had this fight with Old Posey, was the leader of the Paiutes, up north of the San Juan. He was killed during the fight. The Posey War is what it was, the last Indian war in the United States. They rounded them all up, every man, woman, and child, and put them in the stockade up at Blanding and they kept them there for all that summer. Then later, they located them on White Mesa.

The Mormons had kept their word from that meeting at Bluff back the first time John Stevens and I had come out. They were offering the Paiutes new land, and the ones down here had accepted too and were moving up to White Mesa. It had all went through.

And I was glad to see it too, I went back from that trip and I felt pretty good about everything. I knew that if the Paiutes left Monument Valley, it would be thrown open, see, because there'd had to have been some arrangement made about that land just as soon as those Indians moved off.

■   In April 1923, the tension resulted in a skirmish that the local Mormons call the Posey War, after the Paiute leader, and which proved to be climactic in this series of clashes. Three Paiutes held up a sheepherder at gunpoint and took what they wanted from his camp. Two of them were arrested, and during a recess in the trial, one of them seized the sheriff's gun, leaped on Posey's horse, which the Paiutes had ready and waiting for him, and escaped, while managing to put a bullet in the pursuing sheriff's horse as he fled.

The entire towns of Bluff and Blanding were aroused, and the Paiutes fled for safety en masse. After a series of chases through rough canyon country, some remarkable horsemanship, and some good and bad shooting, one Paiute was killed, Posey was wounded and in hiding, where he finally died, and the rest of the Paiutes surrendered and were locked in a stockade in Blanding.[10]

To put an end to the raids, the Indian Bureau finally agreed to give the Paiutes of Allen's Canyon allotments of somewhat better land near Blanding. This was a far cry from the new reservation on the river, surrounding Bluff, which Elfego Baca had unrealistically promised two years before. There were those who said that the government had been too slow in acting on the Baca recommendation. The white settlers did not want to give up their land, and the Paiutes were becoming increasingly impatient and hostile.[11] Nevertheless, the Paiutes accepted the offer,[12] and as Harry saw when he visited the Valley in 1923, most of those who were living in Monument Valley moved up to join them.

Coincidentally, there were larger moves in Washington, having to do with oil, not Indians. The Paiute Strip had originally been "set apart as a reservation for Indian purposes" in 1884 by executive order, together with the land south and east of it. In 1892, it was restored to public land. In 1908, it was again withdrawn by executive order "for the use of various Indians." On June 9, 1922, Secretary of the Interior Fall, who later went to prison for his part in the Teapot Dome oil scandal, signed an executive order again opening the Paiute Strip, along with other executive-order reservations, not, as Harry thought, because the Paiutes had settled on White Mesa, but because oil had been discovered on the Navajo reservation and oil developers were clamoring to get in.[13]

HARRY GOULDING: So then I had to sell the ranch and get things straightened up. Mike and I had been married the winter before, and we were on the headquarters ranch in Aztec where I had the stock. We finally got cleared out and ready and came down to the Valley in September or October of 1925. I got her off down in here where she couldn't get away from me. I wasn't aiming to lose that gal, I tell you. She was a great one, and has been all the years, my goodness.

MIKE GOULDING: That was it. The long voyage began. I didn't know anything about Monument Valley then.

2 ◼ THE TENTS

HARRY GOULDING: It was an old Buick we brought in with us when we first moved to the Valley. I put in a low-speed ring and pinion gear, and it had big balloon tires on it. And I brought in a Graham Brothers truck, and I put these big doughnut wheels on it too, the biggest wheels I could get on the thing, and I got that auxiliary transmission in it. Mike drove the Buick in, and I brought a load in the truck; it had fourteen hundred pounds of merchandise on it. Old José, old Joe, he was with us, he traveled on the truck generally. We put in a bigger tent for the store, a fourteen I think it was, and we brought down a ten-by-twelve for ourselves; that wasn't much room for a home.

Mike drove that Buick all the way, even when we'd get stuck. I'd be first, and I'd get stuck and get on through. Then we'd come back and lay a little stuff in where I dug things up going through with my rig, and she'd come through, and occasionally she'd get stuck. Then we'd jack it up and chock it up and get the road made out ahead of her for a few feet, and she'd get in that old car and take her through just as good as I could. No stopping at all, and go right on out!

MIKE GOULDING: We had a dog and a cat. And old José. *"Por Dios,"* he said, *"mucho lejos."* "Oh my God," I guess is what that is, "so many miles." From nowhere I guess is what he meant. Poor old soul, scared him probably.

We had the tents, but no furniture. There was no room for furniture. Harry had to have a drum of gas, and he had to have water and extra oil, and he had food, dutch ovens, skillets, and all that heavy stuff. It was hanging all over; you'd think you were a John Ford's Joad family going down the road. [Laughs.] I had the bedding and the clothes and stuff like that, as I remember. Stove, there was a little camp stove, what they call a sheepherder's stove, that you can hang on the side of a burro and not break their back. The oven was about a foot square, bake a pan of sourdough biscuits and that was about it, just a little bitty thing. That was mostly what my gear was.

I didn't ever want to go through Snake Canyon again after that first trip. Snake Canyon is between Bluff and Mexican Hat, used to be. Most times you had to get out and move boulders, if it had rained or anything, to get through it all. There weren't any roads, nothin but a nothin! You'd come down Comb Reef, you'd cross Comb Wash down there, and that's where you'd come out and get into Snake Canyon. I can't tell you just how narrow and how awful a place it was, because nobody liked it. It's like a wash, was what it was. But it was very narrow. Of course there wasn't any of it that was a road. Mexican Hat, you crossed that old bridge and then you went right around the edge, hanging out over the river. That old trail, if you know where to look you can still see it. But we didn't fear anything; Harry was ahead, so we just kept going.

Then we got into our tents and settled. José had a little tent of his own. He came along with us, but it was just too lonely for him. We were busy learning Navajo, and he could only speak Spanish. Of course Harry could talk to him in Spanish, and he was teaching me Spanish, which I enjoyed so much until I got started on the Navajo. Then he complained to Harry that I didn't talk to him anymore. I was so sorry. I was in the store all the time; there was somebody around there most of the time. I didn't divide my time right, I guess, and Harry didn't either. We were busy thinking about these other things. It was all new to us, you know. José stayed with us four, five,

The Gouldings' tents, where they lived and traded from 1925 to 1928. Their house tent is in the center of the picture, to the left their Buick with its hood under a summer shade, at the far right the flap of the store tent, and between them the small tent of two visiting Oklahoma artists. (Goulding's Monument Valley Museum)

six months maybe, but then he wanted to go back. We got him back to Durango with Harry's brother Charlie, and then Charlie got him into a rest home. He was real, real old before he died, senile. He always called me *primita*, little cousin.

We'd got down to the Valley before Harry started calling me Mike. And then of course everybody else picked it up. The reason was that he never could spell my name right. When I went to California before we were married, he wrote letters to me and kept spelling it wrong. It's Leone, L-e-o-n-e, but he either left the "e" off or put an "a" on it, and so he said, "Well, I've had enough trouble about this, I guess I'll just have to call you Mike, and then I can spell that." [Laughs.] Bless his heart.

MAURICE KNEE: The first water Harry and Mike had, when they were still in tents, they developed that little spring around up Rock Door Canyon. There's a little side canyon up there, you just keep going left and left and left. That's where they bathed, they'd go up there and get a bucket of water and bathe.

HARRY GOULDING: We fixed the spring up to where you could get a pipe out, because when the water would run there was loose stuff that'd make it dirty. We cleaned it out and put gravel back in behind, and a pipe, and covered it with concrete. I think the pipe is still coming out of the concrete for a ways. It's been twisted with the floods, but it never could pull out of that concrete, because I had her nailed in there with big washers. I made a little trail, worked some footsteps out, and we got up on that bench on this side. It's nice to get up on one of them benches, really, to go up. You can go way up in there.

I came in here to trade. It was the only way, just to trade with the Indians. We couldn't have stayed here otherwise. We traded in the tents, and our corral and things were right down across the wash. Well, I didn't have a corral for quite awhile, but that's where we bedded the sheep, right down in there. And the rains used to come in here, we got a little more moisture than we do now. You wouldn't even know a rain was coming sometimes. These old clouds would start billowing, that's generally the way the rain starts in the desert. Here comes this big old gusher, and then it'll finally even out to a nice drizzle. We used to get drizzles here that'd last all night. That's when the grass was high.

So those clouds would come over, and when the rain comes fast and hits a dry canvas, if it isn't awfully thick, why it'll come right through. Well, we had our shelves in there and we had these yard goods. It'd hit the yard goods, and the color would run, and a terrible mess. So we'd be down where the corrals are down there, and when them clouds would come over and we'd hear that thunder, everybody would come running up and grab a canvas and put over our shelves to protect our merchandise. We had a big twelve ounce duck tarp, and it would shed the water.

MIKE GOULDING: I spent my day just doing whatever there was to do.

I was in the store if there was anybody there—in the tent where the store was. And of course I had to feed everybody. Oh, you'd manage to keep busy. Sometimes I'd walk up to the spring and get a bucket of water, away up in the canyon, take Brownie and go. And then we had sheep at that time, they had to be watered, and you had to get them out early in the morning. We watered the sheep up there at that little spring as long as it held up, and then we'd have to take them down to Oljeto. We bought them from the Navajos, and in the fall they'd take them out to Farmington. We kept them in corrals down there, and we had a herder who took them out, or else we herded them. We always had Navajos around. If you just didn't do whatever there was to do around here, why you would have been sort of lost.

I had a pet lamb, and I had Brownie the dog, and the cat. When we'd haul water, we'd usually go up and get cans of water in the old car. The lamb would get out in front of the car when we were going to go and put her head down and wouldn't move. That lamb had to go. It was an old touring car, so Brownie would sit on one side and the lamb on the other, and away we'd go. Now you wouldn't think of a lamb being a pet like that, but it was just like a dog. It was the cutest thing. You had to amuse yourself as best you could, because sometimes I was here nine, ten months without ever going anywhere. But there were lots of things to do, and I'm not a lonely person anyway.

HARRY GOULDING: Old Brownie depended on that lamb to stop the car. It gave him time to get in the back seat, and then Lambie would get in with him. She was on this side and Brownie on the other side. Whenever we'd come to any bushes that would touch the car, why Brownie would fight them. Then Lambie would want to change places, and she'd butt him. He'd generally give way, and they'd swap sides. Even after she grew up she stayed with us at the camp, there in the tents. Then when she finally got a little older, she went out with the herd, but all Mike had to do was go down around that herd regardless of where it was, and holler, "Lambie, Lambie, Lambie, Lambie!" and here she'd come. She never did forget Mike. Old Lambie's head would come up and listen, and she'd head right up through the herd toward Mike.

MIKE GOULDING: I had that little old camp stove and I used to make sourdough bread and sourdough biscuits. I had a sourdough jug. I'd make several loaves of bread, but it was quite a tedious chore, so mostly it was pancakes and biscuits that I made up. Sourdough, there's none better, you know. It makes just the best bread. And for meat we used lamb and goat. They'd bring it in. I didn't know I was eating goat, but I was. You know how I finally knew how? When they'd bring the carcass in, the goat was already short-tailed and the little tail would go right out to a point, you know, and the lamb's been docked. I finally figured it out, and I went prancing out to Harry and said, "You've bought a goat!"

"Well," he said, "we've been eating it all the time." He knew it, an old sheepman, I guess he did!

HARRY GOULDING: This goat meat out here, well, goat meat anywhere, is the choice meat there is. And yet people won't eat it. The reason for it is that the old billy goat when he's put with the herd, he gets to smell awful. But we always kept a few goats in our herds back home for our camp food, because it was much better than the mutton you could get downtown. Whenever they go in to a water hole, if there's a spring and the water is running down or if it's a watering trough, they'll get up to the head of the trough where the fresh water is coming in or up to the head of the herd when they drink in a creek. They're cleaner, and they're choicey about what they eat. They eat a lot of browse, a goat is a great browser, he's just like a deer in that way, he has a little bit of that flavor of deer meat. He's cleaner, and you'll never get in trouble eating goat meat. It's the top meat there is, and yet we won't have nothing to do with it.

RAY HUNT (a trader in Bluff who later worked for Harry Goulding): When Harry came in to stay, with his wife, I was quite surprised to think that anyone would want to move off down there where they were, so far away from civilization. Living out like that, just in tents, with the sheep, they really had it rough, although they had their tents fixed up that it was awful nice. I dropped in for a meal or two. They had these little lambs all around there and sheep and everything. It was a typical sheep camp.

Mike kept the tents spotless inside, in spite of all the wind storms and everything they had. They were fixed up in those tents just about as good as you could be, especially out in the flats where it was plenty hot in the summertime. I don't know how they put up with it, they went through a lot of misery. But they were all happy. There was no time of day that you'd go by there or stop in, that they didn't ask you to stay and eat with them or have a cup of coffee or something. I didn't give them that much time to stay, but they did, and the longer they stayed, the better they liked it, liked the country. It got too hot down in the flats where they were at; later they moved up under the rim of the hill.

HARRY GOULDING: There were four Navajo families in here when the Paiutes were still here. There were no other Navajos as far west as Nakai Canyon; that I'm sure of. Beyond that there were Paiutes, but I don't know whether there were any Navajos in there then or not. There were Paiutes in Paiute Canyon over there with little farms, and they stayed in over towards Navajo Mountain.

After the Paiutes left Monument Valley and went up to White Mesa, there were still a few families that stayed in here, about six families stayed for about a year, I guess, and then they went on out too. They lived out toward Cedar Springs, that's all east of Train Rock and south of Douglas Mesa. They were camped up in those cedars there. What held them was the spring. The spring was in the lower land, and there were more cedars and some piñon down there. They had built up a dam that wasn't too good, but they could water their stock. You had to let them lay there two or three hours because it would run dry. It was hard on the stock because they was pushing each other, trying to get that water. I put in two troughs when I kept sheep down in there. I kept a bunch of sheep there all the time I was buying lambs.

Well, just as soon as the last Paiutes got out of sight, the Navajos were in here. Katso's family was one of the groups that came in then. He was the one that finally got Cedar Springs. There was about three or four Navajos that went in to Cedar Springs to water after I put the troughs in. Then they could take their herds in and there was plenty of water for them to drink.

At first when I'd go into a place where there were Navajos, you'd see those little old kids running back into the rocks, and the women. It was quite a while before it got to where we'd go into their homes and everybody was at home. They were that way because of the cattlemen. Before we first come in here, the cowboys had started bringing their cattle down for the winter, Mormons and the Colorado cowboys. They ate up the winter feed and the summer feed, and that was hard on these people in here. Then some of them got to being a little bit nasty, and the Navajos didn't like them at all. I think it was mostly that Colorado bunch. I don't know of any of the people around Blanding or up in there that would abuse an Indian in any way.

But they'd push their stock around and run through the Navajo herds. There was never any shooting went on, but there was the fear that it gave them that there might be something. And so they'd have the wife and the children always run back up in the rocks and hide. They used to put their hogans in places where they could do that. The Navajos never tried to drive the cowboys out, they wouldn't hardly have had a chance. Those fellas had rifles and everything. So they just dodged them the best way they could. But when we first come in here we were strangers. We'd go up to those camps, and there was nobody in there if there was no buck around.

It took a little while before they got real friendly. They don't make up their minds in a few minutes about a person. You've got a pretty good test to break through. The only way to do it is to go and act just like you would, and then it finally turns out. Then it was a delightful place.

The Navajos have a great way of feeling a person out. There was one old Navajo that came into the tent, there at the store tent one time, about three or four months after we got in here. It was cold, early morning, and he kicked the tent flap back, and he stood there. He had his robe on, and he brought it up over his face like they have the pictures of the old Indians sometimes. They do that. He pulled his robe over in front of him like that, and he kicks this atmosphere out toward me. He just stood here and eyeballed me. I knew something was on his mind. He didn't do much talking, but he wanted to know if I was going to be there very long; I knew what it was just from his actions. And I couldn't tell him, I didn't have enough Navajo to tell him, not at that time. He was named after a big rock; he lived there by it for so long that he got his name because of the rock.

After he'd looked at me quite a while I thought, well, I'll just look at you too and try to find out something. The air got pretty thick while we was looking. But he finally come over and put his arm up on the counter and shook hands with me.

The Navajos don't have a Dunn and Bradstreet or any way to tell who a person is. They're just like our old folks used to be, they had a way of sizing a person up. The Navajos have an even better way. And I guess he didn't find anything wrong so we went ahead and traded. He was here in the Valley quite a while after we came in, and we got to be good friends.

MIKE GOULDING: We had two Navajo brothers working for us; Little Boy and Big Boy we called them. We had to learn the language, and Big Boy wanted to learn English, so it worked out just great. We'd sit by the campfire at night and make lists of words and whenever they quit laughing at us we figured we had said it pretty good, because they have a jolly good time, you know, if you say it wrong.

The Navajos started coming in right away. They wanted to see who these new people were. We were being looked over, couldn't be no question, but well, it didn't bother me, because I was innocent as that orange. [Laughs.] Tried to learn their language, that was the main thing. Every time one'd come in that wasn't too busy, they had a tutoring job right away. But they enjoyed it too; I'd tell them our words.

HARRY GOULDING: Mr. Heffernan had the little trading post down where the Wetherills used to be at Oljeto. The old Oljeto post, after the Wetherills left, the wash took that store and the biggest part of the wool shed and buildings. When this old fella moved in, he built a new store down below there. That's the new Oljeto. I think his wife died when they were there, and he had a daughter, and so Mr. Heffernan and his daughter were running the trading post. I hadn't met him yet, Mike and I had just moved in, and so I wanted to meet him.

■   The Wetherills left Oljeto in 1910.[1] Joseph Heffernan was the youngest son of Civil War general James J. Heffernan. Born in New York State, he moved to Parrot City, Colorado, with his father's family in 1876. He married and had two daughters: Eleanor, later Mrs. John Ismay, herself the wife of a trader; and Anna, later a nurse in the Indian Service at Fort Defiance. At various times, he had trading posts at Aneth, Four Corners, McElmo,[2] and finally at Oljeto.[3] It was probably his daughter Anna who was with him at Oljeto.

According to Virginia Smith, the wife of the present trader at Oljeto, the Heffernans built the new store in 1921. They were followed by John Taylor. "He was there possibly six or eight years and he sold to a man by the name of Pearson, George Pearson. He was there two years and then he sold it to my brother-in-law, Ruben Heflin. Ruben, I believe, was here six years when he sold it to a cousin of ours, Fred Carson. I believe he had it two years and then my father [O. J. Carson] bought it from Fred Carson."[4] Mrs. Smith's sister, Mildred Heflin, remembers the same sequence of owners, but her dates differ. She and her husband were at Oljeto from 1937 to 1945.[5]

HARRY GOULDING: And then I wanted to go down and see another old fella that had a little farm down below Oljeto. Everybody called him Bidághaa' Nééz—Long Whiskers. He had a mustache like the old saloon keepers, you know, coming out to here, and he twisted them. He lived down there among them Indians, he was farming there, and he wasn't a bit afraid of nothing! "There's fine gold in here," he says, "down in on the San Juan River, lots of it, big heaps of gravel that is loaded with this fine gold." There'd been quite a few people come in there earlier, and they tried it and couldn't do anything with it. It was so fine it would get away from him. He had himself clean out of money and nobody to grubstake him.

Well I wanted to go on down and see if I couldn't get to the river to see what things were like down that way, so I stopped at his place and asked if he'd like to go along with me. "Yeah," he says, "I'll ride down with you." So we did, and then we came on back up, and I let him off where he lived, the other side of Oljeto Wash, and went over to Oljeto to shake hands with Mr. Heffernan.

His girl came to the door. I imagine she was about eighteen or twenty, a very capable girl. She used to haul all of the merchandise in for the old fella. She'd go get it and bring it in and hassle it around. She was quite a person. I says, "I been wanting to come down and meet Mr. Heffernan and get acquainted."

"Oh, he's awful sick," she says, and I could see she was worried.

"I'll tell you," I says, "I haven't had anything to eat. I'll go right here back of the trading post and cook a bite to eat, and if he gets worse or anything, why you just call me."

So I got things started and then I came back up, and she was crying. She says, "I'm afraid my father is going to die. I don't think he's going to live. I'm awful glad you came," she says.

We went in his room, and the pain was getting him, it was just deathly pain he was in. He was about to roll off the bed. I went over and got ahold of him, and about that time whatever this was, something inside of him busted and came out his nose. He threw up all over me. It just came up and smelled the room and everything, and he died, right there, in my arms.

There was nobody there but her and I, I don't know where his wife was, but then by gosh, here come somebody else, and then some more, and here starts people to come in, all of a sudden! There were eleven people just happened to come in there. One thing that was a blessing, there was a fella and his wife came in, and his wife had been a nurse. She knew exactly what to do with a person when they died. That was needed, because things got to be done that's kind of rough. You got to put a plug in there or there'd be a mess. She knew all about that, and we'd do the things that she told us to do. I wouldn't want to tell you what we had to do.

Bidághaa' Nééz could see the cars coming in from down at his place, and he felt there's something wrong up there, so he come on up. I was glad he was there, too, before it was over, because he rode out with me. We'd already driven down with the old truck to look at the river, and that was a rough drive. Then the two of us went to Kayenta and got some boards and built a wood box to take Mr. Heffernan out in, built a coffin to get him out to where he could *get* a coffin. We got it fixed up and a cover for it, and brought it back to Oljeto.

We got him in the box and into the truck, and we was all standing around the truck there. Those eleven people were all still there, they'd all stayed. His daughter said, "This is the biggest crowd of people that ever hit this trading post, right here, now! We've never had over three or four, never like this. God has certainly done something for me."

Then Bidághaa' Nééz and I, we started on out; we were going to have to go clean to Cortez with his body. When we came by our place, Mike come out and looked at the coffin. I had it right up crossways close behind the cab, because there's less jolting up there. Mike says, "Harry you ain't never going to be able to take that coffin up there that way! It'll tear off on them rocks as you go by them!" It was sticking out the sides a ways. So we turned it around and got it back up.

MIKE GOULDING: I was thinking of Snake Canyon, and I had visions of that thing rubbing off. The canyon seemed so narrow to me that I didn't think they'd ever get the casket through. After I went through there again, I realized that there was plenty of room, but that first impression!

HARRY GOULDING: That was just about the longest day's drive I ever had! And then this stuff he threw up had covered me, and I didn't have any way to change. And I hadn't eaten, I had no appetite. That old Bidághaa' Nééz had to ride with it all the way, but he didn't say a word about it. I done all the driving and it was a long trip with the truck, especially in that country; and I didn't want, you know, to hit the bumps. When I got up around Monticello I got pretty near to where I'd fall over on the wheel! Bidághaa' Nééz didn't know nothing about driving a car, leave alone a truck, so I'd tell him, "You just keep me awake. We've got to get this man in or it'll be hard for them to work with him." So he kept shaking me. We got up where there was some cold water in a little stream come out of Monticello. Everybody was in bed, and we didn't want to wake anybody up, but I always packed a bucket and chuck box in that old truck, so we got a bucket of water, and he splashed me with this cold water to keep me alive.

We finally got to Cortez, to the undertaker. We was a day and way into the night, in fact it was close to morning before we got to Cortez. I hit the old hay and give her a good working! I slept for a solid day and a night before I started back home.

We kept it quiet that a person had died in the trading post. The Navajos wouldn't have come back in there or traded at all. I could have got rid of a competition if I'd just let them know. No, we were very careful not to. The girl told them that he went out with me to do some business, and then made it up that he got sick and died out there. Oh no, they wouldn't have even looked at that store!

José Lucero Montoya y Gouldies, he got lonesome and wanted to go up and be with Charlie, so I took him out. Then, after about nine months, I wanted Mike to go out, and if she decided she didn't like it, why we'd stay out. So I took Mike out with me, and I left our tent store and a lot of merchandise in there. Bidághaa' Łibá, Grey Whiskers was his English name, he lived over pretty close to Mitchell Butte there, where we camped when we first come in. I told him that we were going to leave. We thought everything would be all right if I just tied the tent doors up and went out. I says, "I may be gone for five or six days," and he says, "Yes, that would be all right," and he just got word out, I guess, told the Navajos not to go in there. He was responsible, you know, he was watching it so nobody would go in. But there had been sickness and they'd had to have the medicine-man, so they took a sack of flour and coffee and salt and onions and potatoes, stuff like that, that they'd need for the ceremonial sing. But they brought sheep in and paid for it as soon as I got back. So by that time I guess they thought we were all right.

On that first trip we made in to Flagstaff, Mike and I, we went in to get merchandise for the store. We decided Flagstaff and Winslow had a lot better assortment of things that a Navajo would want than any place like Durango or up in there. When we got out the other side of Tuba City there was a couple of trappers in there. I could smell them. They have some awful scented stuff that they put on their bait that draws the coyotes, and they get it all over themselves too.

So we went in, and sure enough, off to the side of the road, about a mile the other side of Tuba City, there they were. They couldn't have got closer than that or Tuba City couldn't have stood it. I could smell it from the road going past. So we drove in to see them. I told them the coyotes were thick up here, killing a lot of the Indians' sheep, and that Utah was paying a bounty on coyotes. I says, "If you're in Utah and you're catching coyotes, they won't pay you your bounty unless you say you caught them coyotes across the river, north of the San Juan." They wouldn't pay bounty on anything south of the San Juan River because there were only Indians in here. "If you just say you got them around John's Canyon, Mexican Hat, or in there somewhere, then you'll get your bounty."

And so they came, by gosh! I told them what it looked like they might could do, and they decided to come out. Oh gracious, I even hesitate to say that wonderful old person's name—Bert, Bert Davis! Bert, and then he had his partner, Laverne. We got our truck loaded up in Flagstaff with everything we wanted and came on back, and they followed us in. It was wintertime so the pelts were good. They trapped all winter.

They had set camp out a ways, and finally I told Bert one day, "Heck," I says, "come on up here with us."

"Oh," he says, "our tent smells pretty bad."

"Well, take a little bit of care, and we'd like to have you in for a meal once in a while. We got plenty of water and stuff around here. Come on up and join us."

And so they did. They kept their tents out where they was mixing the bait up, but they kept theirselves clean so they could come in and eat with us.

One day Laverne came into camp packing a six- or seven-months-old lamb so they'd have some meat. Bert asked him where he got that lamb. He says he caught him in a trap. "Well, you take that lamb back, and you leave him where you got him," he says, and he made Laverne give the lamb back. When they got back over to their bait camp, he told Laverne, "Now just roll up your bedroll and everything, I'm going to take you out. You're going to leave the Valley. I'll have nothing to do with a man that'll take food away from these Indians." The car they was in belonged to Bert.

I asked him, "Where's your partner, Bert?"

"Well," he says, "I took him out. He didn't want to stay here." Finally, Bert told me one time what had happened.

That left Bert here alone, and he came up and stayed with us. He'd work for us, and then when it was trapping time, he would go to trapping. Good old Bert, he was a worker. He was honest as the day is long, and longer than that even.

Dobbie was another fella worked with us. He went to school with Charlie and me when we were kids. He was a little older than I was, but him and I would go hoboing together on our vacations—out on the freight trains with the hoboes. Francis Dobbins. You didn't ever hear his name, he was Dobbie to everybody. He came down here and was with us in the tents.

Dobbie would go up every day for a bath to that spring that we developed up in the canyon. We brought a pipe down and put some canvas around, is all it was. It was down below and we had a little pressure in there, and we had an old bucket with holes in it; that was your shower stall. Dobbie would go up every morning and have a shower.

I was sitting there with Bert one morning when Dobbie came back down from this bath, and Bert says, "Harry, I'm sure worried about that boy. He's going up there, and you know how weak you get when you take a bath?"

I says, "Yeah."

"Well," he says, "he's just going to fade away!"

Yeah, we was going to lose Dobbie.

Dobbie stayed with us for a little while, but he left while we were still in the tents, before we built the house.

We were in the tents about two and a half years. About the end of the second year, some Navajos came in and wondered when we was going to leave. Generally, if you come in to buy stock, it would take you about a month or two, three months at the most, and then you'd be gone out, but we kept staying, so they wanted to know how long we was going to be here. They said that this land around here was all theirs, all belonged to them.

There were six or eight of them. It was kind of their head men that were in there, Grey Whiskers and White Horse were there, and Hugh Black, and Old Man Tom Holiday, and Adikai Yazzie, he was bound to be there. Adikai Yazzie was an agitator. Generally in our little towns some fella makes it his business to check everybody else's business and is always talking to people. Sometimes he'll agitate a little and try to get a little trouble started or something. He was that type of a person. He was a gambler, Adikai Yazzie means Little Gambler. His hogan was right on the trail through Monument Pass, and the Navajos would stay with him and play cards with him. He got to be a pretty good card player, so he got his name, the Little Gambler. It wouldn't surprise me at all but that it was Adikai Yazzie that got that group together to come over.

They came in about ten o'clock one morning when Bert was out. It was in the winter and he was trapping. They wanted to know how long we was going to stay here. Well I didn't feel too easy about it because you could feel the atmosphere strong. There was a .38 Smith and Wesson that I carried clean through the war, it was hanging on the front post of the tent. I stepped right up beside it, I wasn't leaving it too far. A Navajo can put out an atmosphere—oh, it's like a breeze if it's nice, or it's like a terrible whirlwind when they want it to be. They have that ability whenever they want to use it. It was their land, and they had the atmosphere that they was wanting us to leave. They didn't *ask* us to leave, they just wanted to know *when* we was going to leave. They left it so that the atmosphere would tell you, if you're going to leave pretty soon, well it's all right, but don't hang around too long. We had quite a visit about it.

There was one fella, Hugh Black, 'Olta'i Nééz, they called him, Tall Schoolboy. He only went to about third grade, but he remembered enough of his school so that he could interpret just a little. We done quite a lot of talking one way another.

"I'm not going to leave," I said. "When I buy these sheep, every fall I just take them out and sell them. I ain't going to get a big herd and take all the land. I'm just going to buy this stuff off of you folks and take it out in the fall and sell it. And that'll help you."

They came down actually to try to move us out I think. Finally they asked me, "How long you going to stay?"

I didn't talk the best Navajo right then. I didn't know what the word for "hair" was, so I pointed to my hair and went over and put my hand on that white tent, and I says, "When my hair gets as white as that tent, maybe I'll go out."

They laughed at that a little bit. So then it was all fine. We shook hands. I think they seen that the bluff wasn't going to work, and that joke kind of softened the whole thing out.

It wasn't trouble, you couldn't hardly class it as trouble. But I know they had intentions to drive us out because I've had Navajos tell me since then that they were glad I didn't go. We'd buy the sheep and stock and take it out, and buy more and take it out, and that helped them. All of those fellas that were in there, they must have spread the word, because I noticed that the Navajos were a little different when they come in after that. You could notice it a week or ten days afterwards. They came in freer.

■ This visit of the Navajos, foreshadowed by the earlier visit of the single blanket-robed Navajo to Harry's tent, had been prepared and somewhat tempered by the Wetherills' experience. It was not until John Wetherill came to Oljeto in 1906, with his quiet Quaker ways, that these fierce Hoskinini Navajos of the Paiute Strip allowed a trader to settle in their midst. Everyone the Wetherill party encountered on their long and arduous journey from Mancos to Oljeto warned them against the Hoskinini Navajos. When they arrived, Wetherill sent his brother-in-law, John Wade, back to pick up Clyde Colville, who was guarding part of their supplies on the trail. Confronting the Navajos alone at Oljeto, he met a stronger version of the same kind of resistance that Harry did. But after a rabbit hunt and feast, with flour, sugar and coffee provided by Wetherill, and after a long day of discussion and debate, Hoskinini Begay, the son of Hoskinini, told them they could stay.[6]

HARRY GOULDING: I got friendly with White Horse after that. Sometimes he'd come down and tell me about how he kept everybody off his place up on Douglas Mesa. He got a big kick out of it. He kept the Paiutes off of Douglas Mesa even when it was Paiute reservation, and he kept it after the Paiutes left. The Navajo families all had areas where they stayed and where they ranged their sheep. It was just a gentleman's understanding that they worked out. But he had more range than any of them, he had quite a lot of stock, and I'm sure that nobody ever got up there. He'd take his rifle and put them off, even the cattle people that would come down in the winter. Some of the Navajos said he shot at them sometimes; they knew if they'd come any further, why it'd be their necks. No, he was a tough old buzzard. That was his land, Douglas Mesa; his family and him is all that was up there.

I went up to look and see. He'd buy quite a little bit of stuff at the trading post, he had a good-sized family, and I'd just load it up and take it over for him. There was nobody else on there at all. He was a tough character.

Hosteen Cly was a saddle maker. He made squaw and buck saddles, made them out of, oh, generally it was cedar. Cedar grows sometimes in kind of odd shapes, and whenever I'd see anything that would fit a part of one of the saddles, I'd pick it up and bring it in to the old fella, and he always appreciated it very much. He was a very good saddle maker. When they had a trade of that kind and were getting along in years, you can bet that he knew just what he was doing, because he'd done it ever since he was young. I'd run into quite a few of them saddles of his, traveling around.

A man sells those saddles to different Indians and he meets a lot of people and they talk about different things. He gets more of a chance of an education than the ordinary person. Hosteen Cly accumulated a lot of ideas by visiting back and forth with everybody, and he'd kind of cut them apart and string them out and he'd come out with some pretty good ideas of his own. He naturally worked his way to where the Navajos listened to him; all the people in the area listened to old Hosteen Cly. Generally in every little section there will be some fella that is more outstanding.

Old Hosteen Cly lived probably ten years after I got to know him. The Clys were down in Tsé Bighi', all of that area down in around there. His grave is in the North Window. As you go into the Window, you drag in there, and then the Valley's all spread out to look at. Right in there is where he's buried. They always put branches or logs or rocks over the top of a grave so's the animals won't scratch and go in, because they never had coffins or anything. They're buried in their robe. His horse and some stock is buried with him. There was an old-style saddle there, because he was a saddle maker. And a coffee pot; the coffee pot was a nice new pot, and they'd break it, knock in the head, just like they did to the horse. The saddle is cut up. When they break those things, it kills them and they go with him to his happy hunting ground. He's all fixed up there. Got his horse and a few sheep and a cow or two, and they can breed. He'll be well off down there like he was up here.

■   The Navajos' traditional treatment of burial is dictated by their image of the underworld and by their unmitigated terror of ghosts. In their view, man is a mixture of good and evil, and at death these two spirits or energies separate. The good energy transcends all human individuality and identity, and leaves the body as the breath leaves the body, diffusing into the harmony of nature. The evil energy the Navajos call ch'įįdii has been translated as "ghost" or "the contamination of the dead." This ch'įįdii lives on in an underworld of the dead.

After death, the ghosts of the dead return, and bring with them a dreadful power of evil. Traditionally, if a Navajo is near death, he is removed from the hogan and placed outside to die. If he dies inside, a hole is broken through the north wall of the ch'įįdii hogan to allow the ghost access to the underworld, and the hogan is abandoned forever.

The dead are buried, as was Hosteen Cly, with all their wealth and provisions for a good afterlife to placate their ghosts, for their ghosts will surely return, bent on the revenge of wrongs done them in life, or in search of things omitted from the burial. To match the four-day journey to the underworld, there are four days of mourning and purification, after which all mourning for the dead is suppressed.[7]

HARRY GOULDING: I had Big Boy and Little Boy here and we were learning Navajo. We kept wanting to learn not just what the things were in the store but we was more anxious to get the things they talked about and get to visit with them more.

It just kept getting better all the time. They had evidently made up their mind that day when they came to talk to me at the tent, and it was a little different after that. You could feel a friendlier atmosphere they tracked with them.

MIKE GOULDING: We'd go over probably once a month and pick up the mail, after we got it moved over to Kayenta. First we got our mail in Bluff, because Harry was going out that way to get loads of flour and stuff, but finally we moved it over to Kayenta. If everything rolled along all right and we had a gallon of gas, we'd go and get the mail. And then of course Keith Warren was postmaster, and if anybody was coming over our way, why he'd send it to us. I'd usually get several letters from mother at once wondering where in the world was her child. [Laughs.] I was almost afraid to tell her, you know, because she worried.

■   Elizabeth Hegemann, then married to Mike Harrison of the National Park Service at Grand Canyon, recounts the reservation gossip of those days about the Gouldings, some of it accurate, some of it not:

"Where Gouldings is now, there was nothing. Keith Warren knew that a young couple from Bluff were running sheep over the Utah line near the northern part of Monument Valley. He kept their mail for them for weeks at a time until they could drive in for it as well as groceries and household items. The Navvy trade in the store kept Warren informed as to how many sheep were in their flock and at what place they were watering, and in due time relayed the news that the young fellow was doing a little trading from his tent. Just staples like flour, coffee, salt, and sugar in exchange for goatskins, rugs, or a few stray coins. Apparently he did not need a permit as he was over the Arizona state line, on land which Navahos claimed but about which there was some question. They lived in their tents and moved with the flock. Once a hardy tourist who had come down via Bluff told Warren that in the midst of that desolation he had been stopped by the sight of an angelic figure with long blonde hair running down the side of a sand dune, waving something in one hand. This was "Mike" Goulding, the wife of Harry, and she had a note for Warren to please send up their mail by the next car going through as they were camped near the road for the next week. These are the same Harry Gouldings who now live amid their de luxe guest accommodations on their section, more or less, of patented land."[8]

MIKE GOULDING: We went down to Oljeto to see the Taylors when they moved in there. Johnny and his family didn't move in until I think it was some time in January 1926. Mr. Heffernan died just after we got here, and then there wasn't anybody for a few months, until the Taylors moved in. We had real nice times together, they were a lovely family. They'd come up and see us and we'd go down and see them. They had a house, such as it was. [Laughs.] They had to do a lot to it. There were only two rooms and then this little tiny store. The store is still the same as it was then, but they either added onto it or built a whole new room, I can't remember. And they fixed their living room.

We had a social life with the Navajos. It wasn't long before we could talk with them. You can pick it up pretty quick if you're out here with them, if there's nothing else to hear. They didn't sneeze in English. [Laughs.] Leon Bradley was the only one in here that spoke English at that time.

My brother Chet and Lois came out to see us and show us their little yearling daughter, the cutest little thing. They had to see where ol' sissy lived. They were all very interested to know what in the world was taking place out here. And they all liked it. They thought it was pretty lonesome, maybe, but I never was lonesome. Harry was with me all day, unless he had to go get a load of flour or something. He'd leave about four o'clock in the morning so's he'd be back by night. Hard trips. He'd go up to Blanding, that's where the flour mill was, Black's flour mill.

I didn't leave the Valley then for, well, it was almost a year. Went to Kayenta, went after the mail, went on trips out to the hogans to see the people; but my first trip out, it was just about a year, when we went to Flagstaff and brought Bert back with us. I didn't like Snake Canyon, so I avoided any trips that-a-way, and this was Harry's first trip out the other way.

HARRY GOULDING: Folks by the name of Spencer had the trading post at Mexican Hat when we first came in here, an older couple. Then Cord Bowen came down and bought it from him, and Hazel Bowen, Cord Bowen's daughter, was the first company that Mike really had, those little visits with Hazel. Mike put all of her time in trading. She enjoyed that very much. It was long days. When I'd be gone, old José would stay here with her. Then Bert came along, and Bert would stay with Mike while I was gone. So she didn't have real company, not like having another woman, for quite a long time. If she hadn't come down and gritted her teeth and stuck, why I wouldn't have been here. She should get more credit, really, than I do, because she was loyal.

Only one time did I ever see Mike a little bit put out. When we moved down, we had a nice little rocking chair that we took down with us; I poured it in because I knew Mike would enjoy it. One of the squaws came in one day and she had this pretty little blanket on her saddle, so Mike made a deal with her on it, traded her some stuff out of the store, and that was laying over this rocker—decorated and ornamented it up, and softened it too, just like it softened the saddles for them when they was riding. About three or four days after that, why some seam squirrels showed up. Lice. Those oldtimers back yonder, they had nothing to stop that sort of a thing. They didn't have enough water, they just couldn't afford to use it. That all had to go for stock, and then they left a lot of it for the coyotes and other animals, too. They recognize them. Well, that's the only time I ever saw Mike get put out. I was afraid there for a while I was going to have to hide her shoes, she only had that one pair. She come undone on that a little bit, but not too terribly. My gosh, you couldn't blame her. No sir, she was a terrific person. In that day and age women just wasn't going for that kind of life.

MIKE GOULDING: Later on, I hadn't thought about it, but Keith Warren and his wife came over from Kayenta to see us in the tent, and they said, "Do you remember when we brought Hazel over to see you and you hadn't seen a white woman for eleven months?" Then I did remember. But I was so busy, there were a lot of things to do.

HAZEL BOWEN LYMAN (friend of the Gouldings, Blanding, Utah):   Harry and Mike used to go by my dad's trading post, and they'd stop and eat with us, stay with us, and Mike and I became real good friends. I used to go over there and stay with them when they were in the tents, before I was married. It was pretty primitive in the tents at first, but Mike always seemed happy.

They didn't have well water, the water was carried from a spring. I don't know how she managed to wash, I didn't happen to ever be there on wash day. It was a pretty rough life. She traded with the Navajos just the way Harry did. She learned their language, knows it real well, it seems to me.

LYNN LYMAN (Hazel Bowen Lyman's husband):   They had a phonograph there in the tent. I remember some of the records they used to play—"Oh, Them Golden Slippers" and "Roving Gambler." It seems like that was the kind of music that Harry liked. Those two tunes I remember in particular.

3 ▬ Building the Trading Post

HARRY GOULDING: When we came down, we were new to the country, and we didn't want to make a mistake and put a building in the wrong spot, so we decided to put in tents and use them for a couple of years, and then we could look it all over. It just happened that it was such a nice spot up in here where we had already found a little spring water. We were trying to find a nicer place all the time, of course, but I checked this area all over and hadn't found any place that was nicer than right where we were. There's a terrific view from this bench in here that we built on, and the cliff going up in back was a windbreaker; that took care of the wind. All the winds go down through the Gap there, through Rock Door Canyon. We'd come up from the tents a lot of times in the evening and just sit up here on the bench and look across into Monument Pass there.

When I got to looking into it, it turned out that we were sitting on a school section, and that meant you could buy the whole section, you could bid on it, instead of just homesteading a few acres, like them allotments.

Nobody up in Salt Lake knew about this country down here at all, not a thing about it. They didn't know what I was talking about or who I was. So I had quite a time to get this school section put up for bid. J. Bracken Lee was later the governor of Utah, and he helped me an awful lot. I first met Governor Lee before I was in Monument Valley, when I was buying sheep and one thing another. I was always doing business up at Salt Lake then. He took the red side out of the ledger when he was mayor of the town of Price up there. Oh he was a toughie. And he went to battle with the Tax Commission, paid all of his taxes under protest. He was a bear-cat, that fella! He was a tiger! I think he had two tails![1]

Well he was a big lift to me, because he'd get hold of the heads of the Southern Utah Organization. They blew a lot of smoke. They were a good bunch, and they tied together. When they went after anything they just pretty near got what they was after. So I was a long time getting it put up for sale because nobody was interested in it and they didn't know what it was up there.

▬   After the Homestead Act became law in 1862, federal public land was made available in 160-acre allotments to settlers who would occupy and improve them as homesteads, thus regularizing a chaotic legal situation. From colonial times, however, land had been set aside for the support of public schools. Beginning under the Confederation, Section 16 of every township was designated a "school section," to be used for this purpose. Later, new states entering the Union were required to follow the same policy. Additional sections were subsequently added, until, in the case of Arizona, New Mexico, and Utah, the federal government granted sections 2, 16, 32, and 36 in every township to the new states to be set aside as school sections, the income from these sections to be used for the public schools.[2]

According to Donald Adams, a lawyer in Montecello, Utah, and a friend of Harry's who represented him in this matter, Harry was leasing the school section he occupied from the state of Utah. The state could also sell school sections if they were first listed for sale and advertised, and then they were to be sold to the highest bidder. Harry asked several times that the land be sold, and it was advertised, and he bid on it, but the state did not choose to sell it.[3] Meanwhile, the Paiute Strip was finally added to the Navajo reservation in 1933, although the state of Utah continued to hold the school sections, along with the right to sell them.

Finally, in 1937, Harry insisted on a sale, and the state sold it to him, even over the protest of the Indian Service. On November 4, Donald Adams met with the State Land Board at Monticello. According to the minutes of this meeting, "Mr. Adams called attention to activities of Civic Clubs and private citizens as shown by correspondence in our office endorsing the application of Mr. Goulding to purchase this land," and it was agreed that the land be appraised and advertised for sale. On January 21, 1938, the appraisal was accepted, bids were let, and the sale date was set for April 20.[4] Harry's "Application to Purchase State Lands at Public Sale" was signed on April 20, 1938. On the same day, E. R. Fryer, superintendent of the Navajo Agency, sent a telegram to the State Land Board in Monticello: "Suggest proposed land sale today, Section 36, township 43, south range 15 east, be withheld from sale pending negotiation by Government to purchase the tract. This land is within boundary of Navajo Reservation. Wire your decision collect." The executive secretary of the Land Board replied that "the request came so near the hour of sale that it was impossible to present it to the Board for consideration,"[5] and the sale was completed.[6]

According to a map supplied by the Utah Division of State Lands and Forestry, there are several other pieces of privately held land in the Paiute Strip, including but not confined to school sections.[7] At an earlier time, both Lorenzo Hubbell and Anson Damon on the Navajo reservation, and Thomas V. Keam on the Hopi reservation, succeeded in retaining their land after the reservation boundaries were expanded to surround them, in Hubbell's case with considerable difficulty extending over a period of thirty-seven years.[8]

HARRY GOULDING: Bert had worked over in what he called Utah Dixie, southwestern Utah, where he came from, and he was good at rough work, he was a carpenter, anything like that he could do. You talk about an old boy from way back in the hills, that was him. We were sure that he would be awful good help to put up a building after we'd made up our mind what we were going to do.

Then there was Bidághaa' Nééz, old Long Whiskers, panning for gold. He'd come up by the place here sometimes and get some provisions to keep him working in there, but Oljeto was closer to him; he wouldn't have to walk so far. He had an old horse, too, that he rode in on, a horse and an old mule, and when he come up here we visited with him.

"I'm afraid I'm not going to make it," he says, "I'm getting awful short on money." He was kind of trying to get me in shape to grubstake him.

I told him we were going to put up a trading post. It was about a year after we'd come in, and we'd pretty near made up our minds to put it up here.

He says, "California, they're doing a new type of plastering. All their homes now is going in with this new wrinkle on it. If you want to put up your trading post," he says, "I'm pretty handy around that plaster." He built fireplaces too. "You're going to need a fireplace upstairs, ain't you? Well, I can sure fix them! I'm just getting to where I've got to give up out there, and I could use the money."

"Well," I says, "We're about ready to make up our minds. There's one or two places yet I want to go and look at. That's all that's left."

So we finally decided that we wanted to put it right here. We built a little rock cabin, Bert did, up on the bench beside where the trading post was going to be, and we had that to stay in while we was building the trading post. Mike could cook better in there than in the tents. So we moved in there, and Bert stayed down at the tents. And Bert built that cellar behind the trading post. We used it for winter protection for the potatoes, we had to have quite a lot of spuds in here to go through a winter. So those two were both finished before the trading post.

Then I went down where the old fella was panning for gold on the San Juan. I says, "We've had Bert cutting rocks, and the Navajos, and we don't have that done, but there's a lot of work around there that I imagine you could do. We could put you on right away."

"Well, I've got to leave here," he says.

Bert and the Indians that was working with him, I told them we were going to put in two stories. Most of them Indians hadn't even seen a two-story building. They wondered how that could be done. I told them that we wanted the rocks really flat, top and bottom, so's they'd stick together, "But you don't have to do anything with the other two sides, just the two sides flat will be enough." But the next day they went ahead cutting all four sides,

Harry and Mike Goulding in front of their rock cabin, where they lived briefly while building the trading post. Fall 1927. (Goulding's Monument Valley Museum)

all square. And I said again that two was enough, but they said, "Oh no, why they got to be strong!" And that's how come they were cut so well.

If you'll notice up on that cliff there behind the trading post, there was some big old rocks come down and they landed out here in front of the cellar, right handy. So Bert, he was terrific with powder, he could set his powder so it would cut the things out. The biggest part of it came out of those two rocks that was right there, in fact all of it did.

MIKE GOULDING: When we put the cornerstone in, we broke a bottle of water over it. It wasn't champagne, but it was champagne to us!

HARRY GOULDING: We started working in the fall of the year, 1927; it was pretty well through fall into the winter. Then spring came and the rains started to come. Our tents were down on the flat, down there by the corrals, right behind this cliff, Old Baldy; and every time it'd rain, the rains came right over that big old high cliff up there, they came right from Oljeto direction, and we couldn't hear the thunder until it was pretty close. Then it'd come awhooping over and we'd hear it, a clash of thunder, and every-body'd run for the tent. We had to get down there and get everything covered up with tarps or those yard goods would run together, and the Navajos wouldn't have touched them. It just really was a mess. You put your tarps on, you're going to break a glass or two or something, because them old tarps were long and we didn't have enough men sometimes to control them. We had storms, we'd have to stop work and run for our tarps and get them in there. Everybody would have to go down and get them things covered up.

We worked on it all that summer and about halfway through the next winter. Bert could lay a nice wall, so he laid all of the walls in, and the Navajos was packing the mud up. We got that red clay, there was patches of it. When you get into that real old heavy red stuff, it's pretty near as good as concrete for mortar. It was a long time before it wore in enough for us to get cement mortar, I don't know, two or three years. The rains would hit it on the Oljeto side. The other sides it was longer than that, but every once in a while part of the building would clear out and we'd finish it up with a little cement mortar, and of course then there's no more washing in. Bi-dághaa' Nééz really done a beautiful job on that fireplace, he fixed a good draft, and when we got the building up, the old fella plastered it for us and got it all fixed up.

When I paid the Navajos off I gave them extra for cutting those sides all square because they looked so nice for doing that. They thought it was a beautiful building. They talked about it all over the place. And a lot of Indians, every now and then while we was building it, would ride by and come in and look at it.

So we got it all finished and it was fine. Winter had come again, and Bert was ready to go back to trapping, and Bidághaa' Nééz had plenty of money to get on his way.

FRED YAZZIE (Monument Valley):   Harry Goulding, he know it was a

Goulding's Trading Post, its two-story structure unique in local Navajo experience, bull pen and wareroom below, living quarters above. The outdoor stairway, second-story porch, and rail fence were added by John Ford for use as a movie set. (McLaughlin Historical Photo)

school section, and the state is holding the school section, see? He know all about it. So he talk to the Mormon, they put tape in there, you know, they had stake and line, they put these four posts, every corner. Anybody take it out, it cost two hundred, two hundred fifty dollar if anybody pull out. They're still here. I seen one right the other side of my home. That's Harry Goulding, he find the right place. Well, these old Navajo, my father, Adikai Yazzie, they find these places, you know, they think it's their land, they the first Navajos in here. My old daddy, he pick this place, and White Horse, he pick Douglas Mesa, all over that country, and then he think it's his. Old Adikai, he took Cane Valley. And someone else, he take the low country, way down to Mexican Hat, he think it's his, see, his country.

Nowadays his kids living there, and we living here. Well, I think to myself, I still taking care of this land. I been here for maybe sixty years. My old daddy, he pick this country, and I live here for about sixty years, and I know this country pretty well. I used to run horse here, and the trouble with Harry

Goulding, I know all about that.[9] I'm trying to hold this land no matter what moving in here, and some day they might pay me something for this land. That's the way I think sometime, you know, but other time I don't think so. The government getting way ahead. But my country is here, see, I live here, I live here a long time. That's the way it is these days.

These old people, like Adikai and Adikai Yazzie, my old daddy, they know that the country is rich. Old Adikai's place, Cane Valley, they have uranium in that place, they still holding that land. And my old daddy, he hold this land, he going make money. Well, old Adikai, they took everything from there, you know, took all the uranium, make big hole in there, nothing left, took all the money, there's nothing left there. My country, I still have that in mind, but I'm really happy about it, to be on my own land, even if I don't get no money. Because my old daddy, he got the right country, he knows it.

HARRY GOULDING: I know what Fred Yazzie thinks about this land. Just the same as when those old Navajos came over to the tent in the early days. As I got to knowing Adikai Yazzie more, why I could tell him about it. Or Hugh Black would be in and while he was there I'd get Hugh to translate it and let him know I wasn't on his land. But he was the closest Indian to our place, so he naturally thought that it was his. I knew it was a school section, though, and that we were going to buy it. After we'd had our talk at the tent and after Hugh Black had interpreted two or three times, why then he did become friendly. But that's one thing the Navajo has acquired is a memory, they have terrific memories. Fred could very well feel that it's his land, but he has never said anything about it at all.

Adikai Yazzie had an allotment up near Eagle Mesa. After the Paiutes went away and then for a few years there, it was open as public land, and at that time they could go out and take an allotment. That meant they had title to that land. Adikai Yazzie did that, I know he did. But he could not ever have done it on a school section. I think it was 160 acres, and that would be right up in around where his little bit of water was. It didn't come over to our section, not even close to it: 160 acres would just look like a speck out there.

■   The Navajos live a seminomadic life of sheepherding. Reservation land is owned in a legal sense by the tribe and not by individuals, and a family's range is defined in a practical way, by use and mutual agreement with one's neighbors.[10] It was no doubt on this basis that Adikai Yazzie objected to Harry's occupation of his school section. Harry was operating on the basis of white law, Adikai Yazzie on the basis of Navajo tradition.

HARRY GOULDING: And then of course Hugh Black, he kind of figured a little bit that he had an interest in this area where our place is, too, until he found out what it was. I got a map out and showed him exactly where these school sections were and that they didn't belong to the Navajos, they belonged to the State of Utah, they were school sections. We had a little friction over it, but it didn't amount to much.

Adikai pretty near had to accept it because Hugh Black had been to school and he had heard about those things. I could talk to him and it didn't go anywhere like with Adikai Yazzie. It took quite awhile for him to even start to thinking the other way. But of course after I explained it, why they would talk to some of the Navajos that were on allotments up around Blanding and around there and find out if that was the way it was done. They found out that it was, and it settled down a lot.

JULIA HOLIDAY (Fred Yazzie's sister, translated from Navajo):   My husband, Jake Charlie Holiday, helped build the house. After it was finished, he dug a trench so the water would run to the new house. Later, Dibé Nééz dug a well and there was plenty of water for the sheep to drink. Where the road to Tségizh branches off to Oljeto, he made a water trough. He made that for us, for our sheep, and it is still the same today.

4 ■■ THE BULL PEN

HARRY GOULDING: When we moved out of the tents up into the trading post, we was just crazy to see it rain, just to go out and laugh at it, because we wouldn't have to run for the tarpaulins. We was waiting to see when them big rollers would come over and we'd get to say, "Mister rain, we've got you hooked this time!" Well, it was just a year and five days that there was not a drop of water hit the roof of that store! We had to wait that long before we got our laugh. That was a mean year. The Navajos lost probably fifteen percent of their stock. Then we had a good one, and we got a laugh at it. When we get those flash floods, the headwaters come down, they're ugly, and they pack all that debris and foam. That day, we got in the wash there in front of the trading post, crazy nuts, wrap our pants up, Mike with us, the women wore overalls pretty near all the time, and we off and down, and we outrun it. Then we'd get back and we'd take off again and we'd holler. We had a time! The Indians thought we was crazy.

MIKE GOULDING: It was handy living upstairs over the store, because if I had to fix food for people and Harry and Maurice were gone on a trip, why I could pop down and take care of my trading and go back upstairs. I bought whatever the Navajos brought in, or took in pawn, just regular trading. And we had sheep to take care of at first.

MAURICE KNEE: When they built the trading post, there was a little drip of water up behind the building, right up in the shear, up in the V. They built a big cistern, collected water at a fast drip. It filled the cistern and it come down, and we had water in the tap. We didn't waste water. Just above the cistern there was a little tunnel. That's where the water come from, back in that tunnel. Had a little chicken-wire door to keep the varmints out. That's where we kept our butter. I invariably would go upstairs and sit down to eat, and Mike would say, "Maurice, the butter." I could get up that trail, clear around, open the door, get the butter, and run back down in five minutes. Take me an hour to walk up there now.

HARRY GOULDING: A trading post is where the Navajos gather, and everything spreads from there, all the news and gossip. If they get some news that's interesting, on their way home they stop at a couple of hogans. He sits on his horse just a little while and talks. Then he gets off his horse. If he's got something to tell, he's welcome, because they want to hear it too. Often he gets some coffee, maybe a little biscuit.

They liked to get their horses early, the Navajos in those days, and get in to the trading post and get loaded. We'd generally have two or three of them that would be in in the morning, early. They want to get their trading done and get back before the afternoon heat if they can. And then some of them would come in and trade in the evening. We'd be up before sunup always and be ready to go. And the ones that come in late, they want to trade so as to get out early the next morning, so the trading post was always open till after sundown. They were trading to try and get going in the morning, but, well, there's always something they forgot, and they'd come in and do a little trading in the morning and then get arolling. By the time they got done, our local group would start coming in. Your closer Indians could come in almost any time of day, and the real close ones would come up a lot of times in the evening just to visit, because there was always a holdover of the ones that had come in from farther out, and they could visit with those fellas and get the news.

There was never a day we closed. We were open seven days a week. I think there was a regulation that the trading posts had to close on weekends, but we weren't regulated because we were on deeded land. We were busy all the time. It didn't make any difference to the Navajos. They didn't know what Sunday was until they got in to the trading post.

We had a hogan for them to stay overnight, just down off the hill, between the corral and the trading post. They stayed around the camp there, fixed a campfire, and we'd usually give them a coffee pot. The mother, if she came, she'd bring her littlest one, or maybe the two littlest ones, and the rest would stay home.

For years there, you could hear them coming in to the trading post from way down on the flat, if they was in a wagon or on horseback. They sang a lot on the horses when they come in. That's the way they trained their voices. There isn't a Navajo around the Valley here yet that can't chant. Their voices are terrific, control of their voice and everything. They'd come in singing those chants. It would reverberate into the cliff back of the trading post. It was in the early morning when it would impress you. Or in the evening we'd set out in front, and there'd be an old Navajo coming in across the desert. He'll stay all night, and then do his trading in the morning. He'll hobble up his horse and come on up and shake hands and talk a while.

They had a special chant that they sang while they were riding. It's a beautiful chant, just beautiful, especially where you get it from an old Navajo. And then, boom, it echoes back in the rock, and there she is again, it's coming and going. That big old cliff back in there carried the echo right back to us. It changes. It goes along, and then all at once a high, beautiful note, where most people can't go, chanting down low a little bit and then all at once away up she goes. And do it so perfect!

SHONIE HOLIDAY (son of Hosteen Tso, Oljeta, translated from Navajo):

> This girl does a fancy rope trick
> This girl does a fancy rope trick
>
> She learned it from Man-Leading-a-Horse
> She learned it from Man-Leading-a-Horse
>
> She whistles at the horse neatly
> She whistles at the horse neatly
>
> She likes walking the horse
>
> She whistles at the horse neatly
> She whistles at the horse neatly
>
> She learned it from Man-Leading-a-Horse
> She learned it from Man-Leading-a-Horse
>
> This girl does a fancy rope trick
> This girl does a fancy rope trick
>
> She whistles at the horse neatly
> She whistles at the horse neatly

HARRY GOULDING: Then that stops, that winds up, it's the end of that version. They'll come riding on and everything's quiet for maybe five minutes or ten. Then all at once he starts out again, another part.

SHONIE HOLIDAY:

> The girl from Where-Horses-Are-Taken-Out
> whistles at the horse nicely.
> The Girl from Where-Horses-Are-Taken-Out
> whistles at the horse nicely.
>
> Yoo shi yoo shi, yoo shi yoo shi
> Yo shi na ya, shi na aa ya
> Ya a wei ya hei
>
> The girl from Where-Horses-Are-Taken-Out
> whistles at the horse nicely.
> The girl from Where-Horses-Are-Taken-Out
> whistles at the horse nicely.
>
> Yoo shi yoo shi, yoo shi yoo shi
> Yo shi na ya, shi na aa ya
> Ya a wei ya hei[1]

HARRY GOULDING: There's about three parts to it. Then he'll start over and repeat it, and he's still quite a ways out. Before he gets in, he'll go over the whole chant again. Heck, I used to even sing it, try it sometimes. When I was riding I loved to sing. And oh, I could put it out! It's a great loss to the country here for the fact that they don't come in singing like they used to. Nobody will ever know that didn't hear it.

■   Helen Roberts describes the Navajo singing style as follows: "A falsetto . . . together with rapid, pulsing, bounding movement, and restless, beautiful melodies with predominant major triad intervals, may be said to characterize many Navaho tunes. In the most beautiful style (which may be heard in the songs of the Yeibichai ceremony), . . . these particular Navaho melodies tend to employ even wider intervals than Plains tunes, displaying almost acrobatic feats in bounding back and forth between octaves, while the continual downtrend, so conspicuous in the Plains, is here counteracted by the bold upward leaps. Falsetto, prominent in Navaho music, is rather rare in American Indian music as a whole."[2]

HARRY GOULDING: In the morning they'd come in and shake hands all around and then come over and shake hands with any of us that was trading. Then they'd sit down, and I'd back off and sit down behind the counter. The trading posts had high counters, and the floors behind the counters were high. The floor in the middle, in front of the counters was lower. It was called the bull pen.[3] It was kind of a protection in the early days. You had a little advantage if there was any trouble. I suppose that's why they started it. We had a bench inside and outside, and a lot of them sat on the floor. If there wasn't enough of benches, sit on the floor, that didn't mean nothing to them.

They'd come in, maybe four or five of them. One of them would buy a little bit of something, a can of tomatoes, and another one a can of peaches, and then they'd get down there in a circle. The Navajos love canned tomatoes, eat them right out of the can. When they'd come in the store, that was their snack, a can of tomatoes. And of course the sugar was in a bin, and you had a scoop, and you'd put some sugar on the tomatoes for them. That and crackers, that was their lunch. I can understand how hungry they must have been for something fresh. It wasn't fresh, but it was the vitamin C. They probably needed it.

They'd pass them cans around; one spoon goes with it and you get your turn. I tried hard to break that up because it was the best way in the world to carry germs or fevers, but it was hard to break it. I told them that if one of them was sick, the others would get sick with his meal, the same stuff that he's sick with. But they didn't have spoons of their own. It would take them quite a while to visit and eat, to finish up everything in the cans. And then of course, the more of them there was, that spoon took a lot more time, more visiting. Nobody hurried.

The bull pen, Maurice Knee trading over some pawn and joking with Happy Cly.
The Navajos, from left to right, are Willie Cly, Suzie Yazzie, Happy Cly (Willie Cly's
wife), and Frieda Cly (their daughter). Suzie Yazzie has a baby in a cradleboard. (Jim
Orem, Goulding's Monument Valley Museum)

Then one of them would get up and start trading. The rest would go over
and sit down a while. When that fella got done, another one would get up
and come over and trade. If there was two traders there, two of them would
get up.

He'd probably owe something, had something in pawn. Generally the first
thing he'd do is take his pawn out. Then he'd know what he had left.
Whatever he brought with him to trade, maybe it was a blanket, he'd pull
it out of a sack, or maybe just a few skins, or whatever it was, he'd lay it on
the counter. We used to weigh them. They know pretty well what they're
going to get or they won't sell.

They're traders. Listen, you talk about sharp. They're shrewd, shrewd
traders. You don't take an Indian too much. If what he brought in was
enough to take his pawn out, or if he wanted to pay a little on his pawn,
he'd do that first. He'd always ask how much his pawn was in for. He knew
very well what it was, but in case we'd made a mistake and got it down
wrong.

Then he'd say he'd buy some coffee. Well, you'd get that coffee, and you'd always tell him how much money was left. Every time, *"Díkwíí dzih?"* he'd say. "How much is left?" Then he'd want something else, and you'd do that.

Finally, he'd get to where he had to think pretty good, so then another one would come up, and while the first one was thinking, he'd display what he had to sell. As soon as I'd tell this fella how much whatever he had was worth, he'd take his pawn out. Then he'd kind of hesitate and give his friend a chance, and I'd say to the first one, *"Ha'at'ííshą' nínízin?"* "What do you want now?"

He'd have his mind made up, and maybe he'd order a couple of things. But each time, you'd tell him how much was left, and then he'd buy the next thing. Then he'd hesitate again and you could go back to the other fella. When the first fella was done, then another Navvy would get up and stand there and wait. It generally proceeds something on that order.

The last thing they always bought was some candy. They'd whittle it down to where they could take a little stuff home for the kids, either fruits or candy or pop. The kids loved pop. It used to be red or yellow. You couldn't sell Pepsi or Coke, nothing but just red or yellow, strawberry or orange. For years we didn't bring in nothing but those two colors.

■   In making their trades the Navajos used their resources in a fixed order, going from the most expendable to the least expendable, trading at each step along the way, and not using any more resources than necessary. Adams provides a description of the Navajo trading habits at Shonto in the 1950s that is very close to Harry's experience as he describes it here. First they would trade any hides they had, then blankets or wool; then they would use whatever cash they had on hand; and finally, if necessary, they would pawn. They made their purchases in the same way, beginning with necessities such as flour or coffee, being careful at each step not to go beyond their resources, and ending with a bottle of pop.[4]

HARRY GOULDING: If he got something out of pawn, he'd take it home with him. Then he'd bring it back next time, maybe a bracelet or a silver bridle or a belt. If he figured he was going to do quite a little bit of trading, he'd generally have a concho belt or one of those silver bridles, and he'd trade what he wanted. Then he'd come back in later and trade some more on it. Then maybe he'd come in and pay a little on it. We kept the pawn over a year, and lots of times way longer than that. If they wanted you to take care of it, why that's the way they'd do it, because it was safer here than anywhere else. They'd pay a bit and charge a bit, and it just lived here until there was a sing come along and they wanted to wear it. Then they'd come in and pay it off. We had a lot of stuff that was in here year in and year out that way. If they didn't pay anything on it, you'd start dinging on them in about a year. "What're you going to do about it?" If they wanted it, they'd bring in a rug or some wool.

You have to decide how much to loan them on their pawn; you've got to know the value of the thing. If you gave their pawn the value it actually had, they might leave it with you. What you could buy it wholesale for, is how I learned anyway, what it was worth. When the salesmen, which were far between in those days, when one did come in, you'd learn what was what. On certain pieces you can go away over what it's worth, because it's an old piece that's been carried down through and they've had it for years. If it's that kind of a thing, well just let them go. I would give them more on that than I could probably get out of it, but they'd always take it out, they never failed to take it out. Maybe I'd give them a little more or a little less than they were thinking, but they've got you figured out too. And they know what the other traders are doing. You ain't the only one that's figuring all the time. They just about know what they're going to get.

But you don't ever give them more than they can afford to pay back. If you do that, you've lost a customer. It used to be I had Indians in here, you had to know what they had, how many sheep and how much wool you would get off of them and lambs and so forth. If you get them so far over the top that they just can't cut the mustard, "*Doo sohdííl' íil da.* You can't stand that," I'd say. That was a new word I brought in one time. When I was in Gallup I'd hear the Navajos over there. "You can't stand that." But they took care of their credit, they didn't abuse it. They're naturally honest when you know them and they know you and you trade with them. They didn't mean to beat you and generally wouldn't. Every Indian in this Valley had credit with us. You just had to be careful not to overlook it and go clean over his head.[5]

RAY HUNT: They would come upstairs when they had things to discuss with Harry, and a lot of times he would call me in to listen to the conversation. It would be like if someone in the family was not feeling well and they were going to have a sing and needed extra groceries and supplies. I'd say, "It's your business." He'd say, "Well, don't you think he's sincere about it?" and I'd say, "Yes, I do." And that's all it took. Even if I'd have said no, Harry would have gone ahead his own way, because he already knew the Indians a lot better than I did.

Harry did a lot of credit, a lot of bookwork with them. They'd say, "I'll pay you when I shear my sheep or when I sell my lambs." They only had two paydays really, two paydays a year: in the fall when they sold their lambs and in the spring when they sheared their sheep. Them that didn't have too good a credit would come in and pawn, which made it a lot better.

HARRY GOULDING: When they was through trading, they had these bags that they'd pack their stuff into. They'd buy these seamless bags, is what they sold as. They were made of good quality and bigger than a potato sack.

They could hang clean over the horse and spread the weight out; you wouldn't set it just in one spot. It was easier on the horse to do that.

Men done most all of the trading. Once in a while a woman would bring something in but not too often. And sometimes they'd come in the wagon and bring the whole family; then they'd kind of do it together. They'd talk things over and see what they wanted and decide. If one of them come up with something that was superior to the other one's decision, why if it was her that had the better idea, they'd accept that. And vice versa. They listened to each other. They weighed things up. A lot of people think that the squaws have to bend down to the men, but that's not true. Or some of them say that the woman owned all the sheep. Well that's not true either.

There might be three or four staying in the hogan overnight; they'd be men, always. If the women came in, we'd put them in that little shed off the kitchen where we washed things. Strange men and strange women would not sleep in the same hogan together.

MIKE GOULDING: Oh, it was lots of fun to trade with them. That's why I never had any time hanging on my hands, because I enjoyed those people, they were always fun. But when you started to buy that rug, it was business then, you always knew that that was business. If they bought potatoes and you didn't stick two or three onions in there, why you didn't know what you were doing. You could weigh them just the same as the potatoes, it was just the idea that they got the combination.

We tried to give them a fair price to start with, and then you wouldn't have to do all that haggling. After a while they understood that, and then maybe you'd just bargain a dollar or two here and there, but not much. I guess some people haggled a lot, but I think it's easier to tell them what you think it's worth and be straight with them right from the beginning, just like you would with anybody else, because I think you can baby people too much or you can be too cold. Just be yourself. They're good people.

HARRY GOULDING: The traders have been a good influence, but there have been some rotten eggs among the traders too, and nobody to cull them out. There's not very many of them that are not a proper character, darned few on the reservation today, but it used to be that's all you found out here. When we first come out, there was quite a number of traders around over the reservation that their thought was in the pocketbook. Up home there in the San Juan Basin we were right where we could run our stock bordering the reservation, and I could see a lot of stuff going on that the traders was pulling on them.

But nowadays, a Navajo himself, you're not going to tread too hard on him. Listen, them old Navajos, just when you start selling them short, why they're going to get you. You've got to think a little bit like they do. There's no question in my mind at all but what there's a lot of talk all along about this trader or that one. They do a lot of visiting in that direction. And they've been successful, I think, in cleaning up the traders.

Some of the real early traders that had a proper mind, they taught the Navajo, really, what a good trader could do, how he could be of help. It started with those early traders that were real human beings. They had to make a profit to stay in business too, but they at the same time had a feeling for the Navajo, could see a lot of good in him. It was honesty and friendliness; your thought was with them.

When we come out, we studied harder on trying to get the Navajo words to visit with these people than we did finding the names of our merchandise, because we were so anxious to be able to feel this thing out a little bit. Those old Navajos recognize that. They had quite a trail to follow and they just had to have some of the right answers. The Navajos had a big hand in sorting out the traders, because they're sharp. Don't sell them short!

■ It may be that Harry is optimistic in saying that the Navajos have succeeded in "cleaning up the traders," although Gladwell Richardson confirms his view of the earlier traders, those of the early decades of the century. "It is my belief that old-time traders made thieves of their employees. When teaching a new clerk the business, they explained in detail the necessary tricks of beating Navajo customers before they robbed you. Many of the old Navajos were sharp as diamond dust. As trader Joe Lee said, they had nothing else to do but sit around their hogans for days, thinking up a shrewd scheme to take the trader."[6] Sharp practices on both sides seem not to have been the style at Gouldings. As Mike says, "We tried to give them a fair price to start with, and then you wouldn't have to do all that haggling."

HARRY GOULDING: Old White Horse and Grey Whiskers and Hosteen Tso were fellas that we became close friends quicker than with the rest of the Indians. They would give me little pointers if I was doing something that wasn't just right. One time there was a Navajo come in and he'd given me some pawn. Grey Whiskers was there that day, and after this fella went out, he said, "Now don't give him more than that pawn is worth because he's not very good credit." He was a newcomer; he just didn't have any credit in the Valley yet.

One time a fella come in, and I was about to ask him his name. Grey Whiskers, says, "*Dooda, sik'is.* No, my friend, let him go on outside." So he went on outside, and the old fella says, "We never say anyone's name while he's present, it's not polite. You never should say a Navajo's name in front of him." And then he gave me the name. I'd practice those things. If there was somebody come in to get credit and I'd want their name after they went out, maybe another Indian would give it to me. Sometimes at first they wouldn't talk; you're in there new, and they wouldn't say anything: "We don't know." But when one of them old fellas like Hosteen Cly or White Horse or Grey Whiskers would come in, I could describe the fella and they'd tell me who he was.

The old time Navvies, you couldn't get them to change their style of clothes. You could try and try and try; it would just sit there on your shelf till you got tired looking at it. They had a certain garb that they wore and that was that. The women used to wear those tall shoes. They're built well, they're stout shoes, and there's a lot of wear in them. They come clean up to here, all laced up. The women wouldn't wear anything else. Or moccasins, of course, they made them themselves. I thought, well gee, it wouldn't be quite as heavy for them to take a shoe that come just a little ways and wasn't built quite so heavy, but you put them on the shelf and they just sat there, so there wasn't any use.

What happened, they started out on the railroad there. The railroad would bring in new things, and over near the railroad they started to changing; slowly, slowly, they started to changing. Then the wholesalers that we buy from started to handling those things. But we couldn't do a thing with them out here until they had seen other Navajos wearing them. A lot of the old women when we left here still wouldn't hardly take anything but the old style. But finally when it got so that very few were accepting a thing of that kind, why they stopped manufacturing it, and then they had to take whatever the replacement was.

■ Ruth Underhill speculates that the Navajo fashion of the velveteen blouse probably began around 1890. " 'A woman from near the railroad came to visit,' say the women of Chinle, 'and she had such a blouse. So we all wanted one. We told the trader to get us that fine, soft material, so he did. Then the men wanted them too.' It seems very likely that the 'woman from near the railroad' was a returned slave. Thus, the Navajo dress, as we know it today, was started in the late nineteenth century. This date coincides more or less with that when plush 'basques' went out of style in the East. Can it be that the Navajo liking for such soft material was fostered by traders who had a surplus to dump?"[7]

MAURICE KNEE: One winter, Harry came out to the coast. Navajos loved vests, oh they just loved 'em! That's when you got two pair of pants and a coat and a vest, you know? And people didn't wear their vest, so they'd buy a suit without the vest, fifty cents off. We went down to L.A., Fourth or Fifth Street, down where the clothing traders were, and we traded Navajo rugs for four hundred vests. Eeee! We got out to the store with them and those old Navajos . . . ! *"Chaléeko!"* they'd say, is their word for vest. Oh, they just loved 'em. They pulled the buttons off and put dimes on. Sometimes they decorated them all over with dimes and quarters. *"Chaléeko!"* We got two dollars apiece in trade. They came from all over the country, they found out that Dibé Nééz had some *chaléekos*. And they liked these stripe-ed ones, you know, dinner vests, oh boy!

HARRY GOULDING: When we first come in here, there wasn't a stove in
the country. The oil well drillers were down in here, and they brought in
barrel stock, and sometimes they didn't need the barrel. I'd pick it up, and
you could cut that barrel in two and make two stoves. Those oil drillers, I
knew them all, and if they had anything like that, I would bring it over here,
and give it to the Navajos. Then they would have to have stovepipe, so we
introduced stovepipe and dampers. It wasn't hard to persuade them to use
that stuff. They could see it right away. I always told them to just cut a piece
out and save it. "Put it up there and use it as a door for your stove, and do
your cooking on top." And they'd go for it. It didn't cost them anything and
yet it was a little nicer to handle than an open fire. Cedar wood throws
sparks all over the place. It might put a spark out on a Pendleton robe or
something, and they couldn't afford that kind of thing. So that was a big
help to them.

Even before they used stoves it wasn't too smoky inside the hogans. They
had that hole up there in the top, and they build a hogan a lot like we build
a fireplace, so it'll take the smoke away. They built them just the right shape
and respected the prevailing winds. No, as tall as I am, I never got in a hogan
where smoke bothered you any. They worked. But with a stove, they could
cook on it, and then it didn't take as much wood as it did to cook on a fire,
because you had to build your fire hot and have a fire clean across, where
with this you could put the wood in there and it would come up and heat
the top and then go out of the chimney. And it was just nicer.

We put in everything in the store, the regular things they used. I sold many
wagons. They didn't have much use for tools, there isn't a nail in a hogan,
but they've got to have an axe to cut wood, so we carried them all the time.
They'd been buying wagons and axes before we got in here.

They couldn't afford farming tools like hoes or ploughs, they needed too
many other things. What they'd have to do is get some tough old piece of
wood and shape that up as a plough. It was interesting some of the different
arrangements they had. They couldn't find what the other fella'd find, but
they had to have a plough. And the different models they'd work out, it was
a kick! But they ploughed all right, they done what they needed. Of course
they had mostly sand where they farmed and it wasn't like breaking the
prairie.

The stock needed salt. If they don't get it, they'll start to licking the red
shale. There's some alkaline gyp, gypsum stuff in the thing, and it's awful
hard on stock. There was salt sage away down by the river. It wouldn't grow
on these upper heights; down below Oljeto near Organ Rock, down in there
you'd start seeing the salt sage. And so whenever the stock would go to
licking that red shale, they'd have to take them down there to get them salted
up. They'd go sometimes twenty, twenty-five miles, take the sheep down
there to put them on that salt sage. They'd have to stay about a week and

give the sheep time to get enough of salt sage to satisfy them, and then come
back up to the grass; and in about three weeks more they'd have to go back
down.

So I talked to old Grey Whiskers, I talked to him first about it. I told him,
"We've got salt that we use, it's a block salt—the stock lick it." I says, "You
can watch my sheep." I always kept a little herd here, and I had this salt on
my bedground for the sheep. "We're out here where there's a lot of red shale,
and I want you to come down when you're around and see if you ever catch
any of my sheep licking that stuff up."

So he did, he watched them. I said, "Now if you can see what it's doing,
and if you want to, I'll take some of my salt and let you have it, take it over
there to your sheep." He studied about it quite a while, and finally he come
in one day, he'd brought his wagon in, and he says, "I'll take the salt over."
So I give him about six blocks of that sulphurized salt, and that's good for
stock. Well, his sheep went after it. Then he started to telling the Navajos,
and I would talk to them. Then I brought the salt in and put it for sale. It
done the job, it stopped all of this running sheep from away back up in this
upper country down in to that salt sage.

Rugs, in the early years, we'd have to haul our rugs in to Flagstaff and
just take wholesale prices on them. But as the tourist business got better, we
finally got to where we could sell all our rugs, and we'd have to go out and
buy more to take care of it.

I didn't work with the Indians to try to get them to do certain kinds of
designs in their rugs. That's what a lot of people done, and I could take my
rugs in and sell them where they couldn't sell theirs. They'd just suggest it
and suggest it, till it got to where it wasn't Navajo. All the traders wanted
them to make their rugs the same all the time, but the Navajos never would
make two alike, they always had a difference in their rugs. That made them
professional in their choices, and they always kept the Indian idea right in
them. I would take my rugs and sell them to the stores up around Colorado
Springs. I'd come in behind those fellas, where they'd been, and the store
owners would tell me, "You've got some nice rugs here, regular Indian
designs. They've been coming in here with rugs that just weren't Navajo."

I did encourage them to make their rugs better, though. That's a thing
that the early traders done too. I knew all those fellas over there to the east
when I was young. I sold bucks, Dad did, on the reservation, and I'd go in
to the Two Grey Hills store, they were people that were trying to help the
Indian. I'd have to stay overnight, and we'd swap lies there all night pretty
near. I learned a lot about trading. From Uncle Jack too, he was that way,
he had a trading post up Largo Canyon in New Mexico. So when I started
trading, I remembered all that I had learned from those old fellas.

I started at one time to try and get the Navajos to go to the old natural
colors, the old herb colors, but it's a lot harder for them to make their own
dyes, and the buyers wouldn't pay enough. So I decided, until the buyers get

to where they understand what goes on, I just wasn't going to make them do it. I'd always talk natural colors when I sold. Sometimes I'd get a Navajo to make a rug to take with me to show them the difference. The herb dyes are so quiet and very lovely. But until I could persuade the buyers to pay enough money to make it worthwhile, it was brutal, I felt, to force a Navajo to go to all that trouble. It wasn't going to be me to do it.

■ The 1870s and 1880s brought traders and the railroad to the Navajo reservation, a potent combination, and it wasn't long before the traders saw an off-reservation market for Navajo blankets. The classic stripes, borrowed from the Pueblo Indians along with the craft of weaving itself, and the serape designs, borrowed from the Mexicans, began to give way to designs suggested by the traders, largely borrowed from oriental rugs, in an effort to appeal to white customers. Saxony yarns, imported from Germany, and Germantown yarns from Pennsylvania, with bright aniline dyes, supplemented and replaced homespun yarns and natural dyes. The Navajos adopted the Pendleton blanket for themselves, and their own blankets became rugs for export. By the 1890s and the turn of the century, the rugs had become gaudy and tasteless, and their sale fell into decline. Lorenzo Hubbell at Ganado had always insisted on work of high quality, and other traders soon began a new effort in the early decades of the century, encouraging finer workmanship, a return to natural dyes, and in some instances a return to classic design. Beginning in 1940 and reactivated after World War II, the Navajo Arts and Crafts Guild has established galleries for the sale of Navajo crafts and has done a great deal to maintain high standards of workmanship and fair prices for the craftsmen and women.[8]

TED CLY (Hosteen Cly's grandson, Monument Valley):   In the times of my grandfather, my grandmother, they know Harry Goulding pretty well. My mother, my father, my uncles, they all know him. He got the flour, the food, to help my mother and father down here. He give me some sheep, oh maybe twenty. He was a trader. He buy rugs and skin, our wool, and take it to market. He bring something back, give to our folks. And he ordered all kinds of things for the Navajos, like nosebag for the horses, and wheat, barley, horseshoes or collar, wagon, wagon grease, axe, shovel. He traded, and we all have a shovel and a axe. Otherwise we wouldn't have. We got a wagon, and John Cly got one. Ours is gone. The wheels are right up there in front of the trading post in the fence. Bessie, down here in Monument Valley, she still got a wagon. John Cly's wife took his over by Mitchell Butte when John died.

When we went out to work, we still write to him, from Moab or Salt Lake. We get paid and we always sending some money to our mother or father, send it to the store, and then he take it down there to my father's. Or they can trade it if they want something. That's how we arranged our

Ted Cly, son of Willie and Happie Cly, who as a boy showed Harry many of the interesting features of the Valley, and who later became a tour driver for Goulding's lodge. (Samuel Moon)

family, sister and brothers, how I grew up. But we always come back in summertime, we always be up here with them.

He was close to us, like brothers and sisters. He trade with our family the way our own family trade with each other. That's how we're raised. Somebody have a ceremonial, we take the flour and coffee there. He used to do that too. My sister get married, the others come and help each other, you know. Sometime there's a dance, a Squaw Dance ceremonial, they take something over there, a sack of flour, maybe six coffee, six sugar, potatoes, big sack, hundred, two hundred pound. That's how we get together.

■   In a Navajo extended family such as the Cly family, various hogans will have different sources of subsistence. Some will have sales of wool, some farming, railroad wages, or welfare payments, and in the cycle of the year the members of the family develop a pattern of interdependence. The entire extended group may depend for a time on the members who have wool to trade, or farm products to harvest, or who are receiving unemployment compensation. In effect, they "trade" with each other throughout the year. As Adams describes it, "each member household has a duty to produce what it can, and each has a right to consume what it needs."[9] Ted Cly is saying that the Gouldings entered into this kind of family relationship with the Navajos in the Valley.

TED CLY: The other Navajos here in the Valley think the same of the Gouldings. They all come here and trade. He was their friend, just like brothers. He sat down and talked to them. They got old, got sick, and he come around and get ceremonial for them. They pray and they sing, they feel good all the time.

And he goes down here in the Valley, just drive around when snow on the ground, bring some kerosene or something. He gives lots of help to Navajos. And summertime, with the tourists down in there, he take some flour or coffee and giving out for the picture taking, and a little change, dollar, two dollars. And besides, when there were no jobs, sometimes we work up here fixing places, fixing water pipes. Not much, just a little, two or three days, when it's cold and the sun gets down low right away.

Mrs. Goulding was the same as Mr. Goulding. She traded in the store, and helping the others. Found some girls, show them how to sew clothes with sewing machine, with pedal. So we got some sewing machines. She show them how to use it, so they use it. That's what she did. They get all size material to make the good clothes, and she help. She buying some carding things for carding the wool, and she give to the Navajo ladies. She pass them around and show how to use them. They stop by our hogan and come in. She did a lot of extra work, help Mr. Goulding.

We used to bring some meat to their freezer, butcher a goat or a sheep, give him half of it for himself and his wife. And we used to help them in the winter, like chopping wood and bring it to them, chop in little pieces, just big enough for fireplace, help keep them warm. She go to town, bring us some boots to wear in the snow, and heavy clothes, and tee shirt, socks, gloves. Oh, they used to taking good care of us. We all coming and going together, all feeding each other, help each other. That's the way it happen. Get to know her, real good to know.

HARRY GOULDING: Mike made good friends with some of the Navajo ladies. Those old women would go upstairs and talk to her. I'd come up and the visiting would stop just like that. Just as soon as I stuck my head in the door, why no more visiting. She got a lot of pleasure out of the old women here in the Valley. She got all of the news that came in through that channel, anything that happened in any of the homes, all of those things would come through that source.

MIKE GOULDING: Julia Holiday was a particular Navajo friend of mine. They lived right down here in front of the trading post. Her husband helped with the rock work on the house. She and I were about the same age. I had a lot of them I considered real good friends. If I needed them, I could have gone to them, and they came to me, too. Julia, for one, had lost so many babies. And she wasn't supposed to weep or carry on. You know, after four days the mourning was supposed to be all over, that was the custom. So she would come upstairs with me and cry. But if we'd hear anybody starting up that stairway, she'd straighten up right now! They're just as human as can be; you can't knock it off like that, you know. It gave vent to her feelings to come up with me and cry, because they do love their little kids. A lot of them came up. They would sit down on the kitchen floor while I was working and tell me their little stories.

JULIA HOLIDAY (translated from Navajo): When my husband, Jake Charlie, was alive, he used to take care of the store for Dibé Nééz. He wouldn't do the regular work, but he would tell the customers that Dibé Nééz was not there; sometimes he would go back in the evening.

I used to visit Dibé Nééz's wife on the hill. She made dresses for me; I would tell her how to make it and she would do it on the sewing machine. I used to sit with her upstairs in their house. I really didn't understand her language, and she didn't speak Navajo very well, but later on she learned how to speak better with the people. Dibé Nééz liked us visiting together; he called me Shimá (My Mother). We called her Shimá Yázhí (Little Mother, Aunt). She was very young when they first came.

HARRY GOULDING: You've never experienced something nice until you have a Navajo that really thinks a lot of you, and he gives you something. That is the greatest way to experience their atmosphere. And no talk. It's the grandest thing. Leon Bradley had a bow, it was one of the old, old, old ones that came from grandpa and on down the line, and I saw it one time and admired it. It was quite a long time after that, I was coming by one day. His hogan was up on the hill, and he knew I wasn't going to come up there, so here he came down this hill off of where they lived up there, and he had this bow in his hand, out like this. He came on down, on down, on down towards me, and he stopped, and without saying a word, his atmosphere told me to hold my hands out. And he put that bow in my hands. And that's all that was said.

I used to always when I went down into the Valley, I would take extra water. A Navajo don't camp on a water hole. He gets away from that water hole so the birds and the coyotes and the bobcats can come in in the dark and get their drink. So I'd always take this water in and fill their little water tanks every time I went by. And Leon had this bowl that was covered with leather. I think it was goatskin. It made a tough cover. I always wanted one of them, but I never told Leon that. He might have caught me looking at it or something. But one day he came in to the trading post with that bowl, and the way he handed me that bowl, the feelings that passed as we both held onto it for a while, you could see the pleasure it was to him to give it to me, and he could see me just melting because I was getting it. They can do those things so beautifully, gifts of that kind.

Then old White Horse, I knew he always eyed that black horse of mine. Every time the old fella would come into the trading post and I was getting ready to make a pack trip, he'd always go out and look at the horses and he'd walk around this black horse. So I knew darned well he would just give anything to have him.

When four-wheel drive came along and we quit running pack trips, I had no use for the horse. Then one day, it was quite a long time after that, I was in the trading post and Aunt Molly was standing there beside me watching me trade with the Indians. When it was empty, old White Horse came in, and Aunt Molly and I were just standing there visiting. I could see him coming up. He came into the store and he had this beautiful bracelet, and he couldn't have told me any plainer what to do, to put my arm up. He put that bracelet on my arm. And the atmosphere. There was a hesitation, the air was . . . I don't know what you want to call it, but they could throw what you could understand. And he turned around and walked back out, never said a word. Aunt Molly cried. She could feel what was going on. Some way there's a terrific atmosphere builds up between you and a friend. It pretty near speaks, whatever it is.

So then I gave him the horse.

Now a Navajo will do that. If he figures it's a good even trade, if he would like what you have and he figures you'd like what he has, it'll make you both happy and he'll do it. He never mentioned the horse. I just knew it was that kind of thing. I'd seen it happen between Indians. No words were said, but it sealed us harder than ever because we both got what we wanted. When you do that there's an atmosphere that pushes out. If you live enough with those people you don't have to do any talking about it at all. The ability to give a gift to a person, that stays with you for life, the gift of it is in you, and it's going to stay there. It just does the old soul good, both mine and the giver. They have so many beautiful ways of doing things of that kind.

5 ▬ MAURICE

MIKE GOULDING: My brother Paul came out here first in the summer of 1928; he was out here ahead of Maurice. Then he quit school in 1931 and came out to stay. Maurice was still in school, but he started coming every summer.

HARRY GOULDING: When Maurice was a little kid, just the minute school was out, he was out here. He would get the time on what left Van Nuys right after school was out, on that day. Was it a bus? Was it a train? He'd have her set, the quickest way he could get out of that school and get to that bus or train, or maybe someone he knew of was coming out with a car about that time. But if it was a car coming the next day, he wouldn't wait for it. He'd get on that train, and then we'd have to meet him and bring him on out here. Because he wanted to get back to this Valley. He just loved it, and he mixed right with these young Navajo kids.

That's when you want to learn a language. That's when I learned to talk Mexican, and that's the way Maurice was with Navajo. He'd get out here and he'd play with these kids. And the old Navajos liked him. If there's a spark in a kid . . . Now an old medicine man, generally they'd take one of their sons to teach him their medicine, but if they had a nephew that they thought was sharper than one of their boys, or if they knew of another boy that they thought would really fit, why they would take the sharp one. I think they always had one out of their own family but they had lots of family. And that's the way they were with Maurice.

It was a privilege and a great pleasure to watch that kid mix himself in with these Navajos, and then come out the person he really is. He loved to go out and eat with the Navajos. If he didn't have anything else to do, why he might go out with a Navajo herding sheep for a day. He's just a Navajo, and they accept him as such. In these Yeibichai ceremonials they have clowns, and the little kids get a whang out of that. And Maurice has been a clown in the Yeibichai. He joins them in their sings, in their sand paintings, he's just a Navajo and a white man churned up together.

MAURICE KNEE: In '29 Harry and Mike came out to the coast, and school was out, so I caught a ride with them back. I'd never been in the Monuments. And what a road! Took us two days from Flagstaff. One full

day to Red Lake. We stayed there in our sleeping bags, and then next day
all day long. We got into the Monuments just at dark, grinding through
sand.

They all looked the same to me, those Navajos. Somebody told me, "When
you see a Navajo, shake hands," so I shake hands with six Navvies—same
one six times. Then I got to seeing, and I tried to learn the language. Oh
boy, how would you ever learn crap like that? But I already had a lot of
Navajo in my vocabulary that I didn't know what it was. School kids around
Aztec and Farmington and Durango—lots of Navajo words that we used.
We didn't know what they were.

There were three Navajos around the store that spoke English. There was
one called 'Olta'i Sá, which meant the Old Schoolboy, there was 'Olta'i
Nééz, which was the Tall Schoolboy, Schoolboy Tall; and the other one was
Leon Bradley, who was a very dear friend of ours, spoke good English. They
had long hair, and they wouldn't talk English if another Navajo was around.
The Navajos give an ultimatum: you're either a white man or you're an
Indian, we don't like anybody with two tongues. So those were the ones that
would teach me Navajo when I could get them alone. It was real Navajo.
You can get a good course in the Navajo language, and you and the rest of
the students can understand each other perfectly, but a Navajo can't.

I can go out right now, fifty miles from here, into a hogan of Indians, I
don't know a single one of them, and I can sit down on the floor and wait,
and pretty soon, if they're playing cards or something, pretty soon I can just
say a few words, and they will know I'm friendly and they'll accept me.

I'd run off with the Indians and tell Mike I was going hiking up the canyon
and not to worry if I didn't get back. I'd crawl on a horse and go out and
camp with them. Sometimes I'd stay out three or four days.

Got lice, like a good Indian. You're supposed to have lice; the louse is a
very holy thing. If you get rid of old mother louse, how're you going to keep
active in the winter? In the winter months, when it's hot in the hogan and
they stir around, you scratch. That's in their legends. They'd take them all
off but number one. They'd leave one louse.[1]

And then when they'd get so lousy that the kids were just awful, they'd
shave their heads except for one little tuft of hair.

"Why didn't you cut that off?" I'd say.

"The hair would never see to get big again if you went and cut that off."

If you're too clean you wouldn't have any friends, because your friends
would have them and you wouldn't be welcome in their house. If you have
company who are too clean, they're not welcome. When the city Navajos
came in with their sprays, they wouldn't sleep in the hogan, they'd sleep in
their pickup. And they were inhospitable to the old folks when they came
to town. They was smart aleck. That's when something would happen to
them to bring them down to earth.

In 1933 I got out of high school, and I wrote Harry a letter. There was no work there in Van Nuys, in that stinking San Fernando Valley. I'd mow lawns, work in the Safeway and sort rotten potatoes, anything for twenty cents an hour. Times were rough. So I wrote Harry a letter, "If I come out, can you use me?" I had an alternative, I could've went to the CC camp[2] and gone to Brooklyn, New York, is right where I'd have gone to. Well, that didn't appeal, so I wrote Harry a letter, and I says, "I want a job."

He says, "Come on out for room and board, no money. When you learn enough Navajo to where you can trade in the store and relieve Mike or I, then I'll put you on three dollars a month."

I figured that was all right, because I knew I could go out with the herds, and I knew I could go out and wrangle the horses and stuff like that. So that's what happened.

In about a year I got on money. Took me a year to fool Harry into thinking I knew Navajo well enough to trade. This old Navvy came in. He was a tough one to deal with, and I knew Harry was standing in the back room seeing how I was doing. I asked him *"Ha'át'iísh'?"* "What do you want?"

The old man says, *"Nímasiitsoh."* I knew *Nímasiitsoh* was potatoes, and he traded for it.

Pretty soon I says, *"Ha'át'íí dó'?"* "What else?

He says, *"'Akódí,"* "That's all." And I handed him a free pop.

"Well, my friend, thank you, you're sure a good white man!" he said in Navajo.

I knew Harry was listening. Pretty soon he says, "Maurice, I guess you can handle it." I never did tell Harry I gave him a free pop.

My Navajo name is Dichinii, Hungry, the Hungry One. If I had a store full of Indians, and they were standing around visiting and not trading, just buying candy and pop, pretty soon upstairs Mike would hit on the floor. "Dinner's ready, come and get it!"

I'd say, "Hey, I'm going to go eat now, I'm hungry. Go outside."

Well, that's when they all wanted to trade. At two o'clock I'd finally get up to eat. So at ten o'clock in the morning, I started saying, "Well boys, I'm awful hungry, you're going to have to go," and then I got out by noon.

Three o'clock at night [afternoon] I'd say, "Whew, I'm awful hungry, you're going to have to go now," and then they'd trade and I'd get out by six, six-thirty.

"That white man sure eats a lot," they'd say. "He eats all the time! He's *Dichinii*!"

■   The Navajos may have had a double entendre in mind. Gladys Reichard describes a group of mythical beings in her book, *Navaho Religion*, called "Hunger" (*dichin*): "People so called were found by Monster Slayer when he was looking for evils. Their leader was a big, fat man, though he had nothing more than the little brown cactus to eat. [Maurice, it must be said, was certainly not fat.] When Monster Slayer threatened him, he said, 'If we die, people will not relish their food. They will never know the pleasure of cooking and eating nice things, and they will not enjoy hunting.' "[3]

HARRY GOULDING: The Indians would come in, and they'd buy their can of tomatoes and some crackers to eat here in the store, and Paul and Maurice would throw in a can of something else, beans maybe, make some coffee, and they'd sit out there in the bull pen and eat with them Indians. They really just worked right in. And of course Paul talked awful good Navajo too, he could just rip it off.

Listen, this doggone trading post was a-roar in here, kids and everybody was joking. Well, that's your Navajo, they use an awful lot of humor, and the fact of the matter is that I don't believe they could've come through the things that we put them through unless they had had that terrific sense of humor.

We had a quarter on the counter that we had a lot of fun with. Maurice hooked it up.

MAURICE KNEE: I drilled a hole in the counter and took one of these quarters that a Navajo had made into a button and wired it to a telephone magneto. They would come in, and they'd see it laying there. They'd throw their blanket up on the counter over it and hold on so I couldn't take the blanket to look at it. I'd be looking the other way, you know, but I had it mounted right into the counter. And pretty soon his hand would go under the blanket.

"Look, my friend, I got a beautiful blanket. My wife is almost blind from weaving this beautiful blanket. You've got to give me lots of trade for it. The white men will really run to get it."

One side of the magneto I had to the quarter. The other side I had laying on the cement on a piece of steel about eight by eight by a half inch thick. Then I'd throw a cup of water on it, and that would seep around where they'd step in the dampness, see? It made a real good connection. And when you thump it, just one turn hits you about three times, boom, boom, boom.

Well, I'd see that arm going underneath and I'd let him get a death hold. He was trying to pick it up. I knew he'd touched it, and that's when I'd give it to him. All the local ones knew about it, so they would try to get somebody else in there. It'd knock their hand clear off of it. I never would do one Indian alone or he might get mad and come over the counter after me. The old Navajos would try it once in a while just to see what was cooking.

Then I took a wire and I put it right around the edge of the counter, all the way around. When the little girls would bump up against it, with their little titties right against it with their blouses on, the spark would jump. It didn't hurt them, it was just a ping.

This old man came in, Hoskinini Begay, the son of old Hoskinini, and he had a velvet shirt on. He was leaning up against there, and I reached down and pecked him, and he scratched. So I pecked him again, and he said, "The lice are biting." He unbuttoned his shirt and shook it. God, we were just dying, trying to keep from laughing. He looked all through the seams of his shirt trying to find the lice. The third time I pecked him, "Ah," he says, "that's a smart louse!" And he took his shirt off and turned it wrong side out and just shook the hell out of it! I didn't have the heart to get him again.

HARRY GOULDING: Now, when you're trading with a squaw, and her son-in-law, married to one of the girls, would come in, some Navajo would say something, and she'd duck out with a robe over her head and go down over the hill out of sight. I'd ask those old fellas, "What's this?" Well, her son-in-law came in, and they're not supposed to look at each other, son-in-law and mother-in-law. He might go blind. And so I should warn her if I look out the window and see him getting off his horse. If he was right there by the door, let her go out through the back room of the place.

Those old customs are strange to us, but when you understand what they're all about, they're something, by golly. If they can look at each other and talk to each other, there may some trouble arise over it, but if you're going to go blind when you look at her, you shed your son-in-law trouble right there. Not only that, every person is responsible to see that they don't get together, and that starts your little kids to thinking early, because they certainly don't want nothing to happen to their folks. So it just gets that little kid to going, gets his little old head to working, responsibilities early. If you want to call it a superstition, okay, but it's a handle, it's a great handle to have.

MAURICE KNEE: One time I didn't believe it worked. We had a storeful of Indians, a big ceremonial, there must have been six or seven hundred around here milling around. And this Navajo came up, he'd been hiding over the hill, and he sees me and he says, "Hey Hungry, is the old owl in there?"

I knew she was, but I said, "No, she's gone."

So he walked in the door, and she was trading with Harry. Somebody said, "Psst!" She turned around and there he was! She grabbed one of about nine skirts she was wearing, and over her head it went. She screamed. He turned around and screamed and ran outside.

Everything I earned for three months went to pay for a ceremonial to keep them from going blind. I found out they did believe in it.

I remember one time, these Navajos came in and I knew them both, young guys. Things had been pretty quiet, there wasn't anything going on, nobody was trading, they were visiting quietly. There were a few of them back against the walls, and the middle of the bull pen was empty. It was just very quiet—one asking another how his feed was or something like that. The two of them went out, and one of them got him a stick and gave it to the other one as though he was blind, and led him into the store. Here come these two idiots in. Not a word was said. The minute the door opened and they walked in everybody turned around and looked, and sure enough he led him, poker-faced, this Indian hanging on with both hands, right around through—and of course everybody knew them, everybody knew there wasn't a blind Indian hanging on there—and out the door. There wasn't one sound until they had gone out and closed the door. And then them Navvies just hit the ground laughing! It just absolutely was the funniest thing, and me too. Just poker-faced Indians, that's all. Pretty soon they got to buying, and they laughed and laughed and laughed. They went *away* laughing.

They're a happy people if they were just let alone. Every morning you'd hear them at break of day riding their horse through the canyon, just a-singing. Never no more. How can you sing with a government agency yelling at you? They had the perfect life until the white man disturbed it. A very good religious-medical outlook. Everything had its cause, everything had its cure, even though they couldn't cure a lot of stuff that we can today. We cure it with a pill or a shot. If we were smart, we'd have a little psychology and a little religion to go with it.

Things were real rough on that reservation. It was touch and go for a Navajo family to make it. The only thing they did have was sheep, they did have meat. And then if the weather was kind to them they'd have a good corn crop. The guy that had the fields, through the balance of the year when he didn't have corn, he would receive a leg of mutton or something from somebody else, and then later he would repay them with corn traded. You'd see them in the fields and they would make a heyday out of it. They'd usually have a little ceremonial to go with it. They could always find somebody who was not feeling good to have a little squaw dance.

They'd take the ears of corn, and sometimes they'd boil it, but it's very good roasted. They'd lay it on a little grill over the coals and keep turning it until it was cooked. Many a time I've gone to these little gatherings and traded my sandwiches to them for their food.

But what I wanted to say is that they had a tremendous way and they never thought of death. To think of death, why it would strike. To think of rattlesnakes and talk about it, one would come in and get you. To think of lightning was a bad thing to do. You never thought about the bad things in life. You tried to keep your mind on good things. They were starving to death amongst themselves, and yet they were very kind to each other. They could always depend on a clan or a relative to help them if they could.

No, those early days out here, and even today, it's not a happy-go-lucky society, but they're always wide open for a laugh.

6 ■■■ SHEEP TRADING

HARRY GOULDING: In 1933 we had Paul and Maurice and Bert, all three of them, working for us. We had a lot of trade here. The law was that the traders had a month to buy their sheep and take them to shipping points. It was helping the Indians out so they wouldn't be selling off all their sheep. But I bought sheep all winter long, I bought sheep all year, because I was off the reservation. And then we'd take them out in the fall.

MIKE GOULDING: They wanted them to have lots of sheep; they didn't want them to reduce any of that stock. This was just before John Collier came in and changed the policy to stock reduction.

HARRY GOULDING: So I'd buy, but I wouldn't buy many, I wouldn't let only so many come in, because I knew there was an order on the reservation. And besides, I just felt it'd be better to let them bring in up to around four head of sheep at a time and bring them in whenever they needed. Then the sheep would go for food, instead of maybe bring in a big bunch and want a saddle or a wagon, something like that. And so it worked.

RAY HUNT: At the time Harry went in there, nobody had ever been in that area buying sheep. The Blackwater family, the White Horse family, all of them had herds of sheep. I've asked them when I was down there trading how many sheep they had, and they didn't know how many. I'd guess that some of the Indians probably owned five, six, seven thousand head of sheep in those days.

■ This policy in the 1920s of encouraging the Navajos to hold their sheep, if not actually to increase their holdings, was at odds with the facts and with the general understanding of the facts in the field. The Navajo population, and along with it, their sheep, had increased tremendously since their return from Fort Sumner and the Long Walk in 1868. At that time the Navajos numbered 8,354 at Fort Sumner, and an unknown but smaller number who had not been captured and remained free. The returning captives were issued 35,000 sheep and goats by the government, and the free Navajos, like Hoskinini in Monument Valley, with great humanity and foresight, had husbanded their sheep and now shared them with their brothers.[1]

By 1930, the Navajo population had exploded to 40,858. According to a comprehensive report by William Zeh, a forester with the Bureau of Indian Affairs, their stock numbered 1,297,589 sheep and goats, 80,000 horses, and 27,000 cattle, and both people and livestock were continuing this astounding expansion. It was not until Roosevelt became president and John Collier became commissioner of Indian affairs that a genuine stock reduction program, with all its pain and grief and violence, was inaugurated.

MAURICE KNEE: Harry's Navajo name is Dibé Nééz. I always visualize pronouncing it as "t' pay," like you're going to pay your bill, "T' pay nez." Dibé is "sheep" and nééz is "tall." It's not "slim," it's "tall." "Slim is a different Navajo word altogether. I asked a Navajo once why they call Harry Goulding "Dibé Nééz," and he says, "Well, he's a tall man, and he's got lots of sheep."

But I said, "Why do you call him 'Tall *Sheep*'?"

"Well, look," he says, and you could see down in the flats, way out to the northwest was Train Rock, and Red Rock is about five miles out. They were out of water at Red Rock, and here they were, coming in to the trading post to our little trough. Those sheep were strung out for a good two miles in a big long tall string of sheep. He says, "See how long those sheep are?"

That's another meaning of Dibé Nééz, "Long Sheep," he had a long herd of sheep. Because nééz means "long" and "tall" both. And that's how he got his name.

MIKE GOULDING: Bullets came after we were in the house, probably 1929.

HARRY GOULDING: Bullets Hardy. He was a Mormon.

MIKE GOULDING: From Circleville, wasn't it? Just right over here in Jump the Nest?

HARRY GOULDING: Uh huh. Bert stayed on and Bullets come in. Bert developed water and did all sorts of things. Bullets was buying stock all the time, and he would help Mike with the stock when I was gone out to get stuff.

Bullets was with Wetherill's for a while, and he learned a little Navajo. And then when he came over to work for us, he brought his horses with him. He had one horse, I don't believe I ever rode a better horse. But he was mean. He'd buck. You'd have to ride him, all day you had to ride him. If you'd relax just a little bit, he'd go after you. He'd feel it was a good time to start pitching. Bullets was like iron. We all was. You had to be. If you wasn't, you wasn't for this country. Old Bert was as tough as an old boot.

MIKE GOULDING: When winter'd come, Bullets would go with the Wetherills down to Mexico. He was only here a few summers, but Bert stayed on and on.

HARRY GOULDING: Then Bert could help Mike buying sheep down at the store, and working lambs and one thing another, because he'd seen what Bullets done. He'd pick up quick.

MAURICE KNEE: We'd get up at four o'clock in the morning, and we'd all go down and work those lambs. The ones that had lost their mother, we had to find a mother that had lost its lamb, and get them together. Tie her and hold her to where that lamb would eat, squirt her milk all over the lamb to where she'd accept it, because they don't want a strange lamb. If we'd find a lamb that died at birth and another that had lost its mother, or a mother that had twins and not enough milk, we'd skin the dead lamb and put it on the live one, and then cover it with milk. Then the mother would accept it, think it was hers, smelt like it. It'd wear that skin around for three or four weeks until it fell off. By that time she'd got used to it.

HARRY GOULDING: There's a lot of difference in the way the Navajos work their sheep. If they have a lamb without a mother, they have their own way of making another ewe claim that lamb. When a ewe has a lamb, the afterbirth and everything comes with it. And I don't know why we didn't think of it, as simple a thing as that, but they will just roll that orphan lamb around in the afterbirth, so it will get the same smell as her lamb. Then she will take the two lambs and raise them. So then we done that ourselves.

And they train their dogs different. We train our dogs to help us herd the sheep. Well, they go and snap at the sheep's legs, and they're afraid of that dog. Navajos have their dogs to keep the coyotes out of the herds. They just travel right in with the sheep and on all the edges and around like that. They use a dog to keep the coyotes out.

The older dogs will lead the sheep, like if someone was with them, and they will lead them in at night. Here in the Valley, the Navajos will start them out this way or that way. Well, those old dogs get to know, when you turn them out that way, just what ground you cover, and they'll take them on the same route.

The dogs learn from each other, they'll put a pup out there and he'll learn from the old-timers. Then as soon as he's to move up, the Indian himself has got to train him that he goes out ahead that way. Eventually he works himself up to where he's the leader.

The Navajo dogs are a breed off of every dog that ever got lost out here. People come out and lose a dog, and he'll change things around a little.

■   One Navajo practice that is not good for their range is that of bringing their sheep back to the home corral every night. They did it in the early days to protect their flocks from coyotes, but it has resulted in severe overgrazing around the hogan and corral. Another device against the coyote I have seen only once: scattered into the Tódích'íi'nii flocks on Hoskinini Mesa were goats dressed up in castoff sweaters or shirts to make them look like a scarecrow.

MIKE GOULDING: Shearing time was always exciting. The ones that were especially good shearers would come in. We'd cut little cardboard squares, and each time they sheared a sheep you'd give them a square, and at the end of the day you owed them so much money. Real finance! A lot of times I was the one that handed out the little tickets. I'd watch and see what was going on. The wool was to be piled in a certain place. These were our sheep that we had traded for, and then we'd buy theirs too, and truck the whole thing out.

HARRY GOULDING: They sheared their sheep right on the ground, and you've got to figure on a little bit of sand. It's dirty wool anyway to start with, this reservation wool, because they get them old sand storms that blows into their wool. You don't charge as much for wool off of the reservation because it's too dirty.

Then they'd make wool sacks out of their Pendleton blankets. They'd take this yucca plant; that stuff is just tough as tough. I've made a rope out of it, just take them and tie them together. And you can make a halter for a horse, like you catch a horse out where you haven't got a rope. They'd sew the Pendleton blankets together with yucca leaves. You see, it has a sharp point. They'd take two of them and tie the butts together, and then they'd go ahead and tie another one on there, and go on. Finally they'd make a wool sack out of their Pendleton blankets, throw them on the horse and bring them in.

When we first came out here, there was scab in all of those sheep, and they won't let you ship sheep that are scabby, so we had to get something done about it. At that time I didn't have too much Navajo, so I went over to Kayenta, and I got Frank Bradley and brought him back, he could talk both. Then we had a visit with the others, go over this whole thing and see how it would please them. They wanted to get rid of that scab because it's hard on the sheep. A scab is a bug, a little heavier than a louse. They get in there and suck the blood out, and then they pass it. Oh it just gets to be a gummy, terrible mess all over. So they said they would be pleased to dip them, and they would help me.

Then I went up to Salt Lake and talked to the chief inspector of the state. He was ready to do something because it was leaking off of the reservation to the herds of Utah.

I told him that I would build a dip vat if we could really get things done and clean it up down there, but sometimes it's a little hard to get all the sheep in. So he says, "We'll clothe you with authority, and if you can't get them in, why one of us will come down and help you out a little bit."

So Mike and I went in to Flagstaff and got a load of lumber and nails and some other stuff to build the vat with. That was a road that I had to unload four times, whether it was a hill, or sand, or whatever. You'd unload half of your load, take one half through, unload that half load, come back, put this other half on, come through again, and then load the first half back on. You got pretty well acquainted with near every board before you made it out. It took us three loads, three trips into Flagstaff and back, to get our materials.

Frank explained to the Navajos that they'd have to bring in all their sheep. "Don't leave a one back at the hogan, because if you leave that one there, the others will be dipped, and just as soon as they dry up a little bit, the stuff will get off of that one and onto the herds again, and it'll just cause you a lot of trouble, you'll have to keep coming in."

It turned up a little bit the next year and we had to dip them again, and for three straight years we dipped them. Then we'd have to come to a dipping about every two years. We kept cutting it down and down and finally got rid of it all around, and our stock was shipping out. No more scabs. But it took a few years to do it.

I don't think the Navajos had ever seen sheep-dipping before, but they were willing to do it because it was just murder on the sheep. If you leave it on there too long it'll kill a sheep. We was right on the state line, but as far as we reached, why they were willing to bring their sheep in. I didn't say too much about the border. If they'd agree to bring their sheep in, we'd dip all the sheep that came in here. So they did. They brought them in.

Some of the Arizona officials came out and New Mexico, even, and Utah, and we talked it all over. Because if I would've had to do that alone, why they'd be trading stock and one thing another, and after I'd get the stuff cleaned up, they'd trade for some scabby stock and boom would go the whole works. So they decided. They says, "We'll work united, we'll work together, and that'll take all the sheep in the whole country." They never got out this far before. It was off the reservation at that time, too far out.

So I done this area, and then they went ahead and had a vat over the other side of Kayenta and another one the other side of Dinnehotso. And they put one in across the river on the Utah side, they put a couple of them in there, so that anything going into Utah or coming out, either way, they could dip it and clean it up.

A dip vat is about six foot deep. It has sides in it about two feet wide at the bottom and they slope up and out. It gets wider as it gets up to the top. If you have it straight down, it would take too much liquid to fill it up. And it had to be thoroughly waterproof. Then you've got to hold the sheep in there a while, so I built it as long as I could, about twenty-five or thirty feet. I couldn't build it as long as I wanted to, because it would keep us hauling from Flagstaff all the time, but I got it long enough so's we could put in quite a number of sheep and hold them. Then we had to build corrals to hold the bunch that come in till they were all dipped. It was quite a chore before you got through with it. We was a month and a half just building the vat and the outfit. But we had a good deal when we got through; it worked awful good.

We held them in the vat there, and of course the sheep would have to keep swimming. We had to keep them a-going in the medicine to get the action put through. The vat wasn't wide enough to let them turn around. They're anxious to get on. Just the minute you'd open that gate on the other end of the vat, why they was gone.

Some of the Navajos didn't have over forty head, but some of those old fellas had thousands of sheep. We'd be dipping there for twenty days before we got them all through. The Navajos who brought the sheep in helped drive them through the dip. Generally the kids and the mother would come along, and they would get in there. The smell is pretty bad, whee-ew! But you'd get to where you'd get used to it. It's got to be done. And there's where a Navajo is good. It smells bad, and they know it and you know it, but we know it's got to be done and we go ahead and we're all happy. Them old-timers, they were wonderful people.

The chief sheep inspector of the state would pick up one or two local inspectors, and they'd come down to see how things were going. They were having trouble in some places. The Indians balked. They thought it wasn't good for the sheep. The meat wasn't good, you see; you couldn't eat the meat for a little while because it would taste like that dip.

But we got it in our area to where we never had too much trouble. I told Frank that we wanted to tell them everything that's associated with this before we done anything so's they'd know what to expect. So we told them it would make the meat taste different, but just as soon as it dried off it'd be all right again. It's not as bad down in the Valley as it is up in Colorado or Utah. This is a desert and they dry out a lot quicker; it would probably be about fifteen days. If they could have one sheep every fifteen days, why most of these old people with their little herds, they'd have ate theirselves out of sheep.

I had an awful lot of experience with Navajos before I came down here, so we got along just fine dipping sheep. Once in a while I'd kill a couple of my sheep, make some bread, mulligan of some kind, and we'd get together. Then I run a few horse races, got that going. They're having a good time while they're doing the rough stuff, and it passes easier. I never did have any trouble.

We'd buy cattle and sheep the year around, and then ship it out every fall. It would take us sometimes about thirty days on the road getting the stock to the railroad. We'd sell them to the feeders and they'd come in to take over when we got up there.

Mike would have to stay here at the trading post. Bert was here, and Dobbie, they were here to help her. She got along all right, but it was lonesome. She could do anything, she even bought sheep when I was gone. She had to do everything that I'd have done, because we never did quit buying sheep in those years.

When I took the stock out, I always took John and Willie and Leon Cly, and then I'd take two or three other Navajos, because we had cattle and sheep going in together. Old John Cly, he was a comedian, he had an awful lot of humor in him. In October when we took out, we'd get a lot of stormy weather going on up country, sometimes hail, and cold! And when it would go to storming, old John would come loose with one of his jokes. He could just keep the whole crew going all the time. It wasn't like a beautiful day and everything going nice, you know, but with John there, he brought the sunshine.

We took them to Farmington, New Mexico, up over the reservation on the south side of the San Juan River, because there was better feed up that way. I'd look forward to traveling with stock, especially if it was a year when we had plenty of feed. I always went up ahead and rented two or three farmers' fields. It was their last crop, but it had grown up to where it made good pasture. I would put the stock in there. We'd go in to the water holes and water, and then we'd go on out to where the feed would be. We'd rest up for a while and let the stock get a bellyful before we'd go on. We took thirty, thirty-five days, because we drifted through quietly and didn't push our stock, and they actually gained weight on the way up there. If you have good herders and good planning and all, you can do that with stock.

This one fall we were on the road, and I always went ahead to be sure nobody had changed their mind or anything, and here was an old boy hanging in a tree! A Mexican fella was hanging in a tree in one of the fields I had rented. He'd been lynched there. I daresn't let them Navajos see that, because they'd never have gone near that piece of ground at all. There was a fella lived pretty close to where it happened, and he said that the sheriff had got word about it and was coming to take him down. So I went on back and we stopped at a place where there was pretty nice grazing for a day until everything quieted down. Then we went on, and it all went fine.

It took us anywhere from thirty to thirty-eight days to get to Farmington, and then we held them there on those farms until the feeders came in from Nebraska. They would gain a little more while they was there. We wouldn't have to hold them generally over three or four days, because I had the cars ordered and everything; it was just a matter of getting them in. Any stock that was coming from a long distance, they tried pretty hard to get them off first, because they figured we'd had a hard trip, and I didn't let them think anything else.

They went to the feedlots then. The sheep on the reservation were never fat enough to go right to the block. They'd have to go into the feedlots first and top them off there; maybe thirty, forty days later why they'd go in to slaughter.

But I enjoyed those long drives. I loved to be on the road with stock. I enjoyed it so much going out every fall.

After we got rid of the sheep we'd load up and go home. One boy would bring the truck in and we'd come back with a truckload. We'd load up our gear and everything, and we'd always take flour or something back with us, merchandise, and the Navajos in on top of that. And then one of the Navajos would take all the horses back.

Those Navajos were all good singers, and whenever I'd get them on a truck they'd do a lot of singing. We'd come in through town, and these Navajos—there was two of them up in the front seat of the truck and the rest of them were behind—they'd start chanting back there. I'd stop and tell the boys, "Get out and help them out." We'd go up through the upper part of town and oh gosh, everybody was out watching and looking at them.

One time coming back from Durango, we were going to bring in a load of flour, and I had some other stuff that I could get in Durango that I couldn't get in Cortez. I knew there was going to be a fair and a rodeo, and there was one of these outfits that had a merry-go-round, a ferris wheel, and them figure eights, or what they call 'em. I took Leon on that trip and John and Willie Cly, I wanted to take them because they'd always been so nice that way, and then, I believe it was Katso. There was five or six of them. I knew the place where I wanted to camp; it was pretty close to where the rodeo was. I wanted to get them up where there was a nice view. Then we walked around through town and I showed them different things and I bought some ice cream for them.

The next day I went up to buy the tickets to get in at the fair, and this fella had heard about the chanting these Navajos had done coming in the day before. I told him I wanted to get seven tickets. "No," he says, "you don't need them, just go right on in. Take those Navajos right on in with you, we'd just love to have them."

So we went in, and there was this big old ferris wheel was the first thing we came to. I went up and bought seven tickets for the ferris wheel and up we went. She was going round, and them son of a guns started chanting again. They was the chantingest outfit that you ever heard. Beautiful, my gracious! They just turned loose on that thing! Everybody crowded around, so the old boy, he really took us for a ride. And when we come down he had the money that I paid him, and he says, "Here's your money!"

And then every one of the things, we went on everything, every one of them, they'd just say, "Come right on in!" and they would take us for free. And the crowd of people would move right along with the Indians all around the place. Whenever we got on one of those rides, like the merry-go-round, oh that brought the old Indians alive, especially things like the figure eight, or the roller coaster, that's a wicked son of a gun, and they'd have these swinging things, everything we got on, why they'd chant to it.

They had one of the darned good outfits in there. Generally for those smaller towns they wouldn't bring in so many rides, and not so good, but nothing like that ever hit Durango before. So it really touched them off. They did it just because they felt of it. And then they appreciated the people accepting them. They were just feeling so good. You get on horseback and you're making a nice ride, you know, and you've got to sing a little about it.

The next day, after we got the truck loaded up with merchandise, and the Navajos bought quite a little bit of stuff too, to take home with them, I went right down through Main Street with my load. We was on our way home, and those fellas started to chanting again. We'd been on this trip a long time you know, pretty near forty days, with the stock and all, so they really started to singing; they was happy to be heading home. And those doors and windows opened up as we went down the street. They'd hear us coming. They'd phone ahead, some of them after we'd went by. "Get out and see them, here they come!" So they just kept singing till we got out of town, well, even after we got out of town.

One place over in there close to Dove Creek, we came into a bunch of vegetation that none of it ever grew down in the Valley, and it was a medicine weed. They wanted me to stop, they said they'd like to pick some of that and take it home, the medicine man wanted it. So I stopped and they gathered up some of that, and we took it on, went on home. And every now and then they'd start to sing.

7 ■■ HUNTERS AND TRACKERS

HARRY GOULDING: The old Navajos used to come in to the store here in deer season, and the limit would be according to the deer population; sometimes we'd get two deer, sometimes three. One time we got five deer. They used to come in here and ask, "How many deer, my friend?"

"They're letting us have three deer this year," I says.

"Gimme three cartridges."

They'd buy three cartridges for three deer, two cartridges for two deer. I'd break the boxes. They just don't have a chance with those fellas. If you ever want to learn how to hunt for deer, come down here and go out with some of these boys. I never saw such trackers.

We would have a pretty good bunch of sheep by the time we kept on buying. And here would come a Navajo with say four head of sheep to sell, and I'd buy them. Those doggoned sheep would stay together in their little group, they'd try to get away from the big herd, and occasionally they would. Those sheep would go out, and they'd circle round and come back maybe, and maybe they'd hit our sheep tracks and go out through them. There were sheep tracks all over. And that old herder I had could follow those sheep out through all them tracks. There ain't a white man alive, or ever was a white man, that could even start to do that, not even start to do it!

When we had sheep, I kept a little bunch over every winter so's I'd have something to keep my herder, and the rest of them were camped further away, down in a lower area where the feed wasn't so cold. I'd be riding out to camp, and some Navajo would be going that away, why we'd ride on out there together. We'd be visiting along and visiting along, and I knew that these tracks just come up and hit them. They don't have to look, they just come up and hit them, like that. Well, I got to where by watching a little close I could maybe make out some things. We'd be talking about something else, and I'd say, "There's some sheep that are heading on over in towards where so-and-so lives." I wanted to get him to doing it. You wouldn't see him looking down for tracks, but he'd say, "There's some horses are out and they're just grazing." And then, "Here's four or five men coming along horseback," or "Quite a bunch of sheep crossed here." I never caught them looking down towards the ground, them things just came up and recorded.

I wondered if every one of them was as good as the one I was with, but every one I ever rode with had the same ability of that kind. That's a possession!

RAY HUNT: The Indian's newspaper is tracks, which I learned as a kid. An Indian could always tell if a white man had crossed any part of the reservation from the way he rode his horse or the way he got off and walked.

"How did you know they were white men?"

"Well, they don't walk like we do. They didn't ride their horses like we do. Some of the horses had horseshoes on." That was their daily newspaper.

It was pretty hard for any of these desperados doing anything up around Cortez or Mancos to get on out and down into Arizona somewhere. It was impossible to cross the Navajo reservation. This Fowler boy here in McElmo Canyon, he and his father and them got into a jangle, so he just swiped two-thirds or a half of the horse herd they had, took it across the reservation and went right on. Well, all the police had to do was just keep in contact with the Navajos to know exactly where they were at and how many days it would be before they came out on the other side. Sure enough, when they came out, there was the law waiting for them. They didn't have to trail them across.

8 ■■■ EARLY VISITORS

HARRY GOULDING: Just as soon as we got the store up, pretty soon we started to getting more visitors. Some of the people call them "dudes," but we always called them "visitors." They were wonderful people. They'd get stuck coming in, they'd fight their way out of the sand, and while they was here with us they would learn a little more about what to do in sand. But still you had to sweat when you *knew* how to do it. Those folks would come back and come back and come back. They used to stay for five, six, ten days. It was such a chore to get in, they didn't hurry off. Then they'd come back and stay a long time again.

When we were in the tents even, we got a few visitors; the first year we were in here we had two visitors come in. They were artists from Oklahoma, and they stayed about ten days with us. There was a Navajo who told us where there was quite a big arch, a natural rock arch, and so he went with us, and we took the artists in to see it. We had to go up a big high sand bank, and then there was an old trail around the edge that the Indians made, where they could get on through. From there we went up and up, some rough climbing. It was quite an arch. It isn't anything that you can get a picture of because you can't get far enough back from it on either side, but it's something to see.

Mr. Wetherill had been in there; he took Charles Bernheimer, the geologist, in. There was an old Prince Albert can in there with the date that they went in with Mr. Wetherill. Wetherill called it Bernheimer Arch. If you'd ask him about it, he'd say, "Well, we were just going along, and Mr. Bernheimer was there, and he happened to see it first." Something like that.

Coming back out, one of the artists picked some flowers to take back to Mike for the table. This Indian that guided us in, when the sand dune took off, he just let a whoop out of him and down that hill he went, so these two birds took right out after him. I knew better than to run. They got to going so fast down that sand hill that their legs couldn't keep up to them. They had been out for a long time and they had long beards hanging down. They just made a double track right down that sand dune with their beards. The flowers didn't look too good, but we took them along for Mike anyway.

MIKE GOULDING: Just a very few guests would come by when we were in the tents, and we'd all eat together. Artists, mostly. We saw Zane Grey going down with his big pack outfit. He went through with Mr. Wetherill. It was fun to meet those people. He used to take a huge string of mules with him, all packed, with their white canvas packs tied over them, quite a sight to see them go on down there. He was getting stuff for his books. He wrote *Rainbow Trail* about this country; he wrote a book at Kayenta and out of Flagstaff and Red Lake, called *Wild Horse Mesa;* and he wrote *Riders of the Purple Sage,* that was up out of Monticello, I think. That's bean country now.

There's another one that used to come out to Wetherill's, a cartoonist, George Herriman, he drew *Krazy Kat.* He always had his characters by the Elephant's Feet or one of the monuments. He made arrangements that a film would be sent out once a week. It was shown in the old sanitarium in Kayenta, which isn't there any more. We used to get the mail once a week, and we'd go and see the movie.

And Jimmy Swinnerton, another cartoonist. At that time he was over around the Hopis, but he also came to Kayenta. After we got settled, why he came over with us.[1]

HARRY GOULDING: After we got up in the store, we had the little cabin and we had two bedrooms in the upstairs over the store. When visitors started coming in, picking up and picking up, we built another rock cabin, and we'd put our guests in there. When a few more of them came, we'd put them in our bedroom and we'd move to the second room. Our bedroom had a view and it was a little nicer room. When we'd get more still, Mike and I would have to take off and find a clear spot in the wareroom and put out our bedrolls.

TED CLY: In 1928, the Gouldings, they build a house right up here on top. Then we saw some other white people: '28, '29, '30, '31, pretty soon there was a big corral right down here, and he started pack trips on saddle horses. Go down into this monument down here, after that they come across, all day long they stay way up in the canyon. Next morning they go around the arch, way over where the arch is and the Totem Pole, and then come back out here. Two days horseback. Tourists. That was in '29, somewhere along there, 1930. We saw him with the horses and saw white people using little box cameras, some you pull them out, some others regular square. You look right through in there and then you snap. We see that.

Then they got a car and they take tour with it down in the Valley, where the wagon track goes down. We saw the car, just like a spider, it goes like that. Little wagonwheel type, and we saw they got to crank it in front. Little tiny wheels, just like a wagon. Then we saw a different one, a bigger one, wider tires.

MAURICE KNEE: Teddy Cly is Willie Cly's son. Hosteen Cly was his grandfather. When I first saw Teddy he was about eleven or twelve. He was just a little bitty. His arms weren't over that big, just a little bitty old skinny kid, and he used to ride on the front of Harry's car down in the Valley. He'd say, "I'll show you! Go round here by these rock windows. If you can get the car over here I'll show you some old rock pictures where the ancient people lived." Oh he showed Harry lots of stuff in there.

HARRY GOULDING: At first, we didn't have pictures to show people because I didn't own a camera and didn't know nothing about taking pictures. So our entertainment was upstairs, visiting. I'd always get Bert to come up because he had some great stories that he told about where he came from, over in southwestern Utah. He had heard stories about how these rich people loll around a lounge and smoke, so he lolled around too, but he chewed tobacco. He'd sit there all that time with a chew in his mouth, and he'd swallow the juice! I don't know how he stood it! He would have a chew in his mouth, and he'd tell a story, and he'd chew a little bit and swallow, and then he'd tell something else. Oh, he enjoyed that!

PART TWO. THE DEPRESSION YEARS

9 ◼◼ THE PAIUTE STRIP RETURNS
TO RESERVATION

HARRY GOULDING: I and Johnny Taylor down at Oljeto, we had quite a little bit to do with Utah giving this Paiute Strip land to the Navajos. When the Paiutes moved out, there was quite a bit of stock kept coming down in here, even some from up in Colorado, because it was public domain then. We got along with the stock men fine, they were friendly with us. They'd come up by the trading post and we'd play penny-ante poker. But the Navajos started moving in right away, and it could really run into pretty bad trouble. As long as the Anglos were bringing stock in here in the winters, the Navajos felt like they had a right to go and get some of that stock, and it was just keeping a bad situation in here all the time. It could have went ahead and turned into another fracas like the Posey War.

They had given the land to the Paiutes earlier, so Johnny Taylor and I just felt that it should belong to the Indians. It would save a lot of trouble if it was given. There was nobody else that was interested in it. There were no other whites in here, only them cattlemen that would bring a few head down in. John Wetherill was over around Kayenta, he was on the reservation in Arizona, he wasn't interested in it. There was one other trader at Navajo Mountain, but that was far away. There was nobody over to the east in there at all.

There were some Mormons thinking about it too; I know we would talk to some of them and they would agree. Johnny Taylor and I both dealt a lot up in Salt Lake, and we got acquainted with some of the leaders up there. J. Bracken Lee and I were pretty good friends. We worked through him. He gave us different angles that we might try. I told him what had happened down here, the Paiutes leaving, the Navajos and the cattlemen mixing in, and so he worked angles around and gave us different names to write to.

Eventually it fell to the Navajos, in 1933, that's what happened to it. Even Adikai finally accepted my being here because Utah gave the Navajos the Paiute Strip. They all knew that, when they made it back into reservation.

◼◼ The Paiute Strip had been restored to the public domain in 1922 by executive order of Secretary of the Interior Fall, to accommodate the interests of oil developers. By 1929, it was clear that there was no oil in the Paiute

Strip, and the oilmen had left the area. In this year, according to Lawrence C. Kelly, "The strip was temporarily withdrawn from all forms of entry . . . when the Navajos evidenced a desire to incorporate it within their reservation." After all the various interests in Utah were satisfied, the Paiute Strip was finally added to the Navajo reservation in 1933, although Harry Goulding continued to lease his school section of land, now surrounded by reservation, until he was able to buy it in 1938.[1]

HARRY GOULDING: That was when I moved my sheep out. It was in the Depression and you just couldn't sell sheep. I mean if a Navajo would bring them in and give them to you, you couldn't get enough up there at the railroad to pay. You'd lose money on them taking them out. So I quit buying just all they'd bring in. We decided, Mike and I, that we had maybe enough of money to buy two or three off of a family. That way maybe our money'd last until things straightened out. Because during that Depression, I'll tell you, if an Indian would have brought a silver dollar in there, or a rag one, either way, and laid it on that counter, why Mike and I both would have fell over backwards! There wasn't many visitors traveling either. But we kept a-buying sheep, a few at a time, and not selling, and we had a big herd by the time the Depression was getting pretty bad.

Then we got the Paiute Strip made into Navajo reservation, and I had to pull out with my bunch of sheep, had to move them across the river to Mexican Hat and back in that area. We held them in there for about a year and a half, because you couldn't get nothing for them. Instead of taking them to the railroad, I finally sold them to a Mr. Lybrook, who wanted me to buy him a herd of sheep.

FRED YAZZIE: Harry Goulding got a flock of sheep, and my daddy, Adikai Yazzie, he don't like those sheep, he thinks they're taking over the country. Well, he had an argument with Harry Goulding, and he tell the story about Harry Goulding to his brothers. Those two brothers say, "You had better leave him alone," and trying to talk that way to him. They told him not to come up and argue with Harry Goulding, he might do something to him. "He might kill you," they said. Well, my old daddy thinks he's big enough to fight him, he's not going to get killed. He was not afraid to fight, you know. He can do anything quick.

But my old daddy think his brother is talking right not to fight with him, and better do the right way. "Well," he says, "we better go to agency." They used to have agency down at Shiprock. That's the first agency we had. They had a lawyer there, and talk to the lawyer about this country. So he went down to Shiprock to see the judge.

At that time they have no car, no nothing to move fast with. He have a horse he used to ride a long ways. They train them that way. This horse can travel from here to Blanding one day. Night and day they travel. While they're going, he still can eat and take the grass. My daddy, he used to train horse like that.

He started in the evening, he started heading for Shiprock where the judge and all those lawyers are. And Harry Goulding was here, he was right in this corral here. He runs store and flock of sheep and taking all the grazing, you know. The sheep are overgrazing. My daddy, he thinks that way.

Well, he rides all night, and the next morning he was in Shiprock and talk with those chaps, the lawyer, about Harry Goulding, the overgrazing, you know. He trying to be friendly and he going do the right thing.

So the lawyer told him, "You go back, and we'll be over tomorrow night. We want to talk about it, and we'll move the flock out from the reservation to Mexican Hat." They told him that.

Well, he rides home all night again. In the morning he came. I was just a growing boy. It come to me, my daddy's going get killed. And I was ready for it, you know, I'll help my daddy in case something happen. So I conceal myself, and I had arrow and bow and trying to shoot straight. If something happen to my daddy, I can go fight too. My daddy and my brother's uncle, he was training us, run early, exercise, and do those things.

So we get ready for everything, and these judge, by the sundown they be here. My daddy, he started saddling his horse, put gun and pistol and everything on, and he started to ride out. And we took the horse, myself and my brother and my cousin, and we started to follow him, you know, in case something happen. Well, we decided to stay back over there and hide. My old daddy, he was waiting by the junction, waiting for those people to come in. And Harry Goulding right overhead, he was living up there. Well, my old daddy, he do all his best to make good friend with Harry Goulding, but Harry Goulding, sometimes he gets mad, and he think that way.

Then finally, toward sundown, the judge they came. We saw the car coming. We was there too, you know. We got arrow and bow, if something happen we want to shoot, we was all ready. They came in, and we was hiding behind a hill. My old daddy, he got off the horse there, and Harry Goulding saw the car coming. It was them all right. He didn't know they was after him, you know, and he just come friendly, and he talks. "Come on in!" he say.

There was a Navajo judge and a white, and some cops, about six of them, I think, come in, and they started to find out what it's all about. They had talk there, and finally they traded each other to move out right tonight, move his sheep out and take them across the river. This is reservation and belongs to the Navajo. I think Maurice and Paul Knee took the sheep out right that night. They can herd all night and go to Mexican Hat across the river. So they took these sheep across, and they stay there about two years before he sell them.

LYNN LYMAN: Harry was in kind of a predicament there. He'd been trading with the Navajos for sheep, and then they gave that strip south of the San Juan River to the Navajos, made it part of the reservation, and he had to get out. I know that he tried to sell the sheep, and I know the people that he tried to sell them to. While they're good friends of mine, they were hard-headed stockmen, and they thought they had him over a barrel and they could get the sheep really cheap. I think it made Harry a little mad. He was going to hold onto them until he could get a decent price for them. So he had to come across to this side of the river. That's why they were grazing in the Garden of the Gods. He was just trying to hold onto them and get a fair price for them and get out of the sheep business.

This Jimmy Palmer came along just about that time, and Harry got him to look after the sheep. We learned later that he'd already killed one man, and he was down here in strange country. He stayed in Blanding for quite a little while. Then he drifted on down to Bluff and was there for a while. The Jimmy Palmer affair was an unfortunate thing, and it was unfortunate for Harry that he had that kind of a man working for him. It kind of cooled things off between the people here in Blanding and Harry. There's no secret about it, I always stuck up for Harry, and I do yet. I don't think he was to blame any more than I would be if I hired a man to work for me and he killed somebody.

RAY HUNT: Harry needed help with his sheep up north of the San Juan, and Jimmy Palmer was broke, didn't have any money. This young girl was his wife, which they naturally supposed. Only thirteen years old. Probably was his wife. So Harry grubstaked him and gave him a percent of the wool and a percent of the lamb crop and this and that and the other.

I got acquainted with him when he first came into Bluff, and then he talked to me about could he lease these sheep from Harry. I said, "There's only one way to find out and that's go down there and ask him, but I think he will, because I think he needs someone to run them." And I never knew that Jimmy Palmer was the man he was. He didn't seem like that when he was around Bluff, although he was quite edgy, and everybody could see after it all happened that he was that type of fella.

■   Against Harry's orders, Jimmy Palmer took his sheep into John's Canyon, which was cattle range belonging to Bill Oliver of Blanding, who had been sheriff during the Paiute war. Oliver and his nephew, Norris Shumway, confronted Palmer there, who shot and killed them both. The next morning, he and his child wife drove on flat tires to Gouldings and forced Harry at the point of a gun to give him his car and money. They fled to Texas, where they had originally come from, and Palmer was arrested there, tried and convicted of the previous murder of his wife's father. He died in a Texas prison and was never brought to trial for the murder of Oliver and Shumway.

The Olivers and Shumways and many of the people of Blanding, looking for someone upon whom to release the grief and fury of their loss, accused

Harry of giving Palmer permission to use the John's Canyon range, and of delaying to report the murders after Palmer left with his car.

Harry never defended himself to the people of Blanding, and forty years later he would not speak to me on the record about his part in the Jimmy Palmer affair. True to his western values, he believed that a man should be judged by his actions, not by his words, and that his life would have to speak for him. Ultimately, it seems that we must leave it where Harry wanted us to leave it. He did tell me that years after the event, Norris Shumway's mother apologized to him for her earlier opinions.

10 ■■■ STOCK REDUCTION

■ In 1933, President Roosevelt appointed John Collier commissioner of Indian affairs. Like so many of the New Deal appointees, he was a highly controversial figure.[1] In the 1920s Collier had focused his attention on the American Indians, specifically, at first, in defense of the Pueblo Indians' claims to lands that they had long held under Spanish land grants and which were now threatened by congressional action. It was from this background that Roosevelt appointed him commissioner. Collier, the man, was a visionary idealist, ill adapted to bureaucratic governmental life, and yet with a brilliant gift for legal tactics that made him a powerful if not ruthless lobbyist. He came to office at a time when the entire country was suffering the effects of the Great Depression, and was beginning, under Roosevelt's direction, to organize radically new government programs to relieve the situation.

It happened that, coincidentally, the overgrazing of the Navajo range had reached disastrous proportions, and Collier believed that unless drastic measures were taken, the Navajos would be devastated as a people. The centerpiece of his program for the Navajos thus became range management, the most important component of which was a severe reduction in stock to bring it down to the carrying capacity of the range. With some exceptions, most of the traders looking objectively at the condition of the range agreed that it was extremely serious, but they were not at all in agreement that the stock reduction program Collier instituted was the proper approach. The Navajo families out on the range could not understand how taking their sheep away would save them. To this day their bitterness has not faded; they see the stock reduction program as an atrocity equal to the Long Walk of the 1860s.

Harry Goulding felt caught in the middle of this confrontation of the two cultures. He agreed with the logic of stock reduction, but he loved the Navajos and sympathized with the passion of their outrage and their sense of betrayal. His loyalty and his livelihood were both with them. He never argued John Collier's case with the Navajos, and even this long after the events, he would not give me an interview on stock reduction. Among the speakers on this subject, Harry stands silent—not aloof, but torn by the passions of the issue.

MAURICE KNEE: Old John Collier come in and just raped those herds. The Navajos had too many sheep. They told the Navajos that they'd have to keep all the sheep off the range for ten years so the grass'd come back. All it needed was a good rain!

The bad part of it was that they'd come into a hogan, and they'd say, "Mr. Longsheep, we're going to take half your sheep right now." They didn't know the culture, they didn't realize it was a matriarch system. The sheep didn't belong to him, they belonged to his wife, and the herders, each girl, had a certain number of sheep in there.

So Mr. Longsheep would say, "Oh no, they're not my sheep. You'll have to talk to my wife; and that little boy, he's got twenty, because he's herded for five years; and this little girl, she's been with them for ten years and she's got fifty sheep, are hers for when she gets married."

Some herds of a thousand, they took two hundred; some herds of one hundred, they took fifty, and that hurt the little ones, it was just murder on them.

What could the Navajos do? They couldn't do nothing. They promised them jobs, so they give them thirty dollars a month and their food while they went away to work, but they didn't count the five kids setting in the hogan. They didn't get any food. They depended on that mutton, and the wool, and the lambs to sell, and the lambs to keep to revive the herd. One transaction and it's gone. They just came out with police and made them sell.

They gathered the sheep in herds and they was going to ship them out. They'd get orders to move them, and they'd drive them twenty miles, and pretty soon they'd get orders to take them back. There was no grass and there was no water, and they were just walking skeletons. While they were fat, if they'd told those people, "Come and butcher them out," they could've dried the meat, they could've made jerky out of it. But then they finally came in with .22 rifles, and they down had a heyday. I can take you between Goulding's and Oljeto, right down that road to Oljeto, about six niches down, four thousand head of sheep were shot. And you could walk on horse skeletons all the way to Gallup, where they died. Starved to death, or just collapsed, and they'd come along and shoot them. It was just legal murder.

Of course they may have had too many sheep, but if you let nature take its course, it would have equalized out. The Navajos had been through that before.

"John Collier," that's still to this day the name of a dog. "John Collie, he's a dog!" They had a dog they didn't like, they'd call him "John Collie."

■   Collier's first meeting with the Navajos after his appointment as commissioner was at a tribal council meeting at Fort Wingate on July 7, 1933. He spoke in a general way of his plans for the reservation and received approval of the establishment of an erosion experiment station near Mexican Springs, to be built by the Civilian Conservation Corps, which had just been instituted as a part of Roosevelt's assault on the Depression. In October, after he had received funds for his projects, he became more specific. He proposed the unification of the six regional Navajo agencies, with one headquarters and twenty-five subagencies. There would be seventy new day schools, irrigation projects, erosion experiment stations. There would probably be a road-building program. All of these things would provide work for the Navajos.

It was only after this careful preparation that he came to what was basic to the whole program and most controversial: stock reduction.[2] There was strong opposition to the stock reduction program by the Navajos in the council. Above all, the local Navajos needed time to think through the problem and work it out in their own minds. It was not their style to make decisions by majority vote of representatives acting for them in absentia. But Collier had all the charts and figures and money, and he thought he could not wait.

It was decided that the first target would be 100,000 sheep and no goats. The Navajos would be paid two to three dollars for wethers and one to one and a half dollars for ewes. Chee Dodge said that such a low price for ewes would lead the Navajos to sell only their culls, and that the production of lambs would not be reduced. Nevertheless, the plan went forward. The Navajos sold their sheep without protest (in the Depression year of 1933 they were having difficulty in selling their sheep to the traders). As predicted, those with large herds sold their poor ewes, and the productive capacity of the herds remained about the same.

In the second stock reduction of 1934, the quotas were 49,000 sheep and 149,000 goats. Again, as in 1933, although the intention was to protect the small herds by leaving those of less than 100 untouched and taking a larger percentage from the larger stock owners, these wealthier Navajos insisted on equal treatment. The government agents in the field, often no doubt insensitive and looking for the easy way, allowed the Navajos to work out their own differences and took stock where they could get it to fill their quotas. The terrible drought of the 1934 dust bowl left the stock in weakened condition. Many of them died during the drives, and some were killed because they were about to die anyway. The Navajos, whose stock has a profound value to them, not only as the chief measure of their wealth, but also as the center of their entire family activity, were dismayed and sickened at what they took to be the callous slaughter of their sheep and goats.

In 1935, the quotas were again 200,000 sheep and goats. Collier must have been aware of the rising grief and anger among the Navajos, but he apparently did not anticipate any difficulties in this third reduction, for he withdrew the government workers from the field and turned the program over to the traders, who for a commission were to buy and market the stock at government prices. The Navajos disposed of a few culls, and in the end only 16,225 sheep and 14,716 goats were sold, 15 percent of the quota.

In the face of these repeated failures, a more sophisticated approach was undertaken. A detailed survey was made of the condition of the land. In addition, an innovative Human Dependency Survey was begun, in which teams of interviewers from various social science disciplines went from hogan to hogan gathering information on Navajo social institutions; their ideas of property and land use; the distribution of stock ownership; their relations with the traders; their diet, clothing, and housing. On the basis of these studies, land management districts were established in 1936, which followed the terrain, the land holdings of related extended families, and the trading areas around trading posts. Quotas for sheep units were established for each district, varying with the range capacity.

With this system in place, stock reduction was renewed in 1937, and range riders were hired to administer the operation and perform the field work. Unfortunately, most of these men were unemployed cowboys who had no love for the Navajos and no love for sheep. The focus now was on unproductive livestock, especially horses, but in spite of the more rational planning that had gone into the land management districts, the Navajos were in no mood for more stock reduction, and the range riders now became the focus of their grief, pain, anger, and occasional violence.

By 1940, the reservation census showed 621,584 sheep units, which was getting close, but was still not within the carrying capacity of 560,000 units, as required by the regulations. Grazing permits were issued controlling the number of livestock on the range, and in the years that followed, land use varied from 15 percent below to 5 percent above carrying capacity.[3] At the same time, the Navajo dependence on sheep gradually decreased, so that the immediate pressure on the tribe to reduce its stock was somewhat relieved. In 1941, the only real resistance to the selling of horses was in the back country of the northwest—Navajo Mountain, Aneth, and parts of Monument Valley.

On paper the record looked good. From 1935 to 1947, Navajo income from livestock had increased 60 percent. Wool production remained approximately stable in spite of smaller herds, and the average weight of wool per sheep increased 50 percent.[4]

Nevertheless, the searing trauma of stock reduction has never been forgotten. It is clear that the acid still burns in the stomach of Nedra Tódích'íi'nii.

NEDRA TÓDÍCH'íi'NII[5] (Tséyaats'ózí [Narrow Canyon], translated from Navajo):   The problems with the sheep and horses hadn't come up while my grandmother was living. There were no laws to limit the number of sheep, no legal papers that told you how many sheep you could herd. There was nothing like that then. That's how the Navajo people got such great herds of sheep. My older brother had a lot of livestock, sheep and cattle. He had many horses and three wagons.

At Lók'aahnteel (Wide Reeds, or Ganado) stood the only stores. Ten of our people on horses, leading burros carrying wool, traveling in a row like the white people, used to journey there. They had as much stock as some white men do. They used to keep their sheep in three large herds as they traveled.

Then the talk about reducing the stock came up. Our stock was counted over at Tódík'ǫ́ǫ́zh (Sour Water). They took seven of our goats there, although we had a lot of children. I had nine children then, and my younger sister had eight, but when they counted the stock, they didn't think about the number of children we had. We stood and watched them drive our goats away in a cloud of dust. I thought to myself, "I guess it was like that when we had enemies who stole our flocks," because my grandmother used to tell about the enemies they had in her time, the Utes, the Mexicans, and the Pueblos.

They also took seventeen horses. They said the horses were of no use anyway, and we weren't paid for them either. Nothing. Some people said they were going to separate their herds into tiny flocks and hide them. That's how it happened.

The following year talk about children came up. Fine girls and boys were to be picked and sent away to the enemy's territory to school.

They used to say, "Those of you who have no livestock left, kill some here and take the meat with you."

We said, "Why do you take our sheep away from us, kill them, and then tell us to take them back? You take them! You're the ones who were longing to have them! Why don't you eat them yourselves?"

So my family didn't eat any of our sheep. We all said, "Why should we do this, trying to get the last piece, when they make us suffer so much?" But some people came and took meat from the dead ones. They skinned them after they were shot.

They would say to us, "Cut their throats right here. Leave their hooves, horns, and heads on, but take the rest. Skin them like you would skin a buffalo and take the meat for yourselves." My husband skinned one over at Tsék'izi (Rock Door). Then he decided not to, so he took off on his horse. He said, "I don't like the way you have to skin them. It's frightening."

Charley Ashcroft was the one who led in all these bad doings. He was a range rider, a white man married to a Navajo woman. He talked like a Navajo. He married into the Kin Łichíí'níí (Red House) clan, but I know he had enemy blood. That was why we were suspicious of him. He came around with some white men and told them he knew all the Navajos, their livestock, and where they could be located. He took our sheep over to the sheep dip, where they were counted, just like at a regular sheep dip, but as they came up from the vat into the corral, the animals to be killed were divided from the rest of the group. They used to say, "Not this one. We'll have to kill it." They took them to the dip, but they really came around to do their business of reducing our stock for John Collier.

And these were our own people, who lived among us! They didn't even gather them in the sheep corrals; they just chased them against the cliffs or in the corners of rocks. They killed them on this side of Tsé Yaaniichii (Red Rock), and behind Tsé Zhinłeezh (Black Rock Earth), and they divided them up and killed them behind Tsé Łichíí'dah Azkání (Red Rock Butte), where there was an old mine and mine dumps. Then they killed some over at Halgai (White Earth). A lot of sheep were killed right near the foot of Tsék'izi (Rock Door), where the rock wall reaches up. A white man named Dibé Nééz was the only one who lived there then. He used to buy sheep there, but he probably got tired of it. [She laughs.]

Some of the Navajos fought with the rangers when they came around to inspect the flocks. At that time Hastóí Adíl'íní (Imitator) and John Chee fought with a white policeman and almost choked him to death, because of the sheep. They stayed in jail all that winter and the next summer. The following fall, as winter approached again, the people begged the authorities for their release, so they were set free. Now if a white man had been killed, that might have been a good enough reason to send somebody to jail.

At Teec Nos Pos there was a woman who had her sheep in the corral when the rangers told her that they had to be divided in half to be taken away. While her husband attacked the ranger and tied him up, this woman climbed on top of him and tied him up with his own bandanna. When he couldn't hold it any more, his urine came out of him. I understand the woman was in jail for a whole winter with her husband.

If anybody starts doing that kind of thing again, the fight will be so big, they'll all choke from the dust—mainly the white man. That's what I think.

It was all a big waste. At that time there were a lot of coyotes, and they ate some of the sheep. Dogs ate them too. Today, you can still see their bones lying around. Land of ghosts! You can see the bleached bones sticking out of the ground. From here to Kayenta there are graveyards. The horses' bones are scattered there to this day. At Niist'aah, at the foot of the hill near Kayenta, the bones of the horses can be seen gleaming white against the earth.

I don't know where John Collier came from, but he came upon us. They used to say to us that the earth was getting tired and couldn't give any more grass. In the Navajo way of thinking, the sheep are what you live by. You live by the horses and everything around you.

The white men have a God. When the sheep are thirsty they pray to him, saying that their livestock need something to drink. Then the rain will come down to the sheep and the grass will come up on the earth. It is like that on our enemy's land. Their land is thick with grass when it rains.

The Navajo, as they call us, live here in a bad situation. We live in a place where trouble is always nearby. I think at times that's because we don't practice our religion as we used to, we don't receive very much happiness anymore. A long time ago it wasn't like this. There were a lot of sheep with plenty of sunflowers, big fields of hay and mountain rice and rush grass. All around, it was dark with vegetation. When you walked over the land it was hard to walk because of the grass in your path. Now the land has turned to white desert. Our enemy's land is very good. Yesterday I went past Bluff. I saw a lot of black greasewood, sand sage, grasses, mountain rice. I thought to myself, "I wish our land was like that." [Laughter.]

■ Lamar Bedoni—as well as Nedra Tódích'íi'nii—may be exaggerating the numbers of livestock which were killed,[6] but his passion is none the less inflamed, even after so many years have passed.

LAMAR BEDONI[7] (Narrow Canyon, translated from Navajo):   I was born at Navajo Mountain sixty-three years ago. When I was twenty-two years old, the talk of goats began.[8] I still remember what happened when it began. About 160 of our goats were driven into a canyon corner and were shot to death. During the shooting of the goats, one man was shot in the leg. The goats were bought from us for only fifty cents a head, but even then we were not paid right away. About six months later we were paid. Some of us didn't get paid until after three years, and then for our 160 goats we were paid only twenty dollars and a few cents. All of them were killed. From that time on, we herded only a very few sheep and horses. The people suffered from begging for things.

Then they did the same thing again, and this time we fought with some range riders. John Collier was a white cowboy and he had some cowboys with him. They were the range riders, they were the ones who killed the goats here. Some of them were Navajos too. The range riders would chase the horses away and put them in a corral. I was the one who roped the gate of the corral and pulled it open with my horse so the horses in the corral could be chased out. That was why the range riders were after us. If you said no to them, they would just put handcuffs on you right there. Four Navajo men were taken away to Fort Defiance for six months. White Hat was taken, Shorty Yazzie, another man called Hosteen Luke, a cripple, and another named Charley. But they didn't catch me when I sneaked away on a horse to Navajo Mountain.

Later on, seventy-eight cows were cornered against a canyon and shot to death right in front of us. Their bones are still there. This time they didn't pay us anything. Nothing. Then the officials told us not to replace the missing horses, not to replace the missing sheep, not to replace the missing cows! We were told not to expand our land but to try to make it smaller. These were the laws. We felt that we were all tied up and couldn't do anything.

Some people hid their livestock in canyons. When it got really bad, that was the only way out. At that time, my father held some authority at Navajo Mountain; he was a *táá' naaznilí* (one of the three local chapter officials: chairman, vice-chairman, and secretary). He tried to say no to the stock

reduction, but a lot of policemen were against us. That is the way we reacted
to the stock reduction.

■   One range rider, who was an exception to what seems to have been the
rule, who understood the Navajos and could see the problem from both
sides, was Edward Smith, now the trader at Oljeto. He was willing to bend
the rules at times in a common sense way to give the Navajos a break.[9]

EDWARD D. SMITH[10]:   The desire was to have cowpunchers handle the
stock reduction rather than sheepmen, who could have done a better job
because they understood the situation. So I went out into the field as a range
rider, except they made a mistake. I was trained as a stockman rather than
a cattleman, so I had just as much love for a sheep as I did for a cow. I
wasn't at all sympathetic to the policy of destroying the sheep. We had to
reduce the sheep, but you see, some people in the Government Service had
the idea that Indians were something below them. For years that had been
the way the Indian Service looked at it.

When you got in the field you found out that a Navajo has so many head
of sheep; he eats so many head a year and he'll hide so many head. They
don't dock the tails of the sheep they're going to eat; they leave them long.
They dock the tails of the ones they're going to sell or breed, but on the
wether lambs—the castrated buck lambs—they leave the tails long. So when
you count the sheep, as you ride around these different canyons, you look
over there and see all these stones on this far hill hidden over there, except
that they'll be moving. If the stones had long tails, I didn't count them.
Because if you counted the long tails, then the government would come by
and want to confiscate them. They would force them to sell those, and you
knew if they didn't have their sheep to eat that winter, they'd be pretty well
starved by summer. So you had to be enough of an outdoorsman to be
reasonable rather than hold strictly to the record. That didn't go over too
good with John Collier and some of the boys that were trying to put their
finger down on it.

When they have a sing, they might have to butcher twenty-five head of
sheep to feed the people that come to the sing. That takes an awful whack.
If a man is holding out a hundred head of sheep and he explains to you that
he's got to have a squaw dance in the fall, well, you just count it up and
there's your hundred head of sheep. That's why he's holding out. If you
know his customs—and they won't lie to you— then you understand his
thinking. All you're trying to do is reduce the overall number of breeding
sheep that he's going to have during the year. Then you don't have any
complaint and he doesn't have any complaint, because you understand what
the man's thoughts are when he objects. Really, it's simple if you understand
the Navajos.

For instance, I didn't say, "We will meet you and you're going to dip your sheep on such-and-such a day," and then expect that they would be there when we came up. No. If I planned to come rushing up like a big boss and have everybody wait for me, why they'd never have shown up. They didn't expect the white man to keep his word. We would go and camp there the night before. Then they would come in to see if we had kept our word. If we were there, then they would come. My theory was that you were expected to keep your word to them whether they kept their word to you or not. It wasn't wrong for them to break their word, but it was wrong for you to break your word.

They had to reduce. They had tremendous horse herds. A Navajo's wealth was figured by the number of horses he owned. One man might have hundreds of horses that were crippled, knock-kneed, and unusable, but his wealth was determined by the number of horses. When he bought a woman he gave so many horses for that girl. Sometimes he bought three or four girls at one time to marry. To convince him to keep only two or three horses and convert the rest into sheep was very difficult. A person like that was the one who got the maddest of all, because he couldn't change his thinking of Navajo wealth into present-day economy. They really got furious with you. It hurts your pride to be a wealthy man because you have horses, and then to become a poor man because you have sheep. It's like having five wives. You're a better man than if you had one wife . . . Still you'd probably been better off without any to start with!

We had another policy that the government didn't approve of and didn't know about. It was that you, as an Indian, turned in so many of your horses to be sold. These horses were theoretically sold and we would keep them in the corral. But if another man had a worse horse that he didn't have to sell, one which was not as good a horse as the other man had turned in, he had a right to exchange horses, provided that every morning we ended up with the same number of horses in that corral. Our Navajo guides cooperated with us and understood what it was all about. They made sure that if a good horse was picked up, the word got around very shortly: "So-and-so has a good horse in the corral, a better horse than you've got. That horse better disappear pretty soon." The next morning some old cripple would be there. Nobody ever knew what happened to that horse. It could have been a dust storm changed a gray horse to a brown horse.

It was the same way with sheep. If you had only a good sheep to turn in, then someone could come in at night and exchange an old sheep for a good one, because we actually didn't get to branding until after the reduction. Until the time came, they could exchange.

That's why I got into it. I thought somebody that liked stock ought to get out there and help the Navajos. They had enough guys running around trying to boss them without their being undependable on top of that. I thought that if I got out there, maybe I could make them understand what was going on. Reduction had to be. All over the United States on federal land, everything was overstocked. They'd never controlled units per acre. Even a white man was allowed to run as many sheep as he wanted to pay for, and it became overgrazed. It was a conservation movement all over the country, and it was a good deal if it was handled right. I suppose you might call it a crash program that had to be carried out in the United States for conservation of the range. That's just about what it was. It was like the crash program today for ecology, to save our air and our polluted streams. They had to save the range. They didn't just single out the reservation. The only reason it affected the reservation was because it was land under the responsibility of the federal government.

■   Although Harry is silent on this subject, here is the voice of another respected trader in the area.

MILDRED HEFLIN[11] (former trader at Oljeto and Kayenta):   Of course, we couldn't quite see the overall picture either. We were in sympathy with the Indians because this program was just being forced on them. I suppose it was a necessary thing. Yes, it *was* a necessary thing. But it was like all government projects; when you have a big project going and you've got a lot of people involved, some things are unjustly done.

In about 1937, shortly after we moved there, a missionary by the name of Shine Smith came to Oljeto. He was quite a character. The Indians at Oljeto formed a delegation and sent them to Washington to see Eleanor and President Roosevelt, and they got Shine Smith to go along. They'd never been off the reservation in their lives and they had to have a spokesman, so he went with them.

Well, they did get to see Eleanor Roosevelt, but of course they didn't accomplish anything.[12] They stayed back there for about two weeks. The Indian agent, Fryer, was quite upset, of course. Fortunately, he blamed the missionary more than he did us.

The Navajos asked my husband to speak up for them, but we couldn't openly say anything. All we did was listen and sympathize, and that was it. We *couldn't* do any more than that, really, because we were at the mercy of the Indian agent over at Window Rock. Any day they wanted to, they could cancel our lease out.

At that time I was really mad at John Collier. I was just like the Navajos; I thought he was pretty bad. [Laughs.] But as I grew a little more mature and looked over the situation, I thought it was probably for the best. But I do think it was very poorly handled. Whenever you tell a person that he's got to do something, you're going to have problems. He's going to back up and resist.

John Collier did more for the Navajos than any other Indian Commissioner we've ever had. He got schools started on the reservation, even though the day schools at first were pretty frustrating things. He did try, and he really *was* for the Indian. I have great respect for him. I really do.

And from my experience with the few range riders I had anything to do with, I feel that they did the best they could. They were as fair as anybody could be. They were working under very difficult circumstances. These Indians were all upset about this problem, and most of the range riders couldn't speak Navajo. The few I knew were really sympathetic with the Indian and tried to understand his problem. But Washington doesn't always understand the problems way out here, or any other place. You know how Washington is. I'm like the Navajo; he doesn't like Washington.

■   Where does the truth lie in evaluating John Collier's work and its effect on the Navajos? By his own account, the tribal councilmen exhibited extraordinary political courage by facing the facts necessitating stock reduction and acting against the inflamed and anguished will of their own people.[13] But while one does not wish to take their courage away from them, we may also see them as inexperienced in their role as council representatives, required to operate against their own slowly paced consensual cultural style. They acted not on their own ground but on John Collier's ground—a man who, before he became commissioner of Indian affairs, had been an extremely aggressive and effective propagandist in the press and lobbyist of Congress.

The stock reduction program on the Navajo reservation, while it may have come close to meeting its statistical goals in the reduction of livestock, brought little improvement in the range and did little or nothing to replace the income from sheep for those whose herds were reduced or eliminated. What success it did achieve cost the alienation of the Navajo people, the result of a draconian policy forced on them from outside through the instrument of an American-style democratic tribal government and carried out by agents in the field who were often callously unsympathetic to the anguish of the Navajos.

Collier's reforms in land management and conservation, Indian education, reservation medicine, and tribal government, of which we shall see more in subsequent chapters, were all darkened by the shadow of stock reduction. They met with only limited success, but they were destined to find their day of recognition and greater fulfillment following World War II, when Indian veterans returned with a new outlook on reservation life.

The two contrasting views that follow illustrate the range of the Navajos' understanding of the problem. These are elderly Navajos, Tallas Holiday deep in the traditional culture, Buster Whitehorse, though traditional, more exposed to white culture, especially during World War II.[14]

TALLAS HOLIDAY (medicine man, Monument Valley, translated from Navajo):   When I was young, there was a lot of grass; now the grass is gone. Today, the white people don't like the animals, killing sheep and killing horses and taking the sheep away. These animals depend on the rain, and they make the rain come and make more grass. When there is more livestock, then the growing season is longer and more plants can grow. The gods changed this because the white men came and killed our animals when they didn't need to. The gods shortened the rain and made more cold because of the cruelty of the people.

In the beginning, when people, animals, and plants were created, the gods said that there should be no cruelty to animals, no unnecessary killing. If we killed them off, we would have a short growing season and less feed for the animals because the animals had been reduced. That's what the old people have told us, generation to generation, down to this day.

In those days there were fewer Navajos, and they lived in harmony with nature. There was no drinking and no swearing. Life was more orderly and relaxed.

It was part of the teaching that when the people are corrupt, nature will change. That is part of the plan told in the Creation Story. At that time when it rained a lot, it seems to me that every bush grew different kinds of berries and seeds. In those days we picked them and used them for food. There was plenty of food in those days. There were a lot of things to eat when it rained a lot. But now these things are all gone.

BUSTER WHITEHORSE (Monument Valley, translated from Navajo): John Collier told us to kill our sheep, goats, and burros. They were brutal orders. Dibé Nééz seemed to be for the Navajos, but he carried the message to the people in their hogans. They came three times. One time they took fifty sheep from us. Now we are barely improving our stock again. They are just beginning to "turn green" again.

John Collier said that there was not enough room on the land for our livestock. He said that the reason why there was no rain was because we had too many sheep and horses, so we had to reduce our stock in order to make it rain. It seemed reasonable if our land was as small as he said, but the land of this whole country is ours, so we thought somebody was lying to us. We thought it was some kind of a trick.

A lot of Navajos tried to stop the white men in their own Navajo way of praying. They prayed to the different gods to protect their sheep, and a lot of sheep were protected. They prayed with tádídíín (corn pollen) and other offerings in their ceremonies. Like this summer, there was a drought and everyone prayed for rain. I prayed along with the others, and it started to rain.

11 ▰ SHINE'S CHRISTMAS

HARRY GOULDING: The first time I saw Shine Smith was in Monticello. I was going up to get some flour and potatoes. I saw him in a filling station, and just by looking at him . . . I could have gone on a little farther, but I says, "I'm going to go in there." So I went in, and while we were getting gas I talked to him some. He had something about him. And then the outfit he was in wasn't a Rolls Royce. It was an old Ford with stuff stuck all around it. He had a bed and a coffee pot hanging on the thing and this and that and the other, and the way he had them, nobody else could have put them that way. There were holes in the top he could tie the coffee pot to and hang it over the side. He was loaded to the gunnels. I knew he was a drifter, and a lot of those drifters are pretty interesting people.

So I talked to Shine. He preached to the Navajos; he was a preacher but he was a loner, he wasn't tied up to any church. He'd been in here ahead of us even. So we visited quite a little while.

Finally I says, "I haven't had anything to eat for lunch."

"You've got it on me," he says; "I haven't even had breakfast yet!"

"Well, let's go over and eat a bite," I says, so we went over and had a meal and we visited a long time there.

▰   Shine Smith was larger than life. He had the makings of a picaresque comic hero, western style—all heart, and headlong in his dedication. He was born in Rome, Georgia, attended the Presbyterian university at Clarksville, Tennessee, and the theological seminary at Austin, Texas. He was ordained minister in the Presbyterian church of Coleman, Texas, in 1911, where they called him the "Cowboy Preacher." In 1917 he was called to the Navajo reservation as a missionary, where Zane Grey named him "Parson Smith." The church charged him with leaving his post for a trip to Navajo Mountain, dancing in a Hopi ceremony, assisting in a Navajo wedding ceremonial. After four years, he and the church had both had enough of each other, and he went on in his own way.

During the influenza epidemic of the winter of 1921, he carried medicine and food through the snow to the Navajo hogans, and the Navajos called him "Sunshine Smith." He learned to speak Navajo, Hopi, and Paiute, participated in ceremonials, and offered whatever practical help he could. He began to organize Christmas parties each year at different trading posts, where he distributed food, clothing, and other gifts, which he had gathered as donations by whatever means he could find. In the years of the birth of government welfare, he was the spirit incarnate of personal, private charity.[1]

HARRY GOULDING: He said he was coming down into this country. "Well," I says, "if you ever come down our way, why we're pretty close to the road, come right on in, we'd sure be glad to see you." So he came right along back to Monument Valley, and I stayed with him. His old rig didn't go as fast as I wanted to, but I knew he couldn't get through these sand holes down here without a pull. I always packed along chain that I could hook onto people with. It was away into the night when we got into the trading post here.

He wanted to go back out in among the Indians. He would go round to the different trading posts. He'd be at our place, and maybe he'd go over to Hubbell's, and he'd meet a lot of people. A great visitor.

Shine was a Presbyterian is what he was, but he stayed out here so long, and the church wasn't helping him any, so he got to where he wouldn't pay too much attention to them, and they quit associating with him I guess. And I guess he was drinking quite a bit too. But Shine just went on. He just moved from place to place. He never did have a mission.

He got to where he could just go through that Bible backwards pretty near in Navajo. And he would talk religion to them. Most of the time he'd go wherever they had sings, and in those days the Navajos were glad to give a fella like that a chance to talk. I don't think he ever had a place where he sat down. But he'd go to the sings, and of course he had the crowd. He'd preach to them, maybe a half-hour or an hour. All the Navajos knew him, everywhere.

One time he came over and he wanted to go back into the Navajo Mountain country. He wanted to spend maybe a month. I got a couple of burros for him to pack with. I had some horses but he wanted to ride a burro.

"You take this grain along with you." I gave him about sixty pounds. I says, "You feed each one of them a little bit every morning, and those old burros, a few mornings out, they'll be coming right in for you every morning to get that little bit of corn." So he went on out with them and made his trip. That was his joy. He'd go way back in the back country and visit the folks and talk with them about the Lord.

But finally Shine came over one time and said that he had stopped preaching to the Navajos. "There's so many other things they need," he says. "You know, Harry, you can't talk that kind of religion to starving people. It's brutal. If I would keep on talking like this, I'd pull them away from their own religion, and they need their religion."

In all my life, I never have liked the damage that the missionaries were doing, although they were doing kind things out here too. The Navajos have a religion and a way that fits their condition. And to get in there and to spoil that, I say that some day they're going to realize what they've done, and they ain't going to like theirself. But Shine, he quits her!

His headquarters was in the Montevista Hotel there in Flagstaff. They gave him a room. He ate in there. They took care of Shine, was glad to have him. Now that's the kind of man he was. He didn't have an income of his own, and he didn't care about it. What money he had would have to be donations.

And then he went in to Washington with the Navajos during the stock reduction and talked with the big shots over there. He tried to get things done that way, too. He told them about the troubles the Navajos were having.

■ In 1941, in spite of a somewhat more generous limit on sheep units, many were still bitter about the stock program, and a delegation of six Navajos from Monument Valley and Kayenta asked Shine Smith to go to Washington with them to express their grievances. They were unable to see President Roosevelt, but after three weeks of interviews with Interior Secretary Harold L. Ickes, New Mexico Senator Dennis Chavez, and others, Collier finally arranged a meeting with Mrs. Roosevelt. She was moved by the description of their poverty and asked Collier what could be done for them "that's immediate and urgent and will be helpful." Collier, never at a loss, had plans for an 800-acre irrigation development project at Many Farms, which had been rejected by the Department of the Interior. She spoke to the president, and the project was reincluded in the budget and subsequently approved with a budget of $200,000. According to Parman, of the many Navajo delegations to Washington during the New Deal, this was the only one that bore fruit.[2]

HARRY GOULDING: Shine Smith accomplished a lot, yet there were some people that said things against him. They weren't people that I had on my list, but there were some people against him. Some old boy would say that Shine was just doing things for his own benefit. He wasn't doing those things for the Indians at all. But anybody that would say that . . . ! Because everybody loved Shine Smith. He was just what he was and that was it.

One of the great things he started, he started to have Christmas. He'd talk to people, that's the way he'd get his funds to do things for the Navajos. He'd go around and let people know that he needed food and clothes and things, and the stuff would come pouring into Flagstaff! They finally had to make him a storehouse there to hold it, he was so well known. He got to where he could really help a place, I'll tell you! He got a couple of trucks in there, and people would donate their services, drive one of the trucks out, because it was quite an experience to go out with old Shine.

For instance, we had a drought here the year that we moved out of the tents into the trading post, when we wanted so bad to see the water hit on that roof. Shine didn't have any particular place, but he would give his Christmas to the place that needed it worst. So I met him in town, and I told him about the drought that was going on over here. It was just brutal. I says, "Shine, where are you going to have your Christmas this year?"

"Well," he says, "I always try and go the place where they need help." Because he brings in stuff by the truckload.

So he brought it out here that Christmas. He had a cook and everything. He had big bowls, lots of food for the Navajos. He came out early and had them to bring in four or five head of cattle, butchered the cattle. He really put on a feed. That was the first time Barry Goldwater brought his supplies up from Phoenix and played Santa Claus.

Shine took his Christmases to different places every year. Wherever there'd be a hard spot on the reservation—anywhere, that is, in Arizona—he'd take his stuff there to that place. Ours was the only place he ever got into Utah.

After that, we had Christmas on our own here every year there for awhile. We didn't have it right when Christmas came, but the first real cold streak, why we told them that it was Christmas. "Christmas in two days, get to work and get the word out." And they'd all come in.

Visitors would ask what they could send the Indians, and I'd say, "Well, if you've got warm coats and shoes and shirts, or any kind of clothes that's wearable. And if you have any nice old quilts that's served their purpose as far as you folks are concerned. Those are the things we need, because it protects these people when they're out with these little herds of sheep in the winter." So people would get together back home. I'd say, "The way to do maybe is to show the pictures that you made out here and just charge them a shirt or something that you can send out."

We'd get a lot of clothes. Later on, we had a barracks here that we hauled in for the movies from over the other side of Kanab. We had that barracks pretty near full. We would separate it and sort it as it came in. If people gathered up enough to make a good package out of it, why the Navajo Freight Lines would bring it free to Flagstaff. We'd send the word out that it was Christmastime as soon as it come cold, because it was a shame to hold them clothes till the real Christmas when they needed them so bad.

Barry Goldwater would sometimes bring his children in his airplane. He was here for Shine's Christmas, and he loved that. He put his Santa Claus clothes on, and they dished out the toys and things. I always told people, "Any toys your children have that they kind of give up on them, these little old kids out here got to tie a string around a piece of rock and drag it around for a little wagon." Oh we'd get lots of those!

And everybody'd send stockings for Christmas. My gosh, we had stockings! People would send them in already stuffed. The whole corner of that barracks, the two bunks, we had them piled clean to the ceiling with stockings full of stuff.

We fed them all too. Whenever you have a big get-together of any kind, there's always a big feed. That's when we got to eat squaw bread. They'd make it for us and give it to us for our house. The Mexicans call them *buñuelos, dah díníilghaazh* in Navajo. Some people call it fry bread. The way the Mexicans make them is really something, but when I got down to where the old Navajos make them, they made better bread than the Mexicans did. They were handier with their hands. They'd take a hunk of dough and mash it out a little bit, and put it on their hands, and pretty soon it was flipping and flopping around there, just cigarette paper thin. Then they'd drop it in deep fat and bubbles would come up.

We started out pretty early with our Christmas, but it finally got to where it drew so many people that we couldn't handle it any more. I forget when we stopped it. Five or six hundred Navajos were coming in.

Little Christmas, it was Thanksgiving that we called *Little* Christmas. A lot of times later, when the movies were in here, they left us some food you could cook up for a pretty good group. So we built a fire, and we put on two or three of those big pots that we got from the movies, and we would have a Thanksgiving. Just come in and have a Thanksgiving meal. And we'd always have a few horse races with prizes on them, and things for the kids. Jimmy Swinnerton would come, and some others, and they'd bring a lot of stuff to give for prizes. Oh, that's real living!

Whenever Barry Goldwater would get back from Washington and was in a turmoil over things, he'd fly up to the Valley here, and we'd get in that little old jeep and take off into the back country. I'd drive for a couple of hours and then he'd say, "Let me take that outfit, Harry," and he'd drive.

BARRY GOLDWATER: I think the first time I visited the Indian country of the Navajo and Hopi was when I was about seven years old, about 1915. I visited the reservations almost every year from then on. My first recollection of meeting with Harry was after a hunting trip my brother and I made around 1928 or '29 in the Kaibab on the north rim of the [Grand] Canyon. On the way back we drove up to Monument Valley. There are very few men in this world like Harry. I think at one time there were many of them, but they are rare characters today.

I remember the first time we went up on the rim of Monument Valley together. It was an all-day trip and we took our bedrolls and camped out. Another time when my wife and I traveled about a thousand miles around that part of the reservation in a jeep, we came to Harry's one night and he didn't have any extra beds, so Peggy and I slept on the pile of wool which he stored in an old barn after buying it from the Navajos.

Mike and Harry were superb hosts. They would go out of their way to acquaint the tourist with the Navajo, explain the Navajo's way, pointing out that the Navajo had to be treated very carefully because the Navajo believed, and rightly so in my opinion, that they are far superior to the white man.

I remember an Indian named Grey Whiskers, who was a very famous character up around there. Harry was close to him, and through Harry I got to know him very well. You must remember that my trading post, Rainbow Lodge and Trading Post, on the south side of Navajo Mountain, is only about fifty-odd miles in a direct line from Harry's place, but it's well over a hundred miles by road, so we had a lot in common. We knew a lot of Navajos in common even though those Navajos would live as far away from Harry as Navajo Mountain.

I used to play Santa Claus for the Navajos sometimes. In Flagstaff there was an old character named Shine Smith, who was also a close friend of Harry's. Shine was a former minister who I think was sort of ordered out of the church for too much drinking, so he came out to Arizona with an old Model T Ford and later a Model A, and traveled all over the reservation helping the Indians. During the year he would collect toys, clothing, and so forth, and then just before Christmas, he'd collect bread and food. And then he'd have someone show up at a certain place, oh Tuba City, Kayenta, Monument Valley, other places, dressed as Santa Claus, and Santa Claus would stand on a truck and distribute everything.

So one Christmas I flew my airplane up to Monument Valley and was dressed up as Santa Claus, climbed out, and of course the Indians didn't know who the hell I was supposed to be. But we did distribute gifts and of course it made them very, very happy. So I got to be sort of the perpetual Santa Claus. I later did this at Navajo Mountain School and again twice at Tuba City.

BUSTER WHITEHORSE (translated from Navajo): For many years, I re member, Dibé Nééz gave away a lot of things free during Christmas—pants, clothes, quilts, and other things. Santa Claus used to come and give out presents, candies, and cigarettes. He was dressed all in red, with a white hat and a white beard. Sometimes it was one of the Navajos. One time I remember it was a white man.

First we used to have a feast. Then there were different sports like a softball game, races, a tug-of-war with nine men on each side. Dibé Nééz would ask which we wanted to play, a white man's game or a Navajo game, and we would choose. We played any games we felt like playing.

MAURICE KNEE: They always had games and gambling. The gamblers would hit, and down would go their rugs. Maybe they'd come in three days ahead of time and set there in the shade of a rock or put up a little sunshade of some kind, and down would go their blanket and out would come their decks of cards. Cooncan. Cooncan is what they love to play. It's a variation of rummy. And them cards were so worn out from sand gritting in them that you couldn't tell one from the other. I used to sit there, and they'd deal me a hand, and hell, I couldn't no more tell what I had than the man in the moon. Just gone; but they could tell. I'd just throw my cards on the table and leave my quarter in the can. "You won!" they'd say, "you won!" There's always gambling whenever there's a party.

12 ▄▆ SOIL CONSERVATION

▪ Stock reduction, although central to the New Deal program on the Navajo reservation, was only a part of what was needed to restore the land. A massive effort was required to control erosion, restore the range, and improve livestock husbandry. The Civilian Conservation Corps was already in place when Collier took office, and in 1933 projects were begun on the Navajo reservation—building small dams, clearing springs, drilling wells, installing windmills and storage tanks. At first these projects were poorly organized and at times unwisely chosen, but the Navajos, some of whom, according to Parman, "were so undernourished that they collapsed when first put to work," were eager to do the work and receive the critically needed wages of thirty dollars a month.[1]

By far the most ambitious and successful of these projects, at Mexican Springs, was created in the summer of 1933. The Mexican Springs erosion experiment station became the model for all subsequent erosion-control projects on the reservation. A staff of experts was assembled at Mexican Springs, the land was fenced and the livestock removed, and projects were begun in erosion control, range restoration, and improved livestock breeding. The Navajos received fees, in theory allowing them to rent range to replace the range they had vacated; they were given employment on the various ongoing projects; and a day school was built in the vicinity. Under these terms, they agreed to the project, but they remained skeptical, most of them adhering to their traditional belief that the range would improve if they were right with their gods and the gods made the weather change.

By early 1934, the work was already well begun at Mexican Springs, and Collier was encouraged to establish the Navajo Project, which in the next year and a half established twelve additional demonstration areas. Nearest to Monument Valley were the largest of these areas, 39,040 acres at Kayenta, and one of the smallest, an agricultural project of 500 acres at Paiute Canyon on the San Juan River, now called Paiute Farms. By this time the Navajos were feeling the effects of stock reduction, and their embitterment could not be compartmentalized. It turned them against these projects as well, so that their minds, difficult to move from traditional ways at best, were further closed against the visible successes they could see in the fenced areas. Thus, the good advice and successful model projects had little or no influence on the reservation at large.

The relationship between the Navajos and the traders was immediately changed by the wages now paid for government work. Where the traders had been accustomed to the Navajos' bringing in their wool or blankets and canceling any credit they had accumulated before receiving new goods in trade, the Navajos could now take their paychecks anywhere, on or off the reservation, to buy what they wanted, and they began to avoid the trading posts where they had debts to pay. Some of the traders retaliated by requiring the Navajos to sign papers authorizing the government paymasters to send their checks directly to the traders. Government agents, partly because they were unfamiliar with the old established ways of barter, and partly because they began to see abuses, tried in various ways to encourage the Navajos to take their checks elsewhere. In the Southern Navajo District, the superintendent instructed the traders to return at least half of a paycheck in cash. The traders, although they were glad to see the Navajos come in with money to spend, resented government interference, as they saw it. There can be no doubt that the advent of cash wages was the beginning of the end of the pawn and barter system of the trading posts.[2]

HARRY GOULDING: When this Three-C-ID [the Civilian Conservation Corps, Indian Division] came on the reservation and times were hard, the Navajos started to work for the government. They would start buildings, develop springs, or maybe build a dam. Frank and Lee Bradly that were over at Kayenta, their father was a white man, a trader; he married a Navajo woman. When I came into the country here, why Frank and Lee Bradly were coming along just about my age. Both of them became members of the tribal council, representatives from this area through here. We got well acquainted, and we'd go out and find possibilities to build a dam or things like that. Well, the Three-C-ID were furnishing the money, and that changed the trading and the pawn business.

MAURICE KNEE: The government just splattered money galore through here for the Navajo Service, they called it. There was government men running around in V-8 Fords, 1933 and '34 V-8 Fords, pickups, tearing them up, measuring the soil. And the U.S. Soil Conservation Service, they had big groups of people in here, mostly white people, very few Indians, but the money was earmarked for the Indians. Oh they had Soil Conservation, they had the Navajo Service, they had the CCCs, they had the ECW—that's Emergency Conservation Work. According to the newspapers the Indians were getting lots of aid, but they weren't.

HARRY GOULDING: They got some printing out about it, regulations, and of course some of the Navajos would get a hold of that printing. Well, darned few of them knew how to read in those times, and hardly any of them could get the correct meaning out of the way the government writes things. The government wouldn't permit the foremen of the jobs to pay an Indian within five miles of a trading post. I guess they felt they were going to train the Indian how to handle his money and how to take care of things. But instead of doing that, it made them feel as though the government was throwing in with them to get credit and not pay for it. They'd read these pamphlets and they couldn't make anything out of it except that they had to be paid away from the trading post so's the trader couldn't get their money. If you'd pay it in the trading post store, why he'd get the check, see? And that killed the credit. There were just a few Indians that I could credit after that, very few. It was a sad day for the Indians.

MAURICE KNEE: Oh heck yes, we've got some old ledgers that I could go through and tell you the story of every Navajo in there and how he'd get his credit and how he'd buy his stuff and how he'd try to get from paying it. After the government broke them financially with sheep, they owed us big debts. They had run a couple of hundred dollars in debt figuring they'd bring their wool in. No wool to bring in. Old George Cly that lives up the canyon, he was in debt to us eight hundred dollars once. You just couldn't see the guy stand there and starve with nine little kids. They jerked his sheep out from under him and he had nothing. We took him on. He and I'd haul wood, and he'd chop and I'd chop, and whatever there was to do.

HARRY GOULDING: Mrs. Ickes was in the House of Representatives of the state of Ohio when she married Mr. Ickes, so she resigned her job to help him.[3] He had been appointed as secretary of the interior. She was Mr. Ickes's right arm, she was right on the job all the time. I think she put her time in on riding the outskirts to see how things were and report anything to him that wasn't right, and he would stop it right away.

She was interested in the Navajos, but she didn't have any way to go out among them, so we always went out together to look around. If there was anything wrong, I'd show it to her. Anything would go a little stale out here and I'd mention it to her, it was taken care of right away. I was awful careful of what I mentioned, because I know if it had been something foolish and she took my advice on it, it would have hurt her.

I told Mrs. Ickes about a couple of fellas and a woman, white people, up at one of the Three-C camps. It was right up there where you look over into the Mittens. They'd been sent out to teach the Navajo women how to entertain themselves while their husbands were working, and that was so far off scale! Whenever the bucks were out working, doing something for the Three-C, why the women were tied up herding sheep and all that sort of thing. They were going to show them entertainment!

So they were out there, but there weren't no women. And Mrs. Ickes, you could pretty near see her face getting red that night. She says, "Harry, would you drive me over to Kayenta in the morning?"

So we went over to Kayenta the next day. She phoned Mr. Ickes and told him about what was going on. She never even went up to see about it. So the next day he had a car sent out to take them back and get them out of the way.

She was a brilliant woman and an awful nice person.

■   In the summer of 1936, the dust bowl brought a terrible drought to the reservation, adding its misery to the already desperate conditions in which the Navajos found themselves. Because of the Depression, they could only sell about a quarter of their fall lambs, which meant that the burnt-up range would have to support larger flocks over the winter. Agent E. R. Fryer asked the federal government, unsuccessfully, to declare the reservation a drought area. The following winter hit with ten-below-zero temperatures and blizzards of deep snow, covering what little fodder there was and isolating the Navajos in their hogans. Under these conditions, Fryer organized the first reservation-wide welfare relief program on the Navajo reservation. Many of the older Navajos refused to accept it. It offended their dignity, and it went against their deeply traditional way of trading among the members of their family, although they were willing to accept the wages they earned for government work. In April 1937, 5 percent of the Navajos were on relief.[4]

MAURICE KNEE: When I first came out here, it was just for the summer; I was still in school. Then, summer over, I had to go home. In '30, '31, when I had to go back, we had a warehouse full of rugs, and you couldn't sell them, you couldn't give them away hardly. So we loaded our truck with Navajo rugs and jewelry, and we struck out through Durango and picked up Aunt Molly. We went up over the hill to Colorado Springs and into all the curio stores trying to sell rugs for cash, traded for gas. . . .

We couldn't get much for our rugs though. Beautiful things, big as a bedspread, beautiful things. Maybe thirty-five bucks.

13 ◼◣ HORSE RACES

HARRY GOULDING: Horse races, every Sunday we'd have a horse race. Oh, there's nothing like a horse race. They generally just ran two horses, they didn't run a bunch, and then there'd be two more. They'd have these young kids riding, and they were real jockeys! They bet on the races, and the way they handled that, those old-timers, they would lay a saddle blanket over there on one side and a saddle blanket on the other side. One was for one horse, one was for the other, and whatever horse they wanted to bet on, they just put it on the saddle blanket, maybe just a ring, or maybe a couple of dollars, or a concho belt, or anything. Then anyone would come along that wanted to match it. If it was a ring, they would put a ring on the other side that was the same value. And they were so honest with it! Never, never was there any squabbling. When that race was over they'd come and pick up their winnings, and nobody picked up two of anything. It was the nicest thing you ever witnessed.

We had a lot of chicken pulls, but we used money always instead of a chicken. One time we used a couple of chickens, but we never did after that, because, oh there was a bloody bunch of Indians there! You bury a chicken in the sand so the body is down under and just the head and neck are out. They get their fast horses and come by at a run, and they reach down and try to pull that chicken out of the sand. They start to going around, just a little circle, pulling. And that chicken is in the ground fairly tight. You bury it so they can't get it the first time, it's got to be pulled at a few times before it'll come out. And you're not supposed to kill that chicken, it's got to be alive when it comes out of the ground, so they could only pull it just so much.

Then, when it comes out, then comes the race. You had to go round a big circle. When they pull up the chicken, why the old boy that gets it, he takes off, and then here comes the whole bunch of them, trying to head him off and take it away from him. The one comes out with the head of the chicken, he's the winner.

There could be twenty Indians, any number that wanted to join. About twenty is the most we ever had in one of them. But even if you only had ten,

A chicken pull at Goulding's. (Goulding's Monument Valley Museum)

or five, with a chicken it'd be a messy thing. All there is left is the head. The chicken is finally tore apart.

It originated with the old Navajos, and then we put it in our rodeos. There at Durango, in our rodeo we used to have a chicken pull. We had lots of Indians, and there'd be a chicken pull for the Indians and a chicken pull for the whites, because if you'd mix it there'd be fighting. But we never used a chicken at Durango, we used a bag of money, just the neck of the bag sticking out of the sand. That's where the bag of money started, in the rodeos, because even then there were some people that objected to the chicken business. We used a bag of money down here too, after that first time, but when the Indians had it on their own, they always had a chicken. They'd have to sometimes ride clean out to Bluff or somewhere to get one, because they didn't keep chickens. I think they stopped doing it after while, because they would have had to get the chicken, and our society just don't permit that kind of stuff. No, they don't do that any more.

MIKE GOULDING: One time they used my old pet chicken, I always had a pet. Well by golly, he ducked them, he didn't get his head yanked off. And he crowed the next morning. It was a little weak, sounded funny, but I fed him and watered him and petted him, and he was very much alive. His head had been touched, you know, twisted maybe, but it was unusual for one to live through it. I was so mad at everybody! That was one time I really was upset. My old pet chicken.

HARRY GOULDING: When we were having these races and things every Sunday we'd always, to make it handy for them so they wouldn't have to come up and miss some races to get soda pop, we'd have cookies and maybe watermelon and stuff like that down there. These people never had enough of sweet stuff, never, and that's why the soda pop was so popular. Well, Bert would help to build little stands to put this stuff on. The day before they started, we'd put some of the stuff down there so's we'd be ready. They liked to start early in the morning, and would like the cookies and different things, and then we'd bring the melons down later on.

So Bert worked on that, and then he stayed down there to take care of it at night. Well, some one of the Navajos wanted to come on in one time, and Bert wouldn't let him, because old Bert was loyal. I thought if I put him down there nobody would bother him, because they all knew Bert for a long time. But this guy, he kept pushing on in, he was coming in anyhow, and old Bert give him an uppercut. They had a little fight there, and Bert was a little better than the Indian because they never did fight, they didn't know about fighting, so the fight was over pretty quick.

But we had to have a ceremony. Had it right down there in front of the place, where it happened. They told me they thought we ought to have this ceremony. I says, "Well, I know Bert will accept, because he's that kind of a person. And I'd like to see it done. It would be a good thing for both of them." So we done it.

You don't want to attract onlookers at a place of that kind, it's a different thing from ordinary sings, you don't exhibit it. There were about four or five of the older Navajos, that's all, and the two of us, and I translated. I talked to Bert and they'd talk to their man, and I'd repeat what they said to their man, I'd just give it to Bert the same, telling him that it wasn't right to do this. They had a lot of reasons for it; it was not the way a Navajo lived. We talked for fifteen, twenty minutes, and then they'd chant, and then we'd talk a little more. The ceremony lasted, I expect, two or three hours. Then when they come together on the last end of it, Bert had to give the Navajo a dollar. If the Navajo had started it, he'd have had to give Bert the dollar. But there was always that old silver dollar that one would have to give it to the other. That dollar was given ceremoniously, and this fella received it. It was just like shaking hands, like we wind up a fracas sometimes.

And it worked out. Later on, old Bert and that Navajo were very good friends; every time there was a little work to do, Bert would ask for this Navajo.

It wasn't a thing that you wanted to draw a lot of people to, and it happened so seldom—they just didn't fight. They *never* did fight! I'd happen to come by one of those little ceremonies, well, they'd just keep on talking, but I could see what they were doing, so I'd drift on by. Two is all I ever happened to run into. Those old people never fought, and there was never any whiskey in those days, no drinking.

14 ■■ Navajo Children and White Schooling

Harry Goulding: In all the time I've known the Navajos, ever since I was a child when we used Navajos for herders, and I was all around them summer and winter both, I've never seen but one person strike a child. They have a different way of handling things. There's not a child in Monument Valley, the folks only have to say one word, or ask him to do something once, and they're off doing it. Some way they weave that. I could never get next to it exactly. A part of it is that they give the children quite a little bit of authority when they're young, and then when they do something, the family makes them feel as though they're one of the family. It'd be a great asset to have that. We might work it in some way ourselves, because those children, they're different altogether than our folks.

The large families with all the aunts and uncles around, now that has an effect on the children. And not only the uncles and aunts, but friends that come in. If a child tells a lie, maybe they'll get started doing worse things, so the old fellas'll get them in the hogan and visit with them, maybe even make a little medicine if it's necessary. And it works. If you had a boy or girl that was getting off on the wrong track, why a lot of times a friend can penetrate a child or a half-grown kid where the folks can't.

There were a lot of old fellas when I was a kid, close friends of the family. Maybe come a time when a boy spread his oats a bit, and those old fellas would talk to you, a lot like the Navajos. The boy learns that ain't just exactly the proper route. You listen to those old fellas. I used to when I was young.

Uncle Abe, all of us kids liked Uncle Abe. And old Jack McCormick was a great friend, he was the same age as our fathers. We wintered our sheep in adjoining ranges, and when we were out in the winter, I just thought anything he said was absolutely right. If anybody else said something to the contrary, I'd just kind of pity him, because he was on the wrong track, that's all.

If some of those fellas like White Horse happened to be in a friend's hogan and something came up about the children, maybe they'd compliment them. Sometimes an outsider can say something that will help a child; he'll listen better than he will to his own folks. Hosteen Tso and the other old medicine men, if there's something they could say to a child, they would say it. Everybody helped each other raise their children. All the united efforts of friends and family would add or suggest.

When the children are treated like one of the family, they take an interest in what's going on. Maybe they'll make a little rug. They'll bring it into the trading post here, and heck we throw it up on the scales and weigh it just like it was a big Navajo brought it in. We weigh it up and think about it and pretty soon write it down and tell her, "That's two dollars, a dollar and a half." Then she would trade it out. She'd get something she knew the family needed to eat. And at the last, just like the big folks, she would leave enough money, before she spent it all on food, to take her brothers and sisters some candy.

The children are given responsibility. The little children get a sheep or a goat, generally they get a goat. The mother maybe had two and couldn't make enough milk for one of them, so the child would milk other goats that had plenty of milk and feed hers. And of course then that was her property. They start to build up a herd when they're real young.

Those little lambs or kids, when they're feeding them, will follow them around just like they was a mother. Sometimes they play with them a little bit rough, but not bad. They sell their lambs generally in the fall, but occasionally they keep one that has exceptionally good wool to work into rugs, or sometimes they'll eat them after they get older. If it belongs to one of the children, they'll give it up and feel proud of doing it. They don't cry because they lost their little pet. It went into the family, just like any other sheep, and they feel that they're helping, the same as their mother and father.

Things like that I think have a great effect on those children. It just makes them! It would be a great asset to all of us if we could get their methods of raising children.

■ Harry's admiration for the raising of Navajo children touches on themes that are central among those developed in the classic study of children in the Navajo culture, Leighton and Kluckhohn's *Children of the People*.[1] The traditional setting in which Navajo children grow up is an extended family, with mother and father, brothers and sisters, uncles and aunts, cousins, and maternal grandparents all living in close proximity. The Navajos love children, and all the members of the family give them a great deal of attention and affection. There is little distinction in the child's mind between mother and aunt, or between its own brothers or sisters and the other children in the family.

For the first year, an infant spends most of its time wrapped and laced into a cradleboard, with arms and legs confined, and with an arched loop of wood over its head to protect it if dropped. The chief advantage of the cradleboard seems to be the great feeling of security it affords an infant, who, at least for the first six months, cries to be returned to it if left out too long.

A mother will nurse her child whenever it cries and for as long as it shows an interest. If there is not a new baby, nursing will continue for two or even three years, until the child weans itself.

The cradleboard is usually abandoned when the child begins to walk, and the earlier confinement seems not to interfere with the learning of motor skills. Indeed, there is some reason to think that the fact that the infant has spent most of its waking hours in an upright position in the cradleboard contributes to a sense of balance. Everyone in the family group makes a great fuss over the baby, who runs from one to the other for affectionate encouragement.

Surrounded by a permissive attitude, with little or no physical punishment, children eat and sleep when they want to and learn to control their elimination when they are physically ready and in a matter-of-fact way. They are brought into the family activity at an early age with small chores to do and sheep to care for. They are corrected, not by threats or parental authority, but by a realistic pointing to consequences. In this way they are made to feel responsible, participating members of the family group.

In sharp contrast to the American nuclear family and the American emphasis on individualism and competition, the large Navajo family group operates consensually, cooperatively. The model is not a hierarchy of authority with a drive to rise in the ranks, but rather a field of functional interaction with understood roles in an organic whole. Such contrasts lead to conflict when Navajo children are brought into contact with American schooling.

HARRY GOULDING: This one day we went over to Willie and Happy Cly's hogan, where they were doing a sand painting. There was a doctor and another person with top camera equipment to do the job. I'd had them out a couple of days, and they were very much interested in the Navajos.

Katso was the medicine man that was performing the ceremony. He had two or three aides helping in the sand painting, and there were four or five children there. It was a young girl that was sick, and Katso was going through the ceremony, making the sand painting, chanting and all.

The mother asked some of the children to do something, they'd get right up and do it. Then she asked this one child to go and get some water, but she didn't go. They needed some water to mix into an herb that had been dried and powdered. The medicine men like to use something that God made, so he had three or four beautiful seashells there, and he mixed different things in each one and administered it to the little patient. But this little girl wouldn't go and get the water.

Happy talked to her. She says, "You know, you should get up and do this when I ask you." The little girl just fell down there on her head. The mother struck her. "Get up and go do this!" And the little girl didn't move. She just stayed there. So then the mother walked away and went back into the hogan.

I stepped over to this child, because I'd met her many times when I was going through and she'd be herding. I'd always stop and visit with her. So I went over and told her, "Now when you get ready to take the sheep out, you just take them out, and you meet me over on the other side of that Mitten there." There's three or four nice big shade trees in there for her sheep. "You wait for me there and we'll have lunch together."

So we went on and finished up the sand painting, and I seen the mother behind the hogan, sitting there crying.

After the sand painting was over we met the little girl, and we all had something to eat and everybody cheered her up. The folks that were with me had children, and they knew better how to talk to children than I did.

She could talk English, because she was going to school over at Dinne-hotso, and she was a very brilliant scholar. The teacher especially liked this little girl of Happy's, and she took her in and fed her and kept her there. They got to be great friends, and it helped the little girl a lot, but the teacher felt that some of the things the Navajos did, like their medicine, were superstitious, and she oughtn't to believe in it. The little girl told us that her teacher said not to help with the ceremonials because it was just a supersti-tion. That's what caused the whole thing. She didn't know she was telling the child something that was absolutely wrong. It was not superstition. I haven't seen the Indians do anything yet that didn't have a terrific meaning.

So we talked with her and she felt a lot better. We stayed there for a couple of hours. Then we circled on around and came back up and went in for supper.

The first schools they started, they'd come in and get these Navajo children and take them out and keep them for five years! They thought that was the proper thing to do. They got steam heat, and clothes, and good food, but they wouldn't permit them to speak Navajo on the school grounds at all. Never, no place in the school. They thought that was a better way to teach them English.

Well, the thing that happened, when they came back after five years, a lot of their folks had moved and they couldn't find them, and so the traders had to take them out and get them with their folks, or send word by an Indian. I know of quite a number of those children that they brought them out here, dumped them off at the trading post, left them, and went on. There they was, didn't know where their people was, couldn't talk, they pretty near lost their Navajo language, and right out of a steam heat room and all that good food into just coffee, maybe, and some bread, and lucky to have a little meat. Terrible! They couldn't take it. A lot of them, after all that nourishing food, and then to come back to this, why they just died; it made a death trap for a lot of those kids. So you couldn't blame the Navajos for hiding them when anybody came out to take them to school.

■   The treaty of 1868, upon the Navajos' return from Fort Sumner, promised them a teacher and school for every thirty children between the ages of six and sixteen "who can be induced or compelled to attend." There was an underfunded and halfhearted effort to build one school at Fort Defiance, begun in 1880. Several off-reservation boarding schools for Indians were built in the 1880s and 1890s, to which Navajo children were sent, and during the first two decades of the new century, eight boarding schools were built on the reservation. By the mid-twenties there were also nine day schools. The conditions in these schools are described in an impressive study of government policy toward the Indians commissioned by Secretary of the Interior Hubert Work, prepared by the Institute for Government Research, now the Brookings Institution, directed by Lewis Meriam, and published in 1928.[2]

Although the report found a few exceptions, the overwhelming burden of its findings was negative. Teachers were poorly prepared and underpaid, and standards were far below those of the public schools of the nation. Health conditions almost everywhere were appalling: run-down fire-trap buildings, crowded dormitories, poor sanitation, dangerous machinery, malnutrition, child labor abuses, and the destructive effect on mental health of the rigid routine, the confinement to bleak surroundings, the cold removal from family life. The policy of forced assimilation flowered in the "outing system," which placed the Indian children of off-reservation boarding schools in white family homes during vacations, thus keeping them away from home sometimes for as long as seven years and breaking their ties to family and culture. The few day schools that existed, according to the Meriam report, appeared to be the best solution, if only because they had less influence on the children and allowed them to remain in the nurturing environment of their own families, but they too were woefully neglected and inferior to the public schools available to white children.

The thorough and sensitive investigation of the conditions of Indian education in the Meriam report was received with shock. Some reforms were begun, most notably, those allowing the boarding school children to return home in the summer, but improvements were slow in coming, and the report remained the standard for reform of Indian education for decades to come. Nevertheless, the few early reforms that followed its appearance were noted by the Navajos, whose interest in schooling correspondingly increased somewhat, and by traders like Harry, who had the good of the Navajos at heart and who began to encourage their attending school.

HARRY GOULDING: They finally went to just taking them in for a year and let them come home in the summer. That condition pleased them; those kids done well when they'd get to come home and go back again. Then they started to want to go, and then we'd talk it up here. Generally the traders would get out and talk to the people and try and get them to send their kids to school, and when they did, we'd go on out and round them up. I don't know of a trader on the reservation that didn't do the same thing. It gradually worked up to where they needed more and more schools.

■   Here are two Navajos, now middle-aged, who were influenced by Harry
to go to school and experienced the "improved" boarding schools of the
thirties. Ted Cly became a tour guide at Gouldings, and his white education
can be said to have been of some use to him. Fred Yazzie's education, brief
as it was, left him lost between the two cultures. As he says in his striking
way, "Just ride the train, go back and forth."

TED CLY: I went to school, and then all kinds of cars I saw. Harry
Goulding took me to school, to Kayenta. He came down to our hogan, said,
"You go to school." I don't know English. I don't know nothing. [Laughs.]
So he bring me over and I stay at the trading post, next day he took me ride
to Kayenta. Kayenta about five days later take me to Tuba City for school.
Kayenta was just a day school for small kids, so I went to Tuba City for first
grade. I was long hair, that little knot in the back. They just shear it off. I
don't know nothing for a while, about a year. There was Christmas, then
there was Thanksgiving, and New Year. I know a little bit, "yes" or "no."
Then the school let out. Come back with mail truck to Kayenta. Harry
Goulding was over there to pick me up. Bring me back to trading post, and
next day I went down in the Valley and I home. Stay all summer, and next
fall come down again and pick me up. He was just like our own family,
because he talks to my mother and father, so they know each other real well.

He take some other children to school too. He goes up to the school
sometime to visit all the kids from here, see us over there at Tuba City,
Kayenta. Just want to know what you doing, what kind of work are you
doing in school. We do some study and drawing and stuff, and he knows it.

FRED YAZZIE: He done a lot of things for the Navajo, like his own
family, you know. He help us going to school. He says he's been in the
World War and he learn everything right there; he had to train, took the
hard way training. "And your boys going be like that," he say. "You going
put them to school." That's what he talk to my daddy. So he put me to
school, but I never go very far, I went to fourth grade, and then my daddy,
he wants me home and take the old Navajo way. So I learn some songs, a
growing-up boy, you know, but I miss everything. I miss my school, I miss
my old old way of living. Just ride the train, go back and forth. Well, my
old daddy, he knew I was a pretty good boy, my old daddy needs me here,
you know, and I didn't get much education for myself.

Then I raised up, I start thinking, "Well, I can't learn my school, I can't
learn my religion. What I going do?" I raised up now. "I going go to work!"
So I go to work, making a living for myself. I do anything, like stock work,
and making a home, rock mason.

■ It was not until the 1930s, under John Collier, that real reforms began to take shape in Indian education.[3] The situation that confronted him when he took office was the system of boarding schools that we have seen. His plan was to build day schools near the natural gathering places at the larger trading posts.

The introduction of these day schools led to controversy on all sides. Some whites with vested interests defended the off-reservation boarding schools. Even some Navajos argued for the boarding schools because they provided food, clothing, and shelter for their children. Many Navajos saw no use in any white education at all and continued to hide their children, needing their help at home and preferring to raise them in the old ways. They associated the taking of their children with the taking of their sheep, and John Collier was responsible for both.[4] Other Navajos, a group of "returned students" led in the tribal council by J. C. Morgan, fought Collier tooth and nail on this and other issues from an assimilationist point of view. Indeed, the number of Navajo children in school dropped from a high point of 40 percent in 1930 to 33 percent in 1935 and remained at that level until after the war.[5]

15 ■ NAVAJO MEDICINE AND WITCHCRAFT

■ In one sense, the Gouldings' relationship to Navajo religion was quite limited, since they were neither believers who practiced the Navajo way nor anthropologists who studied it professionally. In another sense, however, simply because it is so fundamental a part of Navajo culture, their relationship to it was constant and inescapable. We have already seen many instances where Navajo religious practices, large or small, have figured in this narrative. Harry's respect for Navajo beliefs and practices is manifest, and their influence on his life was deep and pervasive, like a resonance, activating what was already present in his own character.

Medicine—curing or healing—is a central motif in the Navajo ethos.[1] To speak of Navajo medicine is inevitably to speak in terms which we think of as religious. The myths of the Navajo gods sanction and give power to the curing ceremonials of their medicine by providing their supernatural origins. Thus, like all myths, they provide a divine context for human life, an order to which the accidents and tragedies of human life belong, and by example and counter-example they teach proper behavior. Supernatural forces pervade the physical world, creating harmony in nature, society, and the individual mind. Illness is disharmony and disharmony is illness, and the ritual cure is to restore the harmony within and between nature, society, and the individual. Indeed, the proper performance of the correct ritual ceremony compels the restoration of harmony, for the same spirit of mutual obligation or "reciprocity"[2] that informs the trading and gift-giving of the Navajos also informs their relationship to the supernatural. If they do their part in restoring the universal harmony, the other forces involved must and will respond in kind. Their medicine is thus their way of controlling the forces of the world otherwise beyond their control.

The massage and herbal medicines used in these ceremonies are no doubt effective for certain kinds of ailments. Antisocial behavior is also effectively treated as disease, thus substituting medical treatment for punishment and lessening the negative effects of guilt. The small private ceremony for Bert and his Navajo antagonist in which Harry participated exemplifies this attitude.[3] Most importantly, the ceremonials give tremendous pyschological support to the patient by demonstrating the caring attention of the singer and the entire family as well as the spectators. As he sits on the sand painting, at the spiritual center of the Navajo universe, he is identified with the gods whose images are in the painting. The spectators and all who participate in the experience share in this psychological healing and come away testifying to its beneficent effects.

The determination of the cause of a particular illness and the choice of a ceremonial and singer are the responsibility of a diviner, who is thought to have a gift of intuitive powers similar to what we call extrasensory perception. Such diviners also have the ability to find missing persons or lost or stolen property. Depending on the technique used, they may be called hand-tremblers, star-gazers, or crystal-gazers. Ted Cly and Harry both have interesting descriptions of their experiences with hand-tremblers.

TED CLY: If somebody sick and you want to have a ceremonial, first you go to the hand-trembler. They shake their hand some way, I don't know how. Just like holding electricity, it shake you like that. They're called "hand-shakers." They say use that kind of ceremonial or this kind, so we go up there and bring him back, the medicine man for the ceremonial, just like the doctor. He comes down and is with the person who's sick.

The hand-shaker can find things too. Sometimes people steal, and their arm goes this way or the other way, just like some kind of a machine. If you tell the truth it goes one way, if you tell a lie it goes the other way, just like a needle goes. Maybe this one did it, or that one did it, so the shaker point, usually when they kill somebody or they steal. Maybe he's way on the other side of the mountain, and they point that way, and we know who was over there. It's the only way we can find things.

HARRY GOULDING: One time I lost a mare and a colt and another horse, and so I went to a trembler. Some of the women can do it too. They have a little ceremony and they will go into a trance. They have a chanter with them and he chants. This trembler, he ate a little weed before he started in. He shut his eyes and then his hand would start shaking, and this hand tells him. First it goes around, and then he talks. Then the chanter would go to chanting again, and pretty soon the trembler's hand would get back in gear.

He says, "Your horses were driven away, and they went over to a certain water place and were watered." And then he kind of bore down on me while the other old fella started chanting. He says, "Then he started up Black Mesa," and he told me exactly what canyon they was in and where he had put a fence across that canyon so they couldn't come out again.

I sent a fella over after them, and by golly, he met them coming back. A Navajo he knew from Black Mesa told him that he had seen them up there behind this fence. So evidently they'd broke the fence or got around it some way. We knew that there was a fence there or they'd have come back earlier. They wouldn't have stayed over there.

Another time, some Indians lost the government checks that they'd been paid, and they had a shaker to tell them where they was. They told me about it, that this fella had taken the checks. They sent word over to his area that they knew who this fella was, and he'd better bring those checks back or they'd put the police on him. And the checks came back.

TED CLY: Sometimes they look in a glass, like mica, or a little crystal, they look right down in there, like a fortune-teller. You don't know where the man is, he's gone somewhere, way out. They look right in the crystal. "There's going to be a mountain, and he's over there, and he's still alive, he's going to be down in there." They make a river, in the sand. "He's over here on the other side, go across . . ." Maybe we get in the car and go, and then he shows you where it is. "He's right down that way, just follow that way." They find a hole way up in the rock, so they climb up, and there he is in there. Maybe there is a big snake right across the doorway. He don't want you to go in there, see? Maybe a bear in there, see? They just take you in there and bring you right back out, I don't know how.

■   Witchcraft is the natural companion of Navajo medicine, both of which are disciplines of magic, the one compelling a disease and the other a cure, through the invocation of supernatural forces. It is black magic to medicine's white magic. Belief in witchcraft continues strong and persistent among the Navajos, although its actual practice may have waned in recent years with the increasing acculturation of young Navajos.

Kluckhohn describes four categories of witchcraft.[4] One kind of witch takes bits of the flesh, bones, or skin of a corpse and grinds it into a powder called "corpse poison" (a kind of anti-corn pollen, or anti-tádídíín), which he drops down a smoke hole or administers to a sleeping victim or to an individual in a crowd where he will not be noticed. Typically, the witch acts at night dressed in a wolf or coyote skin, and is called a coyote man.

MAURICE KNEE: Your medicine man and your hand-trembler, they're not spoken in the same breath as the werewolf. Or what the Navajos today call the coyote man or the skin-walker. Most of it is imagination today, but before World War II, a Navajo would definitely put on a skin and go out and dig open a grave. They'd go to his house, and there was jewelry from somebody's sister's grave, they'd buried the month before. There was that jewelry laying there, and they'd kill him. He'd robbed the grave. And even today, now and then, up on that high forbidden area of Black Mesa, or Navajo Mountain area . . .

■   A measure of the potency of the Navajos' fear of witchcraft is their reluctance to talk about it. As Kluckhohn points out, a display of too much knowledge of the subject either leaves you vulnerable to attack by the witch whose actions or techniques you are exposing, or it opens you to the suspicion of being a witch yourself. Ted Cly's wonderful description of the coyote man, or "skin-walker," as he calls him, is carefully framed as the uncertain knowledge of a mere spectator. Even if you profess to be a non-believer, as he says, you may be suspected of pretending in order to disguise the fact that you are a witch. It is such a sensitive subject, the fear is so great, that every way you turn there are traps.

TED CLY: The skin-walker, they walk at night, they say. An evil spirit. They run with the coyote skin, they say. There's lots of them here in the Valley. It's a devil, a devil running. It's a human, but well, I don't know. We don't know enough to say. There was a man over here got shot in the leg about two months ago. He was in the hospital, and then about four days later somebody told that he had seen him out there with the coyote skin where they dump the trash, and he shot at him. They found out with the hand-shaking it was the same man. He's an old man, about seventy-five or eighty years old.

If he's got enough power, he give it to the son of somebody; when he die, then the young one take over. That's the way it goes. But the medicine man, they're never witches. They be doctor.

The skin-walker go around at night, and these days they carry a flashlight. They flash way out there, and another one flashing on the other side, so they signal each other. Somebody see a big light like a car coming, way up in the air, and another one coming on the other side, they all link together. Pretty soon the dogs run out, barking. They see it. They're frightened.

Every once in a while I see them. Sometimes you see one use a flashlight right on the ground, goes along, or you see a light across the sky. Just like spotlights. They come way on the other side of the mountain, and another one over here. It's a big light. That's a signal to see each other. They will say, "I'm over here, you over there." They're far away. We're on the other side. But the dogs are barking all around. If it's very close, like somebody walking close, then we just walk out, flash a light, there's nothing. I guess they just hide back there somewhere.

They get together at night and they make some kind of a sand painting. They use maybe snake blood, or some of these dead people from the grave-yard. I don't know how they do. They put the earth here in the sand painting, they put the sunlash[5] in, and put two eyes. Up here maybe the snake blood coming out, like lightning. Then they put you right in the center of the painting. I never seen, but I heard about it.

We got to see medicine man before it gets worse, and we have a ceremonial. We block them both ways, so they can't come through. They go in straight line, they go by the wind, like airplane. So we turn around and put something in the way, like a wall. The witch just kind of jump up and down and fall back. [Laughs.] That's how we taking care of these things. Nowadays it costs us maybe a hundred, two hundred dollars. It's getting high, just like the doctors. [Laughs.]

If you look for the witch, you can't find them. They fly like an owl, maybe they crawl like a snake, they go in a hole. Same way when they running with the mice. They change shape. When they go with the snakes, they work right through the snakes, like a spirit. If a snake come in the hogan, that means a witch is there. That snake don't come in a hogan, see, so you know it's a witch.

We don't know nothing about it, but we know there's witchcraft out there. Like, the teenagers go around, the girls, the boys, they might get drunk, kill somebody, go to jail. That's caused from the witchcraft. Or a lady, trying to love you, and pretty soon she get the knife out and stab you. That's how it is. You never knew that they be a witch. [Laughs.] God talks through the medicine man, a devil talks through a witch, a devil, right in between you. That's how it goes in the Navajo tribe. Some of the folks, they don't know what's going on, they don't believe, they don't use their head. They might be part of the witchcraft, see, and they're just pretending.

■ A second type of witch makes use of spells. He is closely related to the coyote man, or he may be the same person using a different technique. Instead of "corpse poison," he gathers things associated with the victim: a bit of his clothing, some strands of hair, nail clippings, feces, urine. These he buries with flesh from a grave, or he buries them in a grave, or beneath a tree that has been struck by lightning. Then he recites a spell against the victim.

A third type of witchcraft uses the technique of injecting a foreign particle, such as a small stone, a bead, a bone, or a quill into the victim's body, which, it is thought, will move around until it finds a vital spot. The cure for this kind of witchcraft is a sucking cure, administered by a diviner, called a "crystal-gazer" in Ted Cly's story.

TED CLY: Mary Holiday, Teddy Holiday's wife, up on Douglas Mesa, she's a crystal-gazer. There was something in under my skin. It goes around, goes toward your heart. It hurts, you know, like termites in the wood, they go around eating. She see it in the little crystal. The bad people, the witch, they did it from behind me, I don't know how. She look right down in my body, just like xray. There it was, maybe bone, or maybe beads, some kind of stone. Then she suck them out by the mouth and stick them to this napkin or tissue paper. She just suck them out; they come through and she spits them out. There was beads in my back. It was an old man did it to me. I don't know who he was; she didn't tell me. It was because I have this job driving tours at Gouldings. I have this good job and have no problems, work all the time, all kinds of food and things. He was jealous. What we call "witchcraft." There are some witches right down in the Valley, some on Black Mesa, some the other side of Oljeto.

■   Although the belief in witchcraft is clearly much wider than its practice, there is some actual practice, as we have seen. In light of the blasphemous and counter-cultural behavior attributed to witches, it is interesting that sometimes it is directed against the very same rich and powerful who are themselves accused of witchcraft. Suddenly and mysteriously, misfortune may begin to plague a wealthy family, with clear signs that witchcraft is at work, and they will be moved to change their ways. In this manner, the practice of witchcraft, so often beyond the pale of acceptable behavior, joins in support of the cultural values. Ted Cly interpreted the witchcraft directed against him as motivated by jealousy of his good job and comfortable income. This is also the kind of witchcraft that Harry and Maurice describe.

HARRY GOULDING: There was a pretty wealthy family, they had more stock than most of the other Indians; and if for some reason they think he has too much, they'll get after a person and bewitch him. They'll keep after it until he gives a lot of sings to try and break the spell, and that'll cost him a lot of his wealth. But generally the only way he can do is to pile out of the country. One of them one time went way over to Chilchinbito, and another time one of them went in around Navajo Mountain. Other Navajos would tell us that it was being done. I never did talk to one that had actually done it.

MAURICE KNEE: Suppose there's a man who was getting too wealthy and he ignored the big ceremonials. Maybe he would bring some gifts and maybe he wouldn't. So things would happen to him. You use the word "witchcraft," well that's as good a word as any. Something would happen anyway. Forty, fifty head of sheep would die.

Immediately they would get the hand-waver and find out what caused their sheep to die. He would say, "You have not had any ceremonies and you're not helping out with your poorest relatives." So they would have a ceremony. They'd butcher twenty-five head, spit them and roast them and get back in the groove again with their relatives.

Everybody says, "Oh, those Indians are superstitious!" I think that's a stupid word to use. It degrades them. The Navajos had only the elements to guide them. Therefore the owl was the bearer of messages, both good and bad; they respected the hoot of that owl. If a coyote crossed a Navajo riding into town, he'd try to head him off and go round him. If he couldn't, he'd get off his horse and put corn pollen in the coyote's track where it crossed his road. They had many, many taboos in the old days when there was nothing else to bank on but their religion. What we call superstition is their tradition. The word "superstition" gets my goat, makes me unhappy as the devil.

16 ■■ SPEAR POINTS

■ Sometimes a young Navajo, perhaps with some schooling, will violate a taboo that the older Navajos would not dream of violating. Harry's sensitivity and tact in this situation is remarkable.

HARRY GOULDING: This young Navajo was working for us here, and once in a while they'd be having a sing, and he'd go home. So he went to a sing this time, and he came back with these spear points. Oh they were beauties! There were fourteen of them. Some of them were about eight inches and then shorter, but they were all just shiny, they were made out of the best rock. They were top quality, you could see that they were special. So we traded for them, and I gave him quite a little bit, I gave him some food and then I gave him some cash too.

About a month later his folks came over and asked me if he had sold me these spear points. They told me that they had been placed in the ground in a ceremony, buried in the rocks up in a little cave, back in a sheltered spot, and they must go back. The boy was back in the store working, and he knew what they were telling me. You could see that he felt awful bad. So I says, "I'll send the spear points back with him this evening." I felt like I wanted him to take them back. And I knew he would.

Then the old folks wanted to know if they owed me anything. They wanted to know if I paid him for them. I told them, yes, that I gave him some food and he said he was going to take it over home. And they said, "Well, he did."

I says, "You go ahead and keep the food and I'll make a deal with him on the money." They were ready to pay for anything that I'd paid him, but I didn't charge them anything. I didn't even charge them for the food. He paid enough for what he done. Oh, he felt bad!

They knew that he had picked them up. They probably tracked him right into it. You can't fool an Indian when it comes to anything like that. They knew his tracks and they knew what he done, and they just figured that he probably sold them to me. And they were right. He finally said that he knew they'd been buried there, and he studied with himself pretty hard, I guess, whether he should bring them over here or not. He really knew that he shouldn't have, but he did do it.

That's one reason I told them I'd let him bring them home that night. I knew that he'd go through some more agony when he had to deliver them. It would be a better lesson for him to go ahead and take them back himself than for me to give them to his folks. I think it helped him out a little bit to be able to do that.

When they came over another time I asked them if they'd got the spear points, and they said yes.

17 ▰ TRADER MEDICINE

HARRY GOULDING: We were trying to do what we could for the Navajos when they got sick. I knew Dr. Magan at Loma Linda University in California. Dr. Magan cured me when I got some trouble with my plumbing one time back before the war, and we got to be great friends. He gave us a doctor's book that was put out by his father, Percy Magan.[1] It was a book for people who couldn't get a doctor. We were out here, and Mike would run through the way they acted and one thing another, and it tells in that book what to do for them. It was an old-time book, so it had some thinking in it that wasn't so doggoned far from being related to the Navajo, the way he done things. It was a blessing that she got that book. She saved a lot of suffering.

Then doctors that would visit would send us medicine; they get a lot of samples, and they'd send them to us. Vitamins too. If Mike couldn't figure out what it was, she would give them vitamins, and I'll tell you it's surprising what that would do. You'd just kick 'em right up! They don't get enough of the varieties of food, and so you've got a pretty good chance there, thinking like Mike did. They'd come back in looking better, and they'd tell her that was good medicine.

MIKE GOULDING: If they were real sick, we'd have to try and get them to Tuba City, and that was a long, long drive. It took all day long, and a lot of them didn't make it. The little kids dropped off like flies with diarrhea. We always thought it was the melons and things like that, but it wasn't. They can save them now because they give them intravenous. Their poor little hides would be just like onion skin, they were so dehydrated. Of course, we couldn't do anything about that. We'd just do what we could.

▰ The infant diarrhea that Mike describes was caused by the primitive, unsanitary conditions of hogan life. In the 1920s and early 1930s, trachoma, tuberculosis, infant diarrhea, and malnutrition were the most severe threats to the health and survival of the Navajos, and the malnutrition so weakened them that they were helplessly vulnerable to every epidemic that came along—measles, whooping cough, diptheria, meningitis, smallpox, influenza, typhoid. To combat this unending series of crises, there were nine government hospitals on the reservation and three sanatoriums. They shared three X-ray machines, and there were no laboratory facilities at all. The hospitals were ancient, run-down, made-over buildings, and the doctors were mostly failures from the white world, alcoholics, or without accredited medical degrees. Exceptions were two mission hospitals: a small, underendowed, but competent Christian Reformed church hospital at Rehoboth, New Mexico; and the sophisticated and highly successful Sage Memorial Hospital under Dr. Clarence G. Salsbury at Ganado, supported by the Presbyterian church.[2]

Under these circumstances, the traders were faced with an impossible situation, confronted with widespread suffering and death, quite unprepared to deal with it, and finding little to turn to but inadequate help at great distances of brutal travel. They did what they could, and the Gouldings, located in the back country of the reservation, were more isolated and had poorer roads and greater distances to travel than most.

MIKE GOULDING: One time a Navajo woman brought her baby in, the poor little thing, he was just sick as he could be, burning with fever, and I didn't know anything to do, but I gave him some aspirin, and I gave him water, and we sponged him to get the temperature down. It was one of the first experiences that we had with somebody real sick.

That woman still lives up on Navajo Mountain unless she's gone. They were working for us at that time. Her husband was Hastiin Bits'iiní, the skinny man, Mr. Skinny. Poor man, wasn't any bigger around than that, but he was plenty strong.

There wasn't a medicine man around right then, so she brought him up here. We just kept doing what little things, I can't remember all the things we did do, but I know we did sponge that awful temperature down. And I know we used Vicks on his chest. We kept him warm. The mother stayed with him too, we both sat there, I know we were there a couple of days and nights. She probably had a sing after that, I can't remember. Anyway, it broke up, and last I saw of him he was a big strapping man. Bits'iiní Bighe' is what they used to call him, Son of Bitsini.

His mother gave me his cradleboard as soon as he grew out of it. I've still got it. She gave me his first moccasins too, but they got away from me. She knew I tried. When she gave me the cradleboard, she said, "Now he's yours too," so that's my child over there somewhere. He called me Little Mother, Shima Yázhí, he still does. He's a good man as far as I know.

HARRY GOULDING: We asked the Navajos to come if any one was sick and we'd take them in to Tuba City, but the Navajos have an idea that if they're trading and they've got thoughts about sickness in their family, that helps the trader out. There aren't too many Indian traders taking the shirts off of those people. So a lot of times they wouldn't come in for help until the person was just about gone. I had one woman die in the back seat while we were on the way into Tuba, about thirty miles the other side of Kayenta.

Her husband was there and we had to bury her out on the road there, because they don't return toward home after they die or the spirit will come back.

They'd come in with ribs broken, a horse had fallen on them, broken ribs could be awful painful, and that was a drive, those days. You've got a man that you know, he'd sit up there alongside of me in the car, and you could see him grit and grit. I'd see sweat coming off of him whenever I'd hit a bump, but he would *not move* to let me know. He could see that I hated to bump, and rather than to show that it hurt, why he'd just sit there like that. That's the kind of material them old people are.

Sometimes, a mother couldn't deliver her baby, and they used to get these squaw belts and try and squeeze the baby out. Well, they'd get to where it wasn't going to work, and then they'd come to us. I had to take this mother out one time. The medicine men couldn't help her to have the baby, so I took her over to Tuba, but the rooms were all filled up and they just couldn't handle her. I says, "Well, I'm going to have to take her clean over to Ganado." Dr. Salsbury had a Presbyterian mission hospital over there. It was bad weather and a lot of the roads were washed in places. I had to dig my way out of some of them, but we got over there. I told Dr. Salsbury what had happened.

"Well," he says, "we don't have a room left here either, but we'll take her if we have to put her in the hallway."

So he did, he took her, and I says, "Now, whenever she's ready to move, I'll come over and get her."

"No," he says, "I think we'll find a way to get her back all right." So he brought her back over.

I had quite a lot of experiences with Dr. Salsbury after that. He was a man that could get things done; he had a lot of influence. There was a bad sand area between home here and the trading post in Kayenta. Everybody got stuck in it. So Dr. Salsbury was over here one time, and I think I *might* have made it, but I got stuck. I says to him, "It's not so bad when we're like this, just a couple of us fellas. We can take our time getting out of here. If we get to sweating a little, we can slow down and get in the shade. But," I says, "when I've got a patient in the car I'm taking to Tuba, that's something else. It just shakes a person up pretty bad. And it takes you so much time to get through, you could have lost a life by not getting there in time."

"Well," he says, "maybe we can do something about that. We'll see."

One time he came with some visitors that were coming over to our place, and they went around from Ganado all the way up to Shiprock, and then they came down on through Bluff instead of going through that sand. The folks wanted to stay over longer, so I told the doctor, "If it's all right with you, I'll be glad to take you back." So we went back the short way, through the sand—and *that* time, by golly, I made it!

On the way we come by an old sheep corral, and the wind was blowing right towards us. The doctor says, "That open road is just a little more comfortable than this spot right through here."

I says, "Yeah, I expect so."

So we went on, and there was an old fella was sick we was going to pick up. He had this prostate and he had to get into the hospital. With a prostate you get a pretty stout odor. Oh boy, he was staunch! I says, "We come by that old sheep corral back over there and it wasn't too pleasant, but I kind of enjoyed that. Now you're enjoying this!"

"Oh yeah," he says, "this is fine!"

So he did. He took the trouble to write a lot of letters, and he sent me every one he'd write. Finally he got the Arizona road department to come up in there and fix it up.

■ John Collier's medical program for the Navajos received fourth priority, behind stock reduction, soil conservation, and day schools. To the Gouldings, at a trading post in the back country of Monument Valley, the program must have been almost invisible. Nevertheless, some progress was made. A well-qualified medical director was appointed. There was a training program for Navajo nurse's aides, with specialists on trachoma on the staff. The quality of the physicians improved. Monthly in-service training sessions were held, and Depression wages brought good young doctors and nurses to the reservation. In 1936 there were twelve dispensaries with field nurses scattered over the reservation. Two new hospitals were built: 140 beds at Fort Defiance in 1938, and 65 beds at Crownpoint in 1940.[3]

Trachoma was virtually wiped out by the development of sulfanilamide after 1938, but tuberculosis remained a difficult and unsolved problem. Malnutrition made the Navajos particularly vulnerable. In 1938, there were 200 beds for tuberculosis and 900 active cases. For once, however, the Navajos did not refuse medical help as a protest against stock reduction. Although they were slow in finding a way to reconcile white medicine to their own traditional way, even the medicine men gradually became cooperative.[4]

18 ◼️▬ Two Sisters

◼️ The Gouldings had no children, but when they were brought into the personal tragedies of their Navajo neighbors, and when they responded with human kindness and generosity, they sometimes made attachments that were like those of parents to their children.

HARRY GOULDING: There were these two sisters, they were maybe twelve and sixteen, something like that. They were nice little girls. Their father had died, and about five or six months afterwards, why their mother was trying to have a baby. They had the medicine man there, and they were having a ceremony to help her have her baby. And they finally sent word up to me. So I went down there, and they had her hands tied up to the top of the hogan, and they had these woven belts that the women wear. They'd put them around her and tied them up and then they'd pull on them, they'd tighten the belts, to force the child out. And if they can't get it, they then will come to the trader if they know him and ask could she be taken to the hospital.

So I took her over to the hospital in Tuba City, and she died. But the baby was born. The hospital sent a letter to me that this mother had died and the baby was there. I went down and told the two sisters that there was a little boy and he was alive but their mother had died in childbirth. The folks at the hospital had said that they would keep the baby there; they figured it'd be better not to send the baby over yet and let it get a little strength so's the girls could raise it if they wanted to.

So they kept the baby there, and then they sent me word, it was about six months, I guess, that the child was pretty strong and that if the girls wanted to take care of him they could have him. I went down and told the girls, and they did want him, so I took them over and we brought the little baby back.

There were the two girls and this little boy; I always kept track of them. I'd go to their place much more often than I would the others. I tried to scatter the money around that the visitors would spend around a hogan, but I would go to their place two or three times more than I would any of the others. So they raised the little kid, and they hadn't married. They got up to where generally Navajos would marry, but they said they were going to stay single until he was raised to where he could take care of himself.

Then one of the girls fell in love with this Paiute woman's son. There were two brothers, their father was a Navajo and their mother was a Paiute. She was a nice old person. Her husband had died too and she raised those two boys, so they had kind of the same experience as the girls did. They talked to me about it. The other girl said that her sister could get married and she would stay single until the boy was ready, and that they would all live together, right close to each other.

So they did. They lived there and raised this little kid until he got big enough to take care of himself and be of help. Then the other one married the other son of the old Paiute woman, the two sisters married the two brothers. The boys' mother was nice to those girls and they lived close together, always did. They all fell in love with each other and it made a nice situation. That was an interesting thing, to watch that little family grow up, and to help it along.

Then one day the youngest girl was over here with her husband, and they were teasing him in the store there because he was a Paiute. Things got pretty stirred up, and this old Navajo came out and told me. He knew that I had taken care of this little family specially, and he told me that they might be figuring on fighting when they came out of the store. So I watched, and when they came out they started to get ahold of him. This little Paiute guy, he was pretty brave. He walked out there when he knew that he was going to be jumped on. Then I went down and throwed him a rope. I separated them and told them, "Don't you ever! These two girls are our girls, and if you ever get after that man again I'm going to take a hand in it! You stay away from them!" I gave them a good talking to. There was never any more trouble after that. Everything settled and worked out fine. That was the last time that anybody ever teased the Paiute kid.

19 ◼ VISITORS

RAY HUNT: I was living in Bluff when Harry came up and wanted to know if I would come down and watch his store while he went to Albuquerque. I said sure, I'd go down. My brother was living in Bluff, so I said, "You take care of my place; I'm going down to Goulding's for a couple of weeks."

I stayed almost five years, just lacking two weeks of being five years. I never worked for finer people. They treated me just like I was a member of the family.

When I first went there, Harry was just getting started into the dude business, and so I ran the trading post for them. I was paid seventy-five dollars a month and board and room and two percent of the payroll. At that time that was good money. There was no place to go to spend it, that's for sure.

HARRY GOULDING: Ray Hunt was a number one Indian trader. He was born right in a trading post. His dad, John Hunt, started that old trading post east of us, over the other side of Mexican Water, one of the early trading posts in the country. Ray went to the trading business right away. He could talk Navajo just like Maurice can.

RAY HUNT: I ran the store, and Harry started in to have his dudes or whatever you call it. One time some people came in and I asked them, "Did you have a good day?"

They said, "We had a wonderful time watching Harry Goulding getting such a kick out of the country that he sees every day! It just did us so much good to see anyone that thought that much about his own part of the country." Which he did.

That's where I met my wife. She came out there to cook for them and help Mike with the tourists. They would have one big family table, and the tourists would all join for breakfast and dinner. Whenever they fed them, Harry would step out onto the porch and yell "Chow!"

GRACE HUNT (Ray Hunt's wife):   You never knew how many people you were going to have for dinner. There were people who just found their way in there, and Mike took care of them with no more than anyone would have in a normal house, as far as utensils and things to do with. It was just amazing. Every challenge that came up, she handled it so well. She never got ruffled. Where you didn't have trucks bringing in produce and all, she made the most marvelous meals with, really, sometimes it seemed like nothing! Of course they bought fresh mutton from the Indians, and she cooked it so well. She did all these things and yet she didn't seem like a country girl. A lot of hard work.

Another thing I was so impressed with about Mike. They had their own cow for milk. She just took such perfect care of everything, she was so spotless. And her methods of caring for the milk were interesting. I learned a lot from her because I hadn't done anything like that before. They had a screened-in porch that faced the east, and the pans were always washed and put out there to air. And the straining cloth she was so fussy about, we'd wash it, and everything was put out on this screened porch to air. She was so meticulous about keeping the milk in as near perfect condition as we could.

HARRY GOULDING: I'd catch the kids down there herding when I'd go in with a group, and the poor little old things was out there hungry. And boy, a bottle of pop and a drink of water! I'd always have a can of beans or a can of tomatoes and some crackers, something for them to eat. And then we always took plenty of water with us, and if they had anything they could carry water in, we'd fill it for them and give them enough to drink so they'd have a full bottle to take off with when we left. You couldn't do anything that would please them little tykes more than to give them some stuff like that.

We'd take pictures of them and then we'd all chip in, all the guests, whatever we had and pay them. Then I'd give them the candy and stuff.

I had some visitors out one time, and right where we go into Mystery Valley, there was an old fella, he wouldn't live there only in the years that he would plant corn there. He wouldn't plant there every year, and then once in a while he'd plant it. I told the folks about this old fella, and I says, "He's out there planting again. I'd like to take a few minutes and drive up there. I want to find out why he's planting this year, because he doesn't do it only every now and then."

So I went up there and talked to him. "My friend," he says, "the snakes told me to plant this year." And by golly, he got two corn crops. The migration of the snakes told him if it was going to be a wet season; he got his message through the snakes.

And they got messages from the coyotes, too. The Navajos wouldn't kill a coyote unless it was just absolutely necessary. The old-timers would not build a hogan right close to a water hole; they'd either go out around behind a hill or behind a bank, or at least a mile away. They said that their gods had created the coyotes and the badgers and the birds, and that they had also made the Navajos, so they would get back off to where those animals could get in at the water hole and get a break at that water. You know when water is as scarce as it is on this reservation, why a paleface get ahold of that kind of a deal, he'd put a lock on it. He wouldn't let his own kind in there unless they had the dollar.

The Navajos wouldn't kill a coyote unless he made it a habit of killing the lambs. Then when they did go after him, there'd be maybe six or eight of them, horseback. They'd get the old coyote stirred out and they'd run him, they'd tire him out. One horse would run him, and whenever he got tired, why he'd signal another and another would take in after him, maybe a couple of them because they could head that coyote and keep him out in a big round flat. They'd run him out there until they could move right in on him and club him. They didn't like to kill one unless they had to, because coyotes done things for them, good coyotes.

■ Coyote is the subject of many animal tales among the American Indians, where he figures as a superbly gifted trickster god. As Karl Luckert points out, hunting societies admire this trickery and try to imitate it in the hunt, but among pastoral or agricultural people he is a predator against their flocks, and far from being admired, his trickery is endowed with an evil character. Hence the ambiguous status of Coyote among the Navajos, who were a hunting society until their late arrival in the Southwest, where they learned the pastoral arts. And so Coyote is the hero-subject of Coyote Way, a nearly extinct ceremonial, and he also figures prominently as the coyote man of witchcraft.[1]

HARRY GOULDING: I had another group one time, and we went out to see Happy Cly, Willie Cly's wife. She wanted to go and see her relatives who were farming over at the little farms,[2] and as we were coming on down, I could see a real soaker coming. I wanted to get into the Big Hogan to see the headwaters hit in there. The Big Hogan is a big cave with a hole in the top, like the smokehole in a hogan, and the water comes through that hole there in a waterfall when it rains.

We drove right on in. I says, "I can't go in quite as far as I generally do, because I think that spouter is going to get us in trouble if I drive in too far." About that time the headwater hit and came roaring down. It pretty near hit the car. We were getting the splash off of it, and it was exciting, I'll tell you!

Happy went over, off to one side, and I knew she was going over there to say a little prayer, so I didn't mention it at all. Then she came back, and we were all talking about this cave. The visitors would ask me different questions, and she would answer them, and she had a good answer every time. She told us about the Big Hogan. "This is the place where the giants come. They come into this hogan and hold ceremonies, and the coyotes and the foxes and the rabbits and all the different animals come in here and listen to what the giants say. They give the animals a message to give to us, to show us what would be the best for us to do."

The sincerity that went with her, it was the most touching thing, there in that terrific weather, in that cave with the water roaring down and through. There ain't nobody in that group will ever forget that as long as they live. I know I won't.

Living right with the animals when I was a boy, Dad and all of us, there were a few things we could get that would be the same as information from the way an animal was acting, but not like the Navajos.

■ Karl Luckert has commented interestingly on this story: "In Navajo mythical times the giants, gods, animals, and Navajos travelled about as freely as some of these still do now. If they visited Big Hogan—then it probably happened that way. Lady Happy may be as authentic an informant as the rest of them. She prayed. That showed her sincerity. Her explanation is typical of what a Navajo woman would (or might) also tell Navajo children. This anecdote sounds like an example of traditional Navajo piety at elementary school level."[3]

HARRY GOULDING: The Cly family lived right down in the heart of the Valley, right down in Tsé Bighi' there, and old Hosteen Cly was the first one that let us take pictures. The old Navajos weren't too happy about photography. They thought a picture was like a part of themselves, a part of their soul was taken away. But I wanted them to perform so bad so's we could get their story out and let our people know what's going on down here. The Indians needed assistance and I felt, If we can get this thing to going, it won't only help them by the publicity, it will make them some money too. So Hosteen Cly was the first one. I'd go down and take the folks into his place and we'd get the whole ticket, fry bread, and hairdoing, and weaving. I had quite a rigamarole. The other Navajos would see Hosteen Cly, he was just like Grey Whiskers and White Horse and those fellas, and so when *he* accepted me—and then also there was some beans, and one thing another, coffee and flour involved in it too. I'd always take down food, give them a little money and then some food, too.

Anything I had to do, I'd pick the Cly family because of the old fella. He was a brilliant old person, so it was catching; his family were the same. Leon could talk good English; and John, my goodness, anything we done, John would pull something, get up a funny little catch of some kind. And you could depend on them too. So that's the way we got acquainted with the Clys.

TED CLY: Some of them don't want their picture taken. They say, "I shouldn't let the man take photograph of me." They just don't understand. They can't read or they can't write, they can't speak English, that's why. These days the teenager tell them what's happening. They see some of these picture in the newspapers, in magazines like *Arizona Highways,* and they say, "Maybe in the city, way out there in different states in the United States, all the magazines tell the story from here." Like you and me, we're talking into the book. That's what they say. They get a little pay on it, dollar, two dollars, few pictures. They enjoy it.

HARRY GOULDING: Hosteen Tso was a medicine man. He was here at the store a lot, trading with us, and I would go to his place down toward Oljeto. His whole group was sharp, his kids and all, as sharp as could be, every one of them, quite a family. One time there were camera people coming in, would like to get a sand painting and wondered if it was possible. So one day Hosteen Tso came into the trading post and I asked him if he would make a sand painting for these people to get a picture. I said, "They'll be good people. I won't bring anybody in here but what is very good people, and they're the kind of people that have quite a bit of money. I would try to get you a hundred dollars." Then of course, he had helpers to do the chanting and all that goes with the sand painting, and they got so much apiece. And the womenfolks, they got the meals ready and everything to take a breather and eat a bite. I guess it'd cost at least two hundred and fifty dollars, along in there. So he said he would, he said he'd do that.

I used to get him quite a lot of people who'd come in. He told me, "We medicine men go to urgent calls, but we do have folks that want us for something that can wait. They feel bad, but they're not in pain." For instance, one time a little girl had slept on a sheepskin and there was a snake down under it. Well, that had to have a ceremony. The little girl got scared about it and it bothered her, but he knew that she wasn't suffering as much as someone that was really suffering. He'd always have one or two back like that, and when some of these photographers would show up, why he would take care of them, and he'd make the sand painting the same as he would do for Navajos. So they'd have a ceremony. And it straightens those kids out, too, because one of those ceremonies—it's like our old doctors used to be, years ago. You hear the folks tell about them. They'd come in and sit on your bedside and visit with you and no doubt go through very serious things, and well, that probably worked a lot better than the medicine they gave.

We got to doing a lot of that. Our guests were paying the fiddler; and they could well afford it and enjoyed doing it. Never did I have anybody that wouldn't turn around and hand him a fifty dollar bill or something on top of all that. Then Katso started, and there were two or three others in here that would do sand paintings. That way they could get a lot more money out of it, and everybody was happy.

RAY HUNT: As long as I'd been on the reservation, which was all my life from a boy, and I think I was about thirty-three or -four years old, I had heard of the Mud Dance, but I had never seen a Mud Dance until they put this one on at Gouldings, down in the flats where they could make a big wallow full of mud and water.[4] They had a large hogan that they'd worked weeks on, maybe a month, and they'd brought brush and things in to make the shades and the cook shacks and all that it takes to put on a Mud Dance. Harry donated, I don't know how much that he did donate towards it.

At that time there was no one drinking. There were Paiutes, Navajos, there must have been close to three or four thousand people. They were camped all around there, mostly in wagons and horseback, little groups all over, with their little fires where they'd do their own cooking. On anything this large, the relatives of the people that started the Mud Dance donate flour and coffee and sugar. That's what Harry donated, flour and coffee and sugar and canned milk. But then the Indians furnished all the meat and everything like that and done all the cooking. That's why they had these big brush shades; they were the cook shacks. They didn't just take time out for morning, noon, and night; they'd have it agoing all the time. If you were hungry, you went in and got something. The women would take turns.

There were cameramen who wanted to take pictures, and the Navajos came in and asked Harry to tell them that they could take pictures of everything outside but nothing on the inside. But this one fella just kept crowding in so he could get pictures on the inside. Harry had already asked him twice, very nice, and finally they went to Harry for the third time and said, "We're going to have to take action ourselves if you can't stop this man."

Harry jerked the camera from him and threw it down. He took him by the collar and shook him about two feet up off the ground. He said, "This is my deeded property and I want you off of here now, right this minute!"

The fella made some remarks, and I know they must have been pretty peaceful, because he really got with it and got away from there. Harry wouldn't mess with him for a minute.

Then everything went on again, and finally the dancers all came out of the hogan with their hair hanging down loose on their backs, and all painted up. All they had on was just their G-strings, and singing this Mud Dance song, which is a kind of weird song, really. They'd bring the sick people out of the hogan one at a time on their hands, six or eight or ten of them, whichever it took, holding them up in the air on their hands and singing as they came out, and dropped them in the mud, and then go on again.

After that was all taken care of, they would grab anyone at random, they'd reach out and take standers-by, you know. That's part of the Mud Dance. If you run under a shade or run and jump in your car they won't go in after you, because they only take you if you're in the sunlight. You can step under the shade and they won't do anything. They'd take after an Indian, he'd run jump on a horse, they'd run jump on horses and go get him, maybe it'd be thirty minutes, but they'd bring him back and throw him in.

Pretty quick I seen them take after Harry. I was in his car with the doors locked, and he was yelling, "Open the door, open the door!" just astriding as fast as he could. I was a little bit slow in opening the door, intentionally of course, and they got him. Harry had no idea they would take him, because he was partly sponsoring it. But to them, he was the main one that they really wanted.

They took him and spun him around in the air, walked over, and plunk! In he went, clothes and hat and all and everything. Well, he had to get up and get as much mud off of him as he could and get in the car and go home and completely change clothes. I think that was about the comicalest sight I have ever witnessed.

When Harry seen he was doomed, he took it the same as all the rest of them. Really, if he had gotten away . . . , I think it was better it turned out the way it did. Because he was important to them people. They looked to him for loans and for guidance.

But they were really conscientious about the Mud Dance. It was for rain. It was a drought year, and they hadn't had no rain. It's very sacred, and they only do it in extreme drought. Right now to put one on, well I haven't heard of one around over the country for a long, long while.

It wasn't long it started raining, before they even got through with their Mud Dance.

HARRY GOULDING: Professional photographers like Joe Muench, Ray Manley, Allen Reed, all of these photographers we had, I think people are getting to where they'll accept more literature on the bad side of things we have done to the Indians because they see these very interesting things about them that come out in pictures and papers. There were some wonderful people, like Will Rogers, that would come out with things, but I don't think it took. One picture, they say, talks more than words, and those were things that people had never seen, the reality and the beauty of the Navajo's life. They never got as deep into the whole thing because nobody could get a picture of a sand painting or a sing.

JOSEF MUENCH (photographer): In '28 I came across the water from Germany. Two years in Detroit, then struck west. But I came to California from the Northwest down, so I didn't come through the Valley. In '36 then, I came over here for the first time, and I fell immediately in love with it.

And it has developed that of all of the people I have met in my travels around, and particularly in the Four Corners area, that means the Navajo reservation and the big beyond, and I have met a good many of the old-timers, the only one that if I ever wear a hat, I would take it off the head, would be to Harry. It has turned into a close friendship, our association over the years. We just fell in with each other in a natural way. That is Harry's way of doing things.

We would sit outside at the old trading post. It was in the summertime, warm inside, so you go outside when the cool breeze was blowing, and you have breezy conversations, and that is when I just pricked my ears to listen to what he had to say. With little hints, little stories, a few words at times, he would tell you how you should behave toward the Indian, who is his friend. And that has helped me a great deal to understand the Indians. I can approach an Indian today and he accepts me right away because I'm approaching him in his way; like their gentle handshake. Thanks to Harry.

I never stayed directly with the Navajos. And rather than take pictures of them, I'd wait for Harry to come with me, because I oftentimes wanted to associate Harry with the Indians. Shooting him alone with the camera, that was one thing, but to associate him with a family of Indians around the hogan or around the women at the loom, Harry sort of blossomed out when he was with his friends. It came natural. He would maneuver around thinking how would he get the best possible composition out of it. There was always a conversation going on between them, and he was always bringing the Indians in a natural way into the best position for me to take pictures. I never had to teach him how to pose himself in a picture or with his Indian friends. We had a sort of unconscious teamwork going between us.

In the first few years he had caught on to the idea of pictures because I would talk about how I would compose a picture: that it had to have a meaning in it, not only for myself but also for thousands of other people. He would suggest to me, "Before you take this, take a look over from that side, or the other side." He began to suggest what was really natural to me. He would come out with the suggestion, "Let's do it this way," and it would just be my own natural way.

The first thing I try to catch in a picture is the beauty of it, in the rock. Sometimes when I used to sit in front of the trading post looking across that string of monuments, they would change. When you're among them they're not in a row, but from the trading post they appear as if they are in a single lineup. You think they change by the minute. They don't change; the light that falls upon them changes them. You think something is about to happen to them. You sit there and you gaze and gaze. Nothing will change. No rock will fall. But you sit there as if something is going to happen.

Yes, and to me it's still a unique drive, coming up from Kayenta, after you pass Owl Butte on one side and Agathlan on the other side, sort of a natural gateway, you don't see too many monuments, but there's enough of a suggestion there. Once you have been there, you know what's coming. You keep on, something will open up, some curtains will be drawn apart. It has a magnetism to it. You want to get into it quickly.

20 ◼ John Ford Comes to the Valley

HARRY GOULDING: It was along in the Depression and things were terribly tied up on the reservation. You couldn't get any cash. If a Navajo *gave* you sheep or wool you would have lost money. You couldn't afford to take it in, because nobody would buy it. It was terrible. So all it was, you had to trade; trading got pretty good. We took Navajo rugs out every fall, but you couldn't get money for the rugs. Sometimes a person that didn't sell rugs was having trouble moving their stuff, so they would trade for the rugs. They wanted anything they could turn around and trade again. Everybody was trading.

Mike and I didn't want to leave here, and we figured we would put our money in with what we were trading, hoping our money would last long enough and the trading would stay right so's we could make it through this thing. And there was one good thing happened. Ed Bibberman, he was an artist, he came out and was with us for three months, and he paid cash. I think when we squared up with Ed Bibberman, we had about eighty dollars left.

MAURICE KNEE: I stayed here with Harry and Mike until '37. Things were real rough, they just wasn't a crying dime, and I knew that I was on the payroll and would continue to be, and I knew that they didn't have it. I had a chance to go on a trip to the East Coast with my brother and his wife, so I went. Then I quit them and beat my way back.

HARRY GOULDING: This news came in over the radio that Hollywood was looking for a place away out somewhere, a good spot to make this Indian picture. United Artists it was. I had a friend out in California, that he was associated with Hollywood, and he wrote me in his letter that they were looking for a location to film a western. Mike and I figured, "By golly, we're going to head for Hollywood and see if we can't do something about that picture."

So we loaded up. We took our bedroll, coffee pot, grub, and the whole works. We had a lot of pictures of the Valley that visitors had sent, pretty near everybody would send us back nice enlarged pictures, so we gathered up all of those pictures and we took off for Hollywood. We didn't spend any money, only for gasoline. We never told anybody where we were going because there was this Depression and there weren't many people traveling. Whenever anybody come along, those fellas at the gas pumps would wonder what was making you travel, because things were so hard. They thought you might know about a special job or something. So we never said anything to anybody what we was going to do until we got right in close to Los Angeles there.

Then one old boy there asked us where we were going when we stopped to get gas, and when he found out we was from away out on the reservation, why then we told him that Hollywood was wanting to make an Indian picture. "We want to see if we can't induce them to make the picture out there, because we've got a lot of beautiful country and a lot of Indians to go with it."

"Do you know anybody down there at the United Artists studio?"

"No," I says, "we don't know a soul down there."

"Well, you just as well turn around and go home, because you're not going to get into that picture outfit unless you know somebody, and you've got to know them awful well."

"That might be so," I says, "but I'm either going to make that or make the jail. I'm going to make one or the other."

So we went on to stay with Chet, Mike's oldest brother. He had a butcher shop right close to Hollywood, and he flew stunt pilot for the pictures, him and a friend of his. We told him what we were thinking about, and he says, "There ain't a bit of use going down there. You can't get into that place. You got to know somebody to get in," just like this other fella said.

"Well," I says, "that's all right. But I'm going to get in there or go to jail. I know I've got something they need. You just lead me down there and show me where this United Artists place is. You show me the right door to go in down there, their main door, and I'll go on from there."

So he led me there and pointed across the street. I parked the outfit and I went on over and walked in.

It was a pretty good-sized room, and chairs for people to sit on if they came in doing business, and right in the corner of this room, why there was a girl setting in there. She had a glass in front of her and this hole in the front of the glass, and she was answering telephone calls. There was another two or three people so I waited. Then I went up, and she says, "Can I help you out any?"

"Yes, ma'am, you really could." I introduced myself, and I says, "I'm from Monument Valley, out in Arizona, and I hear that the studio here is looking for a location to make an Indian picture. So I brought some pictures in of this country, and I want to talk to somebody about it here at the studio."

"Who do you want to talk to?"

"Well," I says, "just anybody."

"Do you mean you don't know anybody here in the studio?"

"No ma'am," I says. "I'm just a stranger in here and I don't know a soul."

"I can't call anybody unless you know somebody," she says. "Do you have an appointment? These people don't have time to stop and talk to everybody that comes in here. You've got to know people."

"Oh," I says, "that don't worry me a bit. I've got a rig right out here across the street. I've got a bedroll, and I've got a little grub left in there yet. I've weathered a good part of the winter in an Indian hogan," I says, "and this is a much nicer place to stay than that. I'll just go and get my bed, and I'll come on back and wait till they do have time. I come a long ways to see these people," I says. So I started out to get my bedroll.

"Wait! Hey, wait a minute, wait a minute!"

"Oh, never mind," I says, "everything will be just fine."

"No! Come here! You can't bring your bedroll in here!"

"Why, it's a good clean bedroll," I says. "I can take it anywhere. I'm in no hurry, I'll just wait. Don't let it bother you a bit."

She called a fella upstairs and talked to him. Well, I could hear what he said on the phone. "Doesn't he know that we haven't got time to fool around with all the bums that come into town?" And he said some other words that was not too nice.

She turned around and started to tell me what he said.

"Never mind," I says, "I heard pretty well. Just tell him I've got plenty of time. I'll just hang around here. That old bedroll is pretty comfortable. I'll wait until someone will have time to talk to me."

He says, "Tell that SOB to get the hell out of there. Wait a minute, I'll come down and tell him myself!"

So doggone, you couldn't see where there was a door. I tried to see if he was going to come in the front door or what was going to happen. I says, "Where's he going to come from? Is he going to come in there?"

"No," she says, "that door right back of you." They had a door in there that you could hardly tell it was a door.

I stood right there and got my pictures in under my arms. I had a bundle for each side. Pretty soon this damn thing flew open and here comes this guy. It was a small fella, and he was so damned mad his hair was pretty near . . . Oh, he was mad!

He didn't say anything. He started looking me over, because I was a pretty rough-looking character. So I turned around kind of slow-like, like I was going to let him see me all, and as I turned, this nice old picture showed up.

"Where'd you get that picture?"

"One of the visitors that come in out there," I says. "Visitors have sent me a lot of pictures of the Valley. They come in to the trading post, and we've got a lodge out there." It was a beautiful picture of the Mittens with an old Indian setting there looking into it.

"Is that an Indian setting there on that horse?"

"Oh yes," I says, "we got Indians, just all kinds of Indians out there. And we've got beautiful country, and if you're looking for a place to make an Indian picture . . . And those Navajos," I says, "I know them all. They never went through the dole that we shoved out and ruined the rest of the Indians and got them lazy and worthless. The Navajos never took hold of that, so they're still alive."

Well, he turned out to be the location manager for the picture. "Would you mind bringing those pictures upstairs?" he says.

"Yes sir!" I says. "That's just what I come here to do! You can do anything you want with these pictures. It's just up to you folks."

So he went upstairs, and I followed along. There was four office spaces there for the big shots, and there was a door going from one to the other all the way through. He started putting these pictures up to where the light hit them right. He put all he could into that one room, and then the next room, and we pretty near run out of room, I had so many pictures.

We walked around through the darned things for an hour and a half, maybe two hours, and he kept asking me questions about this and that, and how it was. I says, "Well, it's rough country to get into. If you ask me I'm going to tell you what it is; it's rough country. But I've been out there quite a little while and I've been making my way through, and our guests come in there."

"I have a friend upstairs," he says. "Would you mind if he came down and looked at these pictures?" And he brought Mr. Ford down. And we did some talking then! We stayed there until it was getting awful late.

Mr. Ford says, "I have a friend that I'd like to have him look at these pictures. Would it be all right if I called him down?"

I says, "Well, you bet! I got up pretty early this morning, and I've been in your place all day now, pretty near. If he was packing a cup of coffee and a sandwich of some kind, it'd be all right. But it don't make any difference," I says. "I go four or five days without something to eat once in a while, it don't bother me too much."

But he come, with an old colored boy following him, packing a sandwich and some pretty good grub there, a piece of pie. I've lost his name in my memory now, but he was the top man in the studio, the producer.[1] I sat down and swallowed that food up in a hurry. We went on around then and looked at the pictures again, and we all sat down, and they called two or three other fellas in, and they wanted to ask questions of all kinds. We stayed in there until about one o'clock that morning, talking it.

They finally got to where they couldn't make the picture with less than a couple of hundred people. "How long would it take to put some more buildings up there?" he says.

"I'm an Indian trader," I says, "and I was a sheepherder ahead of that for a while. I'm a poor man to ask about those sort of things. But I've got to tell you, I'm pretty short on money myself. We just kind of been going through this Depression. Our Indians out there are getting hungry, and I had to cut into I and Mike's money to keep things at the trading post for them."

"Well," he says, "if we put a barracks in, and we'd have to put in some pretty nice places for our stars, what would be your charges if we came out there?"

"Well now," I says, "I'm stuck again. This is the closest I've ever been to a person that makes moving pictures. I haven't even seen too many. I just got to say that if you folks want to come out there, and you can make that picture, you know more about what I ought to charge than I do." I says, "I'm willing to take you up on that kind of a deal." That surprised them a little, I think. They looked at each other kind of funny.

They wanted me to fly out there with them, but I didn't want to go, in those clothes and everything. And I didn't have a dime to pay for anything.

Well, they'd have to see the place.

"I'll tell you what you do," I says. "Lee Doyle in Flagstaff has handled pictures that have been made around, and I talked to him before I left. He'll take you out to our trading post, and there's a young fella there that you'll meet." That was Maurice. "You're going to think he don't know very much when you first take a look at him, but he knows just as much about that country as if it were me."

So they finally decided they'd go out and take a look at it. About six people, the location manager, and Ford himself, about six of them went out. Maurice done a very good job of putting the place over. They had to help him cook and all that. They must have had quite a time.

When they got back they called me and wanted to know if I could come down to the studio.

"I think I can do it," I says. "The first time, my wife's brother led the way and got me down there in front of your door. He's busy at the butcher shop, and I doubt if I can get him, but I'll be there," I says.

"You just stay right there and we'll send somebody up to get you."

And here comes an old colored boy. He had a rig, a big red limousine, with a window behind him, with just a hole in the window to talk through. I never saw anything like it.

I went out there, and he goes back and opens one of them doors. His driver's place was over there, and he come around and opened the door for me on the other side, one of these back doors.

I says, "No, I ain't going to get in that outfit." I wanted to talk to him. I might find out a little, you know, going down, so I says, "I'd rather ride with you anyway, even if I was used to riding back there." So we got in together, and we got pretty well acquainted. He was a nice old colored fella.

When we got back in the room where we wrastled it out before, they told me they'd decided to make the picture out there. Then they asked me a lot of questions and a lot more questions, and I had to tell them, "It's just like I said before; we used our money up and I'm just up agin it."

"Make him a check out," Mr. Ford told this fella, and he gave him a signal of some kind. Then he says, "What can we expect in the way of weather?"

It was in September or October. "I'd bring some warm clothes along, because it can get a little chilly if you're in there very long. But I've got an old Indian," I says, "a medicine man, Hosteen Tso is his name, and when it gets too dry out there, he makes it rain; he has some ceremonies. I just wouldn't worry about the weather." I says, "You let me know what you want about four o'clock in the evening and he'll fix you up with the weather the next day. If he's not right there, he can do it from quite a ways off even. He'll make enough so's it'll hold you until he gets in there himself."

Well, they didn't question it too much. But they wanted to be making the picture in three days!

"Three days? A hundred people?" I says. "Gosh, them old rocks have been out there an awful long time, and the Indians ain't going to move. Wouldn't a few more days be about as well?"

The location man just whammed on the desk! "One thing, Goulding, you've got to know when you're starting out in this picture business! When we want anything, we don't care what it costs, and we don't care what it is, we want *what* we want *when* we want it!"

"Well, that's all right," I says. "Still, I can only do what I can."

"Who do you deal with over there?"

"Babbitt Brothers," I told him. "They'll have anything that you need, I think. I get everything I want from them."

So they got all the dope they wanted, and they started to visiting around. I says, "If you fellas are going to stand around here all night, I aim to be in Flagstaff pretty near by morning. I just can't stand here and lose the night. I've got to get going. Three days comes awful quick out there!" So I slammed the door and the old colored boy took me back. We had another nice visit.

As soon as I got back to Chet's, it was after one o'clock in the morning, we just piled the stuff in our rig and we started to head out for home.

We only had a little left of our eighty bucks, and pretty soon we used it up. Mike says, "What are we going to do for money to eat on?"

"Oh," I says, "I've got a check here, everything's all right." So we went on, and we were getting hungry. I got to thinking, "Wait a minute, I'd better look at this check." I pulled it out, and it was for five thousand dollars! I couldn't get that cashed nowhere with the clothes I had on! So we slowed down to save gas. We got a ways out of Flagstaff and then we had to stop. I went into a filling station to get some gas, and I told him what had happened. "They're bringing a hundred people," I says, "and we've got rooms to build and everything. I can't pay you," but I showed him the check, and I says, "If you'll fill me up, one tank, that'll get me to Flagstaff, and you'll get your money, don't worry!"

He thought about it a little bit. He pulled out a twenty dollar bill, and he says, "Just send me the money when you get it."

When we got into Flagstaff I went to Babbitt's to talk to them about it, and there was a whole string of eleven trucks lined up out there and cars and one thing another. I thought to myself, I wish I had that outfit. That, by god, is just about what we need to get the job done.

I went upstairs, and Jimmy Babbitt says, "Harry, where in the hell have you been? My god, you've had men down our necks, and this damn phone hasn't had time enough to ring hardly! What have you been doing?"

"I've been out to Hollywood," I says, "and we're going to get a picture in here. They're coming out."

"They're here," he says. "You see all that stuff out there in front of the store? They're just waiting for you and Mike to take them out to Monument Valley." And I think there was eighteen carpenters. So I went out there and whoof! And we were ready.

I figured Mr. Ford would be at the back end of the line in the fancy car, so I walked back there, and he looked down and says, "Well, Harry, how's that old medicine man that makes the weather? Is he still living?"

So we went on out. We started way before daylight out of Flagstaff, and we got in about two o'clock, two-thirty. I come on ahead with the location manager, Mr. John [Ford], and Duke [John Wayne], and as we got pretty close to home, I asked Mr. Ford, "Are you figuring on shooting something tomorrow?"

"Oh you betcha!" he said. "We're going to start right away." It was *Stagecoach,* was the movie they were going to make.

"Well," I says, "we can get a smoke signal off to the medicine man if you let me know what you might want with the weather."

"We'd like to have a few nice theatrical clouds hanging around in the sky."

"I can't send that to him," I says. "I don't know what a theatrical cloud is."

"Just pretty, fluffy clouds."

"We'll get it off," I says.

And sure enough, the next day the clouds were there!

■   *Stagecoach* was the first of John Ford's great westerns. No one can account for the chemistry of greatness, but it does seem that in 1938, director and actor and landscape came together, and that in *Stagecoach* the filming of the American West was raised from "B" western formulas to the moving and haunting stature of an archetype. Before *Stagecoach,* John Wayne had been trapped in the formulas, with a reputation for wooden acting, but the discerning director John Ford had seen something in him that showed promise, and in *Stagecoach* he brought it out.

As the dream landscape of the West,[2] Monument Valley remains an active and unforgettable force on the imagination of those who stray into its atmosphere, and it becomes for them a discovery. John Ford's nephew said, "John had first heard about Monument Valley from Harry Carey, who had stumbled into it while exploring the Navajo country in the 1920s. No other film company had ever worked there, and John had been waiting for years for a chance to do so."[3]

John Wayne also discovered the Valley. "Now I'll tell you something," he said. "It's a secret I've kept for many years. I was the guy who found Monument Valley. And I told Ford about this place.

"I'll tell you how it happened. It was back in '29, and I was proppin' and stuntin' on a George O'Brien location, out in Arizona. One Sunday, I wanted to get away by myself. I took a car and went drivin'. I went out on this Navajo reservation. It was comin' on sunset. Then I came to this valley. I parked the car and got out and looked at it and, well, you know how it looks, and that evening it looked, well, kind of like it was another world.

"I never forgot about it, and when Mr. Ford was talkin' about locations for *Stagecoach* I told him about Monument Valley and he looked at me as if I was stupid because he thought he knew the Arizona and Utah country and he never heard of the Valley. I was with him on a party when he was scoutin' locations in Arizona.

"Well, we were drivin' along and finally came to this reservation and went down the road and came to the Valley and then Mr. Ford pretended to see the buttes and said, 'I have just found the location we are going to use.'

"It was Monument Valley.

"And the old buzzard looked me straight in the eye. I said nothing. He wanted to be the one who found it. I don't know why he never wanted to give me credit for tellin' him about Monument Valley."[4]

When Harry Goulding and John Stevens stood on the rim of Comb Ridge in the fall of 1922, they too had made a discovery, and it was one that touched Harry to his western soul. Sixteen years later, armed with the photographs of Josef Muench and other "discoverers" of the Valley, he connected with John Ford in Hollywood.

The question of the "discovery" of Monument Valley for the movies will probably never be settled. The Harry Carey version is not incompatible with either John Wayne's or Harry Goulding's story, but it is more difficult to reconcile the latter two with each other. Perhaps what Harry Goulding did was to offer the practical possibility of setting up a complex movie location in such a desolate place.

Stagecoach was released in 1939. Following its success, Dick Rossen directed three films in the Valley, with headquarters at Gouldings, in the early forties: *Kit Carson*, 1940; *Billy the Kid*, 1941; and *The Harvey Girls*, 1944. Immediately after the end of the war, John Ford returned and established Monument Valley as his own territory with the shooting of *My Darling Clementine*, released in 1946; *Fort Apache*, 1948; *She Wore a Yellow Ribbon*, 1949; *Wagon Master*, 1950; *The Searchers*, 1956; *Sergeant Rutledge*, 1960; and *Cheyenne Autumn*, 1964.[5] With these films he indelibly stamped Monument Valley on the world's imagination as the archetypal image of the American West.

21 ■■■ Making Weather for the Movies

Harry Goulding: The medicine man, Hosteen Tso, didn't get in that first night. Getting pretty close to four o'clock, and nobody interfered if Mr. John was busy; you'd wait until every now and then he stops and there's a little time.

So I went in, and he says, "Just about the same weather as it was today. That was fine. No, wait a minute," he says. "Right out beyond that crossroad, the main road goes by and your road crosses it and heads for down in the Valley. The stagecoach will go out that road, and then we're going to have some action on this other road, and we'd like to have a cloud to follow us along right there."

"About what time of day will you be wanting this to happen on the crossroad?" I says. He told me, and by golly, if there wasn't a darned cloud, a pretty good-sized cloud, come right in there and showed a shadow. They were in this stagecoach, and there was a high wind and the clouds were moving along pretty good. They were just what he wanted exactly.

That evening Hosteen Tso got back. I didn't actually send Mr. Ford's orders out to him; I took a shot at those first two days myself. So when he got back I took him right up to Mr. Ford's room. We'd go to his room at four o'clock every afternoon and he'd give the message and I'd interpret. The old Navajo was really paying attention to what was going on. You could see he was.

If you'd see General Ford, if he was alive, *he'd* tell you that Hosteen Tso made the weather. And if you would say that couldn't be, you'd get piled on! Mr. Ford would give me the signal coming in, and the medicine man and I would come to his room. He always had some real good whiskey, and he asked me if it would be all right if he'd give the old fella a drink. "Yeah," I says, "one drink, not too big, that'd be fine, because he's a one-drink man." Mr. Ford talked about what he wanted, and I'd tell Hosteen Tso—Tso means big; Mr. John called him Fatso—I'd give Fatso the message, and sure enough, the weather would be there the next day.

One day Mr. Ford said to me, "They tell me that you get some real jim-dandy sandstorms in here."

"Yeah, we probably could cook that up any time you want."

Hosteen Tso, the medicine man whom John Ford hired to make the weather for his Monument Valley films. (Goulding's Monument Valley Museum)

"Well, tell him to cook us up a good one." They wanted to take some pictures of the stagecoach running.

"He can do it," I says.

"And we want it just about right after lunch."

That day we went out and done some shooting in the morning, and then we shut down for lunch. I looked down toward Oljeto, and I see this doggone sandstorm coming in. You could tell it was a bugger of a thing coming. So I went over, they were sitting there eating, and I said to Mr. Ford, "Mr. John, just what do you want this sandstorm for, right after lunch?"

He says, "We want to get the stagecoach along the rim of the skyline there, and we want to get the Monuments in the side."

Well, in order to do that, they had to get up on a high trestle there, and they had all the material out there to build it. I said, "Mr. John, you ordered a good sandstorm, and you see that down there? Here it comes, and it ain't going to take it too long to make its way up through here. You better just stop this eating and get out there and get that trestle up, because that thing is going to *be* here!"

"Oh," he says, "we can wait, we can get at it right after lunch."

"If you do," I says, "if you stop and eat this meal, you see them monuments out there that you want to get in your picture? You ain't going to be able to even see them! You wanted a good one and you're going to get it!"

So by golly, he stopped. He turned over to the location man and he says, "That old medicine man has done it! Let's get going!" And they was some activity going on, I'll tell you right now! No eating!

They finally got set up, and about that time comes the sandstorm right down to the old lake bed down there. They made two runs, just two, and the sandstorm got so bad, by the time they wanted the third run they just couldn't make it. They like to make several runs, but you couldn't see a thing, they had to wrap up and come in.

We always took care of Mr. John and Duke and all the actors and actresses up on the bench, and down below they took care of everybody else. They had big circus tents, huge things, for the folks to sleep in, one for the women and one for the men. And one day, here comes a sandstorm from the Monuments, this way, coming right for us. I told the location man, "You'd better get someone down on them tents with hammers and ropes to hold them, because that thing is really going to tear those tents down. They can't stand it."

Somebody says, "Go get the old medicine man to get busy," you know, kind of sarcastically like.

"By gosh," I says, "that's what we'll have to do!" Hosteen Tso stayed down with the folks, so I beat it down and talked to the old fella, and he got his stuff out and got over there on a little ridge, and he started shaking his rattle and chanting, chanting. And I'll be doggoned, with all them people out watching, because it was a vicious thing, if it didn't turn and go down towards Train Rock. Yessir, turned and missed those tents.

Now, if Mr. Ford was alive, and if you ever questioned that! You couldn't say nothing agin that old medicine man. He was ticklish about that.

Well, finally they were finishing up on *Stagecoach,* and we were coming in that evening. Out on location they'd work right up as long as they could, and they generally ate around seven. "Mr. John," I says, "you haven't given me a message for that old medicine man yet."

"Well, Harry," he says, "there's only one more thing we could possibly use, and there just wouldn't be any use in it, because this is the wrong time of year for snow."

"What have you got in mind?"

"Well, that's all we need. We'd stay over if we could get some snow."

It was October, and no snow ever gets here until close to Christmas.

"You getting worried about that old medicine man? Didn't he cut up in pretty good shape around here?"

"Oh, yes, he has!"

So I brought old Hosteen up to his room right quick there, before supper, and I give him the message, and we both had our little drink.

I always got up very early in the mornings to see how things were going, and there was the snow!

I knew just about when Mr. John got up, and that morning I wanted to be there. He slept upstairs over the trading post. He kept his shades down and he never would put them up before breakfast. So I was setting in the old sofa in the living room. I hear him rambling in there in the bedroom. I had a paper in my hand and I was waiting for him to come out. All the shades were open in that room. When he came around the bend into the living room, he looked out, and he came right over there in front of me, and he says, "My goodness, Harry, I owe you an apology! I thought you were just kidding me about that old medicine man!" He believed in him, really, but not that much. To get snow, in October! And so they stayed another day.

The Navajos were paid once a week, five dollars a day. If he had his horse he got eight dollars a day and the horse was fed and he was fed. That was big wages at that time. Hosteen Tso's pay was fifteen dollars a day. He was on the payroll, he got his check like anybody else working there. And when he left, Mr. Ford gave him quite a roll of money and shook hands with him. I know it was big, I could see it. Old Hosteen Tso said, "He sure give me a lot of money," but I didn't ask him just how much.

Mr. Ford hired him for later movies too. That message was in ahead: it was Hosteen Tso or no picture. Ward Bond and Duke said if anybody

questioned Pappy, if they called him, about the old medicine man, why Mr.
John would really get mad about it. He didn't like it at all.

SHONIE HOLIDAY (translated from Navajo):   My father, Hosteen Tso,
was an important medicine man. He knew 'Anaají (Enemy Way), Hózhǫ́ǫ́jí
(Blessing Way), Na'at'ojí (Male Shooting Way), five different kinds of special
prayers, and Hochǫ́'ǫ́jí (Evil Way).

He could also make the clouds come or go for the movies. Sometimes he
made the rain and wind go away, sometimes he brought them in, it would
just come and go according to his prayers. When he was finished, there was
a Hózhǫ́ǫ́jí ceremony for purification and to get back in harmony with
nature.

TALLAS HOLIDAY (half-brother of Shonie Holiday, translated from Navajo):   Hosteen Tso was my father too. One time when the movies were here,
they were all ready to go, but day after day there were thick clouds that just
settled and stayed there. The movie director gave him a hundred dollars and
asked him to make the clouds go away.

But I think he made a mistake. That kind of ceremony is dangerous,
because you can't control nature. Year after year after that, when there was
drought the people blamed him. "You're the one!" they said. I told him, as
soon as the movie was over he should have done another ceremony to
bring the clouds back, but he didn't. He didn't know the other part of the
ceremony. That's what killed him. The first big rain we had after a long dry
spell killed him. He couldn't bring the rain back, but when other people's
prayers and sings brought rain, the moisture affected him and he died. I told
him that if he didn't know how to bring the rain back, he never should have
done it in the first place.

SHONIE HOLIDAY (translated from Navajo):   One time my father was
chasing a jackrabbit on horseback and the cinch of the saddle broke. He fell
off the horse and injured his liver. He got sick from that fall, and just recently
he died. He was over eighty years old. Some people say that the reason why
he died was because he made the rain go away when the movies were here,
but I know for a fact that he fell off a horse and injured his liver. He didn't
say anything about the rain.

22 ■■■ On Location

HARRY GOULDING: Before we ever went out to Hollywood, people used to say, "You'll hate the day the movies come in here, because they're terrible. They drink, they tear a place up." But things were happening so wonderful when Mr. Ford came in, and did for a couple of times, that I asked him, "Mr. John, why did I hear that, and here we've had nothing but good happening?"

"Well," he says, "when you start for a location away from Hollywood, you go through your help with a fine-tooth comb and you pick the very best there is, that you are sure would be able to enjoy a thing of this kind." That's why they all took to the Indians. In the most of the crew there'd be only a few strangers. Even his horsemen and things of that kind, there'd be very few that were people we didn't know. It wasn't like having other shows in here. You looked forward to Mr. John's coming back because he brought the family with him. We got to know all of them and we'd get kind of lonesome to see them ourselves.

He had this fella, Danny Borzage, that used to play an accordion for him. He was a little fella, and everybody liked him; he was just a prince to have around. He'd been working for Mr. Ford a long time and he knew him like a book. He studied the picture before they came out here, just like one of the actors, that little guy, and then he could pick out what was worrying Mr. John and the type of music that he should give him. And it worked every time. Every once in a while when they'd be setting up a scene, the little guy'd go over and give the actors a piece of music too. Everybody loved the guy.

The thing is, Mr. Ford out on the set working, it's kind of rough on the person that makes a mistake, because he's all business. He's awful nice to his people coming in, but boy when he was out there they were working and no monkey business. If somebody made a mistake, he'd lower the beam on him! He'd tromp him down! And the little musician knew if music would help or not.

But Mr. John had the nicest way. I noticed that he'd catch that fella in the evenings after work was over, even if he had to make a little trip down to the lower part where all the horsebackers were and everything. He'd run into this boy, and he could sweep the kind of a broom that would just spread out and make a fella feel good.

When Danny played the squeeze-box, he could wheel it off! He'd play for all of our dances. They would work hard all day, and every evening we'd kick the tables back and something was agoing on. And he played all the music.

And this crazy little nut! The Navajos used to come in to the trading post chanting in those days, and you'd see Danny paying attention. He'd get the swing of one of those chants, and darn if he wouldn't surprise some Navajos with it. He'd go over and play this chant to them on this crazy squeeze-box. And that raised the clouds in the sky! The Navajos liked him. Bihózhǫ́ they named him. *Nizhóní* is pretty. *Bihózhǫ́,* that is way better than pretty, and that's what his name was, Bihózhǫ́.

MAURICE KNEE: I got back to Gouldings just about the time they were making *Stagecoach.* Beat it, took a year, salesman in New York, come back, and helped make *Stagecoach.* I rode a pony in that movie, in the cavalry. One of the cowboys they brought in as a cavalry man got appendicitis, and they asked me if I wanted to be a cavalry man. I said, "If I can have old Ned."

The reason I wanted that horse was because he was a biter. He'd bite you or bite another horse in front of you. I knew that if I got him, there would be nobody else in front of me, so I could find myself in the movie. And it worked. Got five bucks a day. I tried to get room and board out of it, but they says, "You live here."

JACK SLEETH (Mike Goulding's brother-in-law):   The movies were just a big party to the Navajos. They whooped a lot when they had card games going, everybody visiting. It was a big social thing. They'd all work as extras during the day, and at night they were busy socializing. They camped all over here, watered a thousand head of sheep and cattle. They needed the cattle a lot of times for the movie, or horses, and then sometimes the family was working in as extras and they'd just bring their sheep with them. There was a steady stream of sheep coming in to this little trough of ours all day long, and we hauled water where they had troughs for the other horses wherever they corralled them.

This whole area down here was Navajo country, camps all over, and then this section right over here was a tent city for the people they brought in. They set up two long strings of tents, I think four men to a tent, some eight men, and then a big mess hall and a laundry set up.

HARRY GOULDING: When the first pictures came in out here, I suggested to the fella who was in charge of everything that he ease up on them fellas packing stuff around, high-priced from California. Get these Navajos, get them more reasonable, and have an interpreter or two around. There's nothing lazy about a Navajo if he can get work, especially if he can get it on the reservation. They get awful lonesome if they go off the reservation, but this deal was just what they liked, helping these fellas, like electricians and plumbers.

For two pictures they didn't use quite so many of them; they had to have their own electricians and all that. But the third picture, when they came in, they had Navajos with belts of electrical stuff around them, and they'd learn right straight! *Clementine* was quite a long picture and they done a lot of building in here, put a duplicate town of Tombstone in, and that was a lot of work for the Navajos. They were up there hammering nails and doing everything.

One time, here comes the union men out. They insisted that the Navajo couldn't work for these outfits because he didn't belong to the union. I told the Navajos, "We've got these union men in here because they want the work you're doing. Now I'm going to be talking to them, and I want you fellas to come up there." These two union men, one of them was a smaller fella, but he had a big old boy to do the hard work for him if it came to a fight. The Navajos were standing there, and some of them were interpreting to the others what our conversation was. And mister, you've never got into as thick an atmosphere, I don't care where you'd *ever* go, as those people can sew together!

It was raining and storming, it was cold. These union boys darned near hadn't made it in here. I wouldn't give them no rooms. And they could just see that those Navajos were finally going to get on the warpath. Oh, it was tremendous! "We've got to get back tonight," they finally said, "and we don't know that road well enough. We'd like to have you send a man along to show us the road."

"I wouldn't send nothing along with you," I says. "You get out of here and get out on your own, I don't care if you fall in one of them damn washes!" And so they took off.

One time, it was a big picture and they had forty or fifty prairie schooners. And there was an old lake bed. Cliffs came in, and it was a beautiful spot. The sand blows in against the cliff, and in flash floods the water falls off and cuts a little canyon right back between the cliffs. The Indians were supposed to come down through that canyon and then come over the top of the sand dune into the old lake bed and attack the wagon train. There was about four hundred Indians hid behind them rocks in the canyon while we was getting ready.

There were three big trucks came down in there, backed in as close as they could get to that sand. They were carrying—there'd have to be somebody down there left dead after the fight—they were carrying dead men and horses, dummies made out of some kind of rubber. So this truck backed in there and threw a horse out, and that old horse hit and wobbled, you know. Pretty soon here comes a paleface out, and he wobbles and rolls off over there. And here comes an Indian out. They had them there so's they could turn the camera on the damage the Indians had done in the fight.

The leader of the Indians was old Chee. He got a little extra money for being chief because he had a beautiful little horse. He could always go up to that horse anywhere, any place, any time, but they'd been feeding them hay and oats, and so the little horse got kind of wild. That morning it was chilly, and he didn't want to be caught, the old fella couldn't catch him. So they kept waiting, wondering what had happened.

I says, "I think what's happened is, that old Indian pony is feeling his oats. You better send some of them riders down and help him out." So they did, and pretty soon here they come back. They was about an hour finding him and his horse, but they finally got him hid over in there and got everything ready.

They told me what to tell the Indians. Let the old chief be in ahead of them. Give him a horse daylight between the rest of them and the chief. And stay right with him, stay right there, just let him be in the lead.

I says, "Don't you think maybe we ought to let a few of them make the ride and see what's going on?"

"That old man has cost enough already!" says the location manager. "Go up there and get him to going!" They'd lost a lot of money because they had a lot of high-priced actresses and actors in there.

Well, you do what they tell you. So I went up and told him. "You got to go right up between those two bushes and down in on the other side," I says. "That's where you'll meet the protectors of the wagon train."

So they shot the gun off to go, and out comes the old chief, and the others were staying right behind him. The old chief went up over the top of that sand dune, and here were these palefaces down in there, a whole great huge bunch of them, and they had these rifles! All those wagons in there, and here were all these dead men and horses lying around! When he sees all that, why he stampedes. He leaves Cheyenne! He came right on down through the camera gang. They had to spread to get out of the way. And I tried to get out of the way, but I didn't quite make it, I fell, and all these horses jumped over me. He led the whole bunch right through there with one horse daylight between them. That was his best way out. He took on off down the draw, and away they went. They was gone!

Well, I was so darn tickled, I rolled on the ground I was laughing so hard. I just tumbled over, that's all.

Pretty soon somebody kicked me in the back. It was the location manager. "My God, man, get up and get in that car of yours and catch that old fella!"

I took out after him and headed him off. They'd got clean down to the Totem Pole.

He says, "Oh, no, I'm not going back! All of them white men down there with them rifles! Here, look at what I've got," and he pulled one of his arrows out and showed it to me, and it had a rubber point on there. He says,

"I ain't going down there and try to fight them white men with this thing! Let me go home and get my rifle, and I'll come on back."

Finally some of the other Navajos came and helped me out on it, and we went on back up. Well I'll tell you, it doubled me up.

The Navajos wanted to make Mr. Ford a member of the tribe. It was when they were making *The Searchers* in 1956. That was one of their big pictures, and they had a lot more people in, and so that's when they decided.

Frank and Lee Bradley came to me. They were the Navajo interpreters for the movies. Well, they were Mr. Ford's boys. They'd always come to me if they wanted something, and we'd visit it out. So they said they'd like to make him a member of the Navajo tribe.

"That'd be fine!" I says. "I'm just sure he'd want to have a squaw dance or something; he'd want to have something nice going on that you folks would enjoy." I says, "Try to set a day; he might want to let the folks rest or something."

So they did. And he picked the day, he got three beef in here, and a truckload of watermelons. There was everything the Navajos liked. It was quite a day. About ten o'clock in the morning it started out with horse races, and he had very nice presents for the winners. And then foot races. And old man's races. He run in it, doggone, that was a kick! He was getting along in years, but he took good care of himself. He come in right behind the leader, he didn't quite make the money. But him and that bunch of old men! He put it on, he was just using everything he had. Oh, that was a dandy!

Finally about eleven o'clock or eleven-thirty they wanted Mr. John to come down, and they wanted Duke and Ward to be with him, they knew they were very close. They had a deerskin just like they have in their ceremonies. It's got to have all its feet and the hoofs, and not a thing, not even a hair, is supposed to leave that skin. There wasn't anybody that could print too good, but Shine Smith was there that day, so they told him what they wanted on this deerskin, and he done the printing.

They chanted and they had a very nice ceremony and everything in it. It was a sincere thing. I could see that Ward and Duke and Mr. John felt a lot of atmosphere coming in, and they reacted a little to it too. It was a lovely thing.

Now, when Mr. Ford came in here in 1938 with *Stagecoach*, the Depression was on, and that was a great help out of the blue sky. Then there were two times that he came in here just before a bad winter and saved a lot of Navajos. They had the money, so they got a lot of food in the hogans, they got clothes, maybe new saddles, and their hogans were filled up just before this bad weather hit.

The summer before that second bad winter, the snakes had told the Navajos it was going to be bad, so I got in touch with Ford, and be darned if he didn't cook up one of these pictures and he came in. The old Indians

A working conference on location for The Searchers, *1956. From left, John Wayne as Ethan Edwards, John Ford, Harry Goulding, Ward Bond as Samuel Clayton; standing, Henry Brandon as Chief Scar; in the foreground, a young man holding the script.* (McLaughlin Historical Photo)

always knew what the weather was going to be, and so I just dropped him a note and told him what they said. I didn't know whether he'd come or not, but he wanted to make this picture, and so my letter urged him. He told me that it was getting about time he wanted to make another picture. He didn't measure his times, but he said that he read that letter and he got to thinking, "Maybe we'll try to get out there." And did; he come out in the late fall and made the picture. So the Navajos just felt that the gods had something to do with this man coming in here. Mr. John loved those Navajos.

When they made the TV documentary about Mr. Ford in 1971, they brought Duke and Ward Bond, there was about eight of them that came in with him. "Directed by John Ford," it was called, and a lot of Navajos gathered in here to see him. We went down in the Valley and shot pictures down in there. He was here two days.

Mr. Ford was showing his age a little. He was a little weaker, but he was glad to get back to Monument Valley. In fact, they stayed over an extra day, Ward and Duke and Mr. Ford. We wandered around in the Valley, but mostly we sat and visited a lot. And then Mr. Ford, he rested some too. He had the same cabin. He always took that end cabin, the farthest one out, he was always in there.

SETH BIGMAN (Navajo, Monument Valley): The last time Mr. Ford came back out here, we had our last big feast down here at my father-in-law's place, Jake Charlie Holiday, just below Goulding's. John Ford and John Wayne came out, and also another character, he always played comedy, I forget his name. The three of them came out, and this is where they had their last feast. Then we heard about Mr. Ford was passed away. Before that my father-in-law passed away, but they had a happy last meeting. They fed a lot of people and they gave a lot of money away. Everybody went home happy.

PART THREE. THE WAR AND BEYOND

23 ■■■ THE NAVAJOS GO TO WAR

HARRY GOULDING: We were closed up during the war, didn't have gas enough to do anything, but I was recruiting Navajos for the railroad. That's one thing you could do, and it was pretty necessary they got those people, so they gave us a ration card that told any filling station we got all the gas we wanted. I never overdone it. One thing I did do, though; we never took a visitor out in the Valley for money, but a lot of times a soldier would get back on furlough and would come in to the place, and I'd always take him down in, a little skip down around the Valley and a visit with him. But that's the only extent that I ever disobeyed the rules.

■■ Large numbers of Navajos played an active and effective part in the war effort, both in military service and as civilians in defense work of various kinds. There had always been a few Navajos doing section work for the Santa Fe Railroad, but by mid-1941, the number had increased to 200, and other railroads were also hiring them. At peak employment, 800 Navajos were working on the construction of an ordnance depot at Fort Wingate. Following this, 500 were employed in building the Navajo Ordnance Depot at Bellemont, near Flagstaff. Hundreds became migratory farm workers. There was a huge exodus of Navajos to defense factories on the West Coast. There were even Navajo waitresses at the Fred Harvey restaurants, located at depots along the Santa Fe Railroad. In 1945, according to an Indian Service estimate, 10,000 Navajos were employed in war work.[1]

HARRY GOULDING: In the early treaties, they promised the Navajos a school and a teacher for every thirty children. Well, the school that we gave them was the section crew on the railroad. That picked them up at about the seventh grade and took them on up to the twelfth. Instead of a school and a teacher for every thirty children, why that was their schooling.

Now their college, they go on those work trains. The fellas on the section crew are pretty rough, but when you get on that work train, mister, they are terrible, and especially on payday—fight and butcher one another! Those fellas on the work trains were mean and nasty, but it never rubbed off on the Navajos.

They'd lost their society. The minute a Navajo goes off the reservation to work, and especially in those early days, there was nothing out there for him at all. It was just like the boys over at Vietnam, just heartsick to get home. When I'd take a new group in to the railroad, I'd take them to a place away from the other Navajos, where they wouldn't know I was in around. Otherwise they'd pile on the truck and go back, even if they lost their money.

When I was taking those Indians in, I'd get as many as thirty people in the truck. They'd have to stand up all the way to Salt Lake City, but they didn't complain. And our government now, anything they done they furnished buses for, but they wouldn't furnish buses for us to haul those Indians out—they're just Indians!

When we got into Salt Lake, I'd take them into the depot, and we had to cross the street, so they'd come behind me, thirty Indians in single file, thirty and one, going into the depot. Well, some of us got across the street and then the light changed red. So I waited. I thought the Navajos would let the cars get by. I didn't think they would hang to it like that. The cars crowded them to get through, but they just stayed right in their line. Ay golly, we got across the street!

When we went in the depot, it had a lobby with a marble floor, a beautiful floor. At first I just walked in, but I see those Indians was walking on it like it was ice. They just walked like they was walking on eggs! Everybody in the doggoned waiting room, we had to go clean through it to go upstairs, they was all getting a heck of a bang out of it, and so I walked like they did after that. And then go around and take them upstairs.

I hauled the Navajos up to the defense plants too during the war. Just this side of Green River, there's a drive down about five or six miles, and there's a little gusher, a geyser, and there's another one that shoots up a little over two hundred feet, down close to the river there.[2] The first few bunches I took up, we stopped at the little one, and they gave that a lot of attention, so I thought, the next bunch I get, I'm going to go in to the big geyser. So I took them in there, and it gushes every half-hour. I had been in to it only once, I think, but I'd seen it, and it kind of slowed *my* clock down a little. It's a beautiful thing. So we stopped and got out. I wanted to space them kind of close to it, but not where they'd get wet or anything, and so we was all standing there and visiting and waiting for the thing to gush. Pretty soon it started growling and growling, and boy they straightened up right now. Heard that noise and started chanting. And then that thing come up. And my!

After they chanted, each one of them took out their *tádídíín*, their corn pollen, and put a pinch of it on their head, a little deerskin pouch with *tádídíín* in it, and the one that was standing next to me put it on me. When I see his hand moving toward me, I jerked my hat off. And so he put it. Then the chant stopped, and they all moved over. He motioned me and we came around, and there was a breeze blowing. Go around to where the breeze would blow a little spray on them, and stood there until it give up. That's an experience, I'll tell you! I had the great privilege of being counted in.

BUSTER WHITEHORSE (translated from Navajo): It was the beginning of World War II and they made a draft card for me. My brother, Joe Whitehorse, and I hitchhiked to Shash Bitoo (Fort Wingate). We worked for the army there for a year building a new ammo dump. After that we were moved to Kin Łání (Flagstaff) to build another ammo dump at Bellemont. We mixed cement to build the walls. It was shaped like a barrel and was bigger than a house. We had a Navajo supervisor. The weather was very cold, but we did a good job.

We were still working there when they wanted us to go to Los Angeles to work on the railroad. There must have been a train wreck. We cleaned up the mess and repaired the rails, which took us about two months. Then we went back to Kin Łání, still working on the railroad, near a place called Tsiizizii (Leupp). This was a place where they kept prisoners of war; they

Buster Whitehorse, builder of hogans, brick mason, and defense worker during World War II, nearly blind, with his mother, Fast Woman, deaf and over 100. In 1974 they lived alone in this summer shade and their hogan (seen in the background) in back country near Agathlan. (Samuel Moon)

were guarded very carefully. We also worked right in the middle of town in Kin Łání for about a month repairing broken rails. Then two months at Béésh Sinil (Winslow) and a month over towards Na'nízhoozhí (Gallup) at a place called 'Atiin Hóchǫ' (Bad Road), then past Na'nízhoozhí at Tsinyaadootł'izh (Green under the Trees) for a month and a half, and Kin Deelk'id (Houses on a Hill) near Shash Bitoo for three months. There were sixty-some workers.

Then we went back to Kin Łání again to settle our wages. They paid us, but they wanted us to stay and do some more work. One night all of a sudden we heard that the United States had won the war. The war was over. People were shouting and running around and cars were honking. They told us there was no more to be done and that we could go home to our families.

■ Military service got a mixed response from the Navajos. Many were reluctant to register for the draft or to report when drafted. Living in remote and isolated places, and far removed from the affairs of the white world, they were not at all clear about the issues of the war. And there was the pervasive distrust of Wáashindoon that still lingered from stock reduction.[3]

On the other hand, the Navajo tradition, inactive only since the Long Walk, was that of the warrior. Young boys were still trained by their elders to endure hardship in that spirit. The Enemy Way ceremonial, whose purpose was to heal the effects of contamination by contact with non-Navajos, began as a purification rite for returning warriors, and the mythic drama of its performance still involved the burying of a scalp and the welcoming back of the warrior to the community. In that tradition, even before the draft, young men and old men cleaned and oiled their rifles, packed their saddle bags, and rode in to volunteer. In spite of the fact that many Navajos had to be rejected for military service because they could not read or write English, 3,600 of them served in the Army, Navy, Marine Corps, and even in the Women's Army Corps, and in every theatre of operation.[4]

The Navajos had the same kind of combat experience as any other soldier and suffered the same traumas, but in general they accepted military life better than most. The deprivations and hardships were certainly nothing new to them, and they had learned endurance. Ruth Underhill writes, "White officers have told me that no man in their commands took the stress of war with greater calm than the Indian."[5]

One of the most remarkable stories of the war is that of the Navajo code talkers.[6] Philip Johnston, who had grown up on the Navajo reservation as the son of a missionary, conceived the idea that the Navajo language might make an unbreakable code. Indians of other tribes had in fact been used for this purpose before—eight Choctaws in World War I; and Comanche, Creek, Choctaw, Menominee, Chippewa, and Hopi Indians in World War II. In each case, however, their usefulness had been limited by the limitations of their native vocabularies. Johnston's idea was to use the Navajo language as the basis for a code. Twenty-nine Navajos were recruited, and together they worked out Navajo equivalents for a basic military vocabulary of 211 words and 26 words to represent the English alphabet, so that they could spell out other words as needed.

They were sent with the marines to the Pacific islands, where they served many different communications functions, depending on the needs of their commanding officers. Frequently, they were in the thick of the action, directing air and artillery strikes, where immediate coordination of movement was required in direct contact with the enemy. Under such conditions, simple codes that could be quickly transmitted were essential. The Japanese, who had been routinely breaking these codes, never succeeded in penetrating the Navajos or even guessing who they were listening to or what they were hearing. They were such a success that others were quickly recruited and trained, and eventually 420 Navajos served as code talkers, mostly in the Pacific, but also in Sicily and Italy.[7]

A NAVAJO CODE TALKER: We used several types of radio sets. The TBX unit was the one that we used most. It weighed about eighty pounds— very heavy to lug around. We had two sets: a transmitter and a receiver, connected with a junky cable. We tried to set the generator on a bench of some kind when we could, so we could straddle the bench and crank the thing. But this didn't work on a location where it was sandy. So the coconut tree came in very handy. We hooked the generator to the trunk, straddled the tree and cranked. It took two men—one to crank the generator and get the juice going into the mike, and the other to transmit the message. We got information off the ship [the transport] after a landing, and kept those in charge of the operation informed.

One thing we learned in school was not to be on the air longer than was absolutely necessary. We had to be careful not to repeat words in a sentence—that is, if the message had to go through more than once, we tried to say it differently every time. We were also told not to use the same word too often in a sentence, and that we had to be *accurate* the first time! If a message has to be corrected or repeated too often, you are giving the enemy a better chance to locate you. On Guadalcanal we had to move our equipment in a hurry because the Japs started to shell the very spot where we were operating.[8]

MAJ. HOWARD M. CONNER: Were it not for the Navajos, the Marines would never have taken Iwo Jima. . . . The entire operation was directed by Navajo code. Our corps command post was on a battleship from which orders went to the three division command posts on the beachhead, and went on down to the lower echelons. I was signal officer of the Fifth Division. During the first forty-eight hours, while we were landing and consolidating our shore positions, I had six Navajo radio nets operating around the clock.

In that period alone they sent and received over eight hundred messages without error.

Weeks later, when our flag was raised over Mount Suribachi, word of that event came in the Navajo code. The commanding general was amazed. How, he wanted to know, could a Japanese name be sent in the Navajo language?[9]

■   The transliterated name would have been spelled out, using the Navajo words that had been agreed upon to represent the letters of the English alphabet: for example, Sheep-Uncle-Ram-Ice-Bear-Ant-Cat-Horse-Itch.

JACK SLEETH: We were in Marsh Pass just past Tsegi Canyon in '42. Maurice was going overseas, the Japs, you see, he figured on going that way. He'd finished training and he was on his way. So we got down in Marsh Pass and the Navajos said, "Stop the truck." They broke out the corn pollen and did the whole thing. They took Maurice off to the side, took the corn pollen, sprinkled some on his head, sprinkled some to the four winds, sing and chant and prayers. That was supposed to bring him back safe.

MAURICE KNEE: It was the Going to War ceremony. The blessing that they gave me was supposed to put a shield around me, an invisible shield, that the bullet would come right for my nose and hit that shield and go away. And it worked. I come back. If it hadn't worked I wouldn't be here! "Blessing." That's all they said it was. "Make me blessed." It lasted thirty minutes. They grabbed a Navajo too that was going.

■   This was probably a shortened version of the War Prophylactic ceremony, a blessing ceremonial similar to Blessingway in its precautionary and protective purpose, but not a part of it. This ceremonial and Blessingway itself were sometimes used during both world wars for Navajos going to war and returning.[10] Gladys Reichard describes their emphasis as "transformation from neutral to sanctified" or "attraction of good," and contrasts them with the Evil Way ceremonials, including Enemy Way, whose emphasis is on "exorcism."[11] They are thus more appropriate, it would seem, for embarking than returning warriors. Enemy Way, with its popular Squaw Dance, was by far the most widely used ceremony for the returning Navajo veterans. We have seen the deep psychological effect of the Navajo ceremonials in chapter 15, "Navajo Medicine and Witchcraft," above, and there is testimony everywhere you look for their power to heal the psychological traumas of the Navajos. One can only admire the rich resources of the Navajo culture in this regard, in contrast to our own poverty in rituals of healing, especially after the Vietnam War, when veterans met to improvise their own healing process without support from the community at large.

JACK SLEETH: A lot of them went into the marines, they killed a lot of people and seen a lot of killing. They'd also been around the white man a lot. I've seen some big sings for those guys when they came back, to drive out this influence. It seemed to really help some of them. They believed they were straightened out.

■   Seth Bigman's ability to accept the Anglo world that he experienced on shipboard, the wide range of cultures he encountered in the Pacific ports he touched, and the rainbow teachings of his Navajo medicine man bespeak a good measure of intelligence and sophistication on his part. Like so many Navajos, he too seems to have found personal value in the prayers sung over him when he returned from the war.

SETH BIGMAN: The war broke out in 1941 when I was still in school, but I stayed until the early part of 1943. Then I had to volunteer to get my choice, to get into different branches. So I went into the United States Navy and I spent three years there. I came out December 23, 1945.

It was a good experience. It was a lot of change from the dry land to a floor of water, but I didn't have any difficulty since I had been among the white boys a lot. I went to school with them and I didn't have any difficulty aboard ship. We went through quite a few hard times, close calls with the enemy, but still we came back without a scratch. I was top deckhand, which was bosun mate rate, and I also had a petty officer position.

I saw a lot of places I hadn't seen before, different tribes, like Hawaiian, Fiji Island, the Philippines, part of China. When I came back, my old *hataałii,* my medicine man, said, "You covered quite a bit of the territory on Mother Earth, and you saw places with high standard of living. When you were on the warpath abroad, you saw more places than any warrior, you have contact more people than any warrior. That's the way you know," he said.

"The mother has sent out her child to go on the warpath," he said, "the same way as Mother Earth sent out her warriors to defend her. The rainbow is the defense of Mother Earth, where the land and water meet. One of the rainbows is sitting vertically, that's the rain, and one is sitting horizontally, that is the ocean. When you go through the rainbow to war, that's the defense of Mother Earth." And of course the weapons that the warriors defend her with would be the colors of the rainbow.

My old medicine man said to me, "We have only seen the rainbow where the land and water meet vertically, but you have seen both horizontal and vertical, you have gone to war through both rainbows."

I experienced quite a few things in the Marine Corps. I heard my language over there, the Navajo code talkers, they directed a lot of our targets that way, I experienced it. In the Philippines and at Okinawa and Iwo Jima, those three places, I have stepped on the pedal and let a gun go off by their direction. We were going by their information, by their directing targets.

The medicine man prayed for me when I'm going over and coming back. I was back three times on leave, once before we went overseas and twice coming back from overseas and then after the war. He prayed that I'll be coming home safe, come back through that rainbow. So I did, I came home safe.

24 ■■■ URANIUM

■ Uranium mining began in the Southwest during the war, but it was a strict military secret until after Hiroshima. The first mining company on the Navajo reservation was the Vanadium Corporation of America (VCA), with a mine in the Lukachukai Mountains before coming to Monument Valley, and the public were told that these were vanadium mines, a mineral used in steel alloys. Only relatively small amounts were taken during the war, but shortly afterward, production leaped ahead. The tribal income from uranium was $65,755 in 1950, $151,204 in 1951, and over $650,000 per year by 1954, and there were processing mills built at Mexican Hat, Shiprock, and Tuba City.[1] In subsequent years, the early mines, with relatively low-grade ore, became unprofitable. New rich fields were discovered, especially in the Grants Uranium Belt, running from the checkerboard area into the Navajo reservation on the east. Other, larger mining companies moved into the field, such as Kerr-McGee, United Nuclear, and Exxon. The VCA merged with Foote Mineral Company of Pennsylvania in 1967.[2]

HARRY GOULDING: During the war we found uranium in here. There had been some found here years ago, but all they used it for was the numbers on your watch, like radium, a little bit of stuff, and there was no market for it till after the war got to using it.

I went ahead and found about eight different deposits in here, but I couldn't get in on it because I didn't have equipment to mine it with. At that time, you could bid for it at Window Rock if you had the equipment to mine it, but the fella that found it didn't get any royalty. It was all between the mining company and the tribe. My idea was to get it started down in here and it would maybe give the Navajos a pony to ride out on after the war was over. It worked out that way too.[3]

The first one that I run into was Monument Number One. It had been worked before. Mr. Wetherill probably knew where it was, I don't know. I learned later that he and Preston Redd from Blanding were trying to make a claim on a uranium mine in the Valley. But I run into it, and I decided to get the biggest outfit that I could.

One of the boys from the Vanadium Corporation of America happened

to come through, so I told him that I had found uranium down in the Valley
and that I wanted to get in touch with somebody that could handle whatever
amount, even if it's big. I wanted whatever I could get opened up so that the
Navajos would still be working in here after the war, and they wouldn't
have to sit here and starve.

He said, "Denny Viles is the vice-president and field manager. He manages
everything, all the countries."

"Well," I says, "if he comes down any time I'd be glad to show him where
it is."

They were the biggest uranium people by far, and I figured that we might
as well jump on the king, ain't any use fooling around with any less than
that. I would get Denny Viles out here. So it all started out from there, the
whole thing.

I wanted to let him know why I picked him. When we went out to the
deposit I says, "Now on the way, I want you to see the condition of these
Indians, because if a person can throw these Navajos a rope like I think you
will be doing . . . If you ever wake up in the night on account of you've done
something kind of off-gate a little bit, you can think of what you've done
for this bunch of poor old Indians, and that'll just fix you up!"

So I took him into a hogan. I says, "Now I want you to look all around,
inside and out, because what they've got here is all they've got. And then a
little bunch of sheep." We went to about four or five hogans, and I could
see him thinking that I was just salting something up on him, like the old
prospectors would salt up a mine that they found. They'd place some ore
around and then hook somebody, see, and the mine wouldn't amount to
anything.

"You're thinking that I've got this place all salted up for you," I says. "I'm
not after your money, I'm after help for these Indians, and I want you to get
that down good! So from now on there's going to be quite a number of
hogans show up, and you're going to have to point to them, because I can't
salt them all, and then we'll go and look at the ones you point at."

So he'd point at one and we'd go look at it, and another one and we'd go
look at it. I went away around so's we'd get plenty of them. We'd go into
a hogan, and they had a sack, a half sack of flour and a little coffee and
nothing else sometimes in some of those hogans. And sometimes there'd be
that old jerky hanging up, that they'd killed a goat.

"There's some jerky," I says. "I want you to see how many sheep they've
got. They can only have a little jerky because if they would eat all they want,
they would eat the herd up in about three or four months, a year at most,
and then they'd be out of meat. You talk about our ration tickets," I says,
"they're on it all the time, and have been! You measure up what you're going
to see with the terrible war conditions we think we've got. These people are
up against it."

He was a big two hundred and thirty, forty pound man, and tough as an
old boot. And by golly I started to see a little flush come up in him. We kept

going into them and going into them, and it finally reacted so strong that there was no question how he felt.

"My God, Harry," he says, "I don't need to see any more! I can see what it is!" To see him break down that way was quite a thing. So then I showed him the deposits.

It wasn't a very big mine, so instead of putting this big machinery in there, he took it out with wheelbarrows. Number One never had a piece of machinery like you know would go in; he took just the Navajos, he kept it that way so's they'd get more pay. Denny was the guy; he had a heart in him. . . . There was quite a strike over at Lukachukai. They found the uranium over there before we did here, and they weren't paying the Navajos too much. But when Denny started in here he paid the same wages as he paid the white men or anybody. Everything I found after that, I showed it to Denny. But that was the first one was that little mine.

A little later I found Monument Number Two, they called it. Monument Number One was a good one, but this Number Two, there was millions of dollars went out of that mine. Number Two was probably the biggest mine in this whole country. I called Denny Viles in again.

FRED YAZZIE: Two Indian, I think it was Little John, he's the one that saw the uranium, Little John and Luke Yazzie, two men. They showed him that mine. I think he getting pay from that, but these two Indian, the ones that show, was only give them two dollars. They ought to pay, they ought to pay them every month. . . . But Harry Goulding got it. Harry Goulding, he pay two dollar to Luke Yazzie and Little John.

LUKE YAZZIE (Monument Valley, translated from Navajo): I'm about seventy-two years old now. I was born here where I still live. As a child I herded sheep. By the time I was ten years old I had explored the cliffs, the hills, the trees around here. By fifteen I knew where the water and trails were. I realized that plants and trees grew, got old, and died of old age. I observed these things.

I also collected rocks and stones, and I kept some of them for a long time. Among them I found some uranium. I didn't know what it was; it just felt heavy to me. I drew pictures of animals, and I painted them with these rocks. Finally, I found a place where there was a lot of uranium. I found a strange heavy stone. Then I found another one. I discovered a yellow strip in the rocks. I had heard people talk about gold, and they said gold was different from the natural rocks, so I was very curious. I thought these rocks might be gold, so I hid them carefully and checked on them to be sure they were still there, sometimes every two weeks. I kept it up till I was twenty years old.

Then, many years later, during the war, I heard there were some minerals among the Navajos that might be used to make ammunition. When I was in Goulding's Trading Post I noticed that there were all kinds of rocks lying on the counter, and I asked Dibé Nééz about them. He said they could be

Luke Yazzie (right), who brought the uranium ore sample to Goulding's that resulted in Monument Mine Number 2. He is seen here with his wife and family in their summer shade. (Samuel Moon)

used in many ways, to make automobiles and airplanes. He said they cost a lot of money. "If you find these rocks, bring them in."

I was in no hurry to reveal my secret information. I was a young married man.

One day I went over on a horse and climbed up to the place where I had hidden the rocks. They looked like the ones at the trading post. Dibé Nééz had told me these rocks were the valuable ones. Then I remembered that there were some more of the same colored rocks nearby. I used to mark on my clothes with them. I went there and took them, along with the two rocks I had hidden, back to my hogan, wrapped them in a cloth, and put the bundle of rocks in a bush. I didn't pay any attention to them for months.

One day while I was at the trading post I remembered putting the rocks in the bushes, and I asked Dibé Nééz again which rocks were the most valuable that were lying on the counter. He said only a few of them had much value, but these few cost a great deal of money.

A few weeks later I took the rocks I'd been keeping to Dibé Nééz. He looked at them very carefully and said, "That's it! These are the rocks. They're worth a lot of money!" I didn't have any idea what they were.

He put them on a scale to weigh them. He was amazed. He asked where I had found the rocks and if there was as a road leading to the place. There was only a horse trail. I was kind of hesitant to tell him where I had found them because I thought he might get all the glory and money from it. He alreay knew what they were and I didn't.

In the meantime, he gave me free pop and asked me to have lunch with him in his house. He told me that if I showed him where the rocks were, I would not have to do any of the work, that I'd probably just get paid for showing them, that starting today I would receive payment for the rocks. Up to this day I have never received any payments from those rocks or the place where the rocks were.

He told me to be back in seven days and that the next day we would travel out to where I had found the rocks. An Anglo by the name of Denny Viles was interested in those rocks, and he would go out with us to explore the area. There might be a large site, or it might just be a small strip, but he said the rocks that I had were worth a lot of money and that I would get most of the money from the minerals. He told me there would be a policy on this and that he would also tell Denny Viles about the agreement. My name would be first, he said, and his would be second as a witness. He also told me that Window Rock would be notified if there was a big site. I went back to the trading post in seven days. I got there in the evening on horseback, and they gave my horse some hay. The Anglo who was interested was also there, and we slept in the same room. Early in the morning we had coffee and took off for the place where I'd found the rocks. We traveled in a car over rough places where there were no roads, only some wagon trails. When we couldn't drive any more, we walked into a canyon and climbed up on a ridge.

When we got to the place we were looking for, sure enough, there were strips of yellow lines along in the rocks. They had an instrument with a gauge, and they tested all these rocks and put some of them in gunny sacks. They took my picture and pictures of each other, and they told me that our pictures would be on the claim papers if the site should ever be developed. Then we left and brought the sacks down to the bottom. It seemed like they didn't want to leave. They looked astonished. I was tired and hungry by that time, and I had no idea what they were thinking about. We arrived back at the trading post that evening. I never thought how big the mine would be or what could be made from the minerals.

In about two years they started preparing the site for mining. I was asked to help in the surveying. After this, they sort of ignored me. In another year they started mining. They gave me a pick, a shovel, a big jackhammer, and a wheelbarrow. Instead of being one of the owners, I was just one of the laborers. I worked hard digging and hauling out the ore. I also worked as a driller, hammering and shoveling rocks. I worked with the drilling for five years. After that I worked as a helper to the men who blast rocks with dynamite. Altogether, I must have worked for about fifteen years.

What they promised me at the beginning was a lie. I was told that I'd get paid for the mine discovery, which I never did. Instead I worked hard for the money I was given from the mine. My salary was about $130 a month. What Dibé Nééz and Denny Viles did was they took advantage of me. It seems like they profited the most from the mine. Many Navajos from here and other parts of the country worked here. Yes, they benefited from the uranium mine. They bought food, homes, and livestock with the money they earned. But I still feel that I was taken advantage of. I feel like I helped everyone else, including Window Rock and the United States Army.

HARRY GOULDING: No, Luke Yazzie wasn't with Denny Viles. Might have been some other fella at the VCA went over with us that first time. After the mine started, sometimes I'd go over and see how it looked, and then Luke was working there. Denny's promise to me was that he would keep that fella on the job all the time. I says, "He showed me the uranium and I think that he ought to be able to work there as long as you're working." And he says, "Well, that we'll do."

See, that mine had to go up to bid, no matter who found it, and they had to give the tribe so many months to advertise it around. Everybody could come in there and bid on it. Later on they changed it so that if a Navajo found some uranium he could get a royalty on it. The Navajo's royalties would have run from two percent up to about eleven or twelve. One percent out of that Monument Number Two mine would have made anybody rich. But that was later on. When Luke Yazzie brought in his ore, everybody could bid on it, and whoever bid the highest got it. They weren't obligated to anyone, only the tribe. They had to pay the tribe a royalty.

I never asked Denny for nothing on Monument Number One or Number Two. I wanted to get that uranium opened up if it was in there. I always said, if I can do that, it might be a wonderful little old pony for the Navajos to ride out on after this war's over, and like all wars, you get a depression afterwards. So that was the way I looked at it. I wanted to get as much of it opened up as I could.

■   The specific agreement between the Vanadium Corporation of America and Navajo tribe for Monument Mine Number Two could not be located either in the Navajo tribal files or the National Archives. However, the royalty arrangements for uranium at the time Luke Yazzie brought his ore sample in to Goulding's appear to have followed the model of oil royalties, which typically stipulated only "that Navajo Indians shall be given preference in all labor performed in the mining operations, except for those in the skilled and technical category."[4]

In 1946, Chee Dodge, then chairman of the Navajo Tribal Council, discussed with the Bureau of Indian Affairs the possibility of authorizing a procedure by which Navajos who discovered valuable ore deposits might receive some benefit, and at that time the bureau gave him some suggestions.[5] The change in royalty arrangements for individual Navajos was made official in a resolution of December 8, 1948, when three categories of individual Navajo claims were established "in order to interest our Navajo people in the mineral deposits that may be found on the reservation, and as an aid in the search for and development of such minerals." First, a Navajo who discovers a deposit, the development of which is within his technical skill and financial capacity, will be issued a "simple permit," paying a "reasonable royalty" to the tribe. Second, a "Navajo permittee who gains experience in mining and establishes by his record that he is a qualified and responsible operator, and who finds that he requires financial assistance for further development and operation," may be issued a regular mining lease and may take another Indian or non-Indian as partner. Third, a Navajo who discovers minerals but is unable to develop them may negotiate a lease with outside parties and is entitled to a percentage of the tribe's royalties and other incomes.[6]

Unfortunately, Luke Yazzie's discovery was too early for these enlightened changes, but as we shall see later in this chapter, Harvey Blackwater and Seth Bigman are two Navajos who benefited from the new arangements.

HARRY GOULDING: When Denny looked over Monument Number Two, he says, "This is really something! It's going to be a big one!" And there was just trucks and trucks agoing in.

And these old Navajos . . . ! Every weekend they'd bring the Navajos in to trade. I'd keep the newspapers, and I'd tell them anything I found about the war. Enough of the Monument Valley Indians were in that fracas that they wanted to know what was doing all the time. I'd tell them about the airplanes, that our bombs would do a lot more than the enemy's bombs. Oh I'd tell them whatever I could think of.

And then if Denny had anything that come up over at the mine, he would talk to the Navajos and tell them how he appreciated what they were doing. He told them there one day, "You folks are taking more vanadium out of this mine per man in those wheelbarrows than the white people and Mexicans are taking out where they have big equipment!" They called it vanadium then, of course, before the bomb, to keep it secret. We all called it vanadium, didn't know it was really uranium until later, when it all came out.

And these fellas would bring it out in their wheelbarrows. They was sweating! It was really something, the interest they took in getting that stuff out to help their people in this war.

One day he showed me a telegram he had got from General Eisenhower.

Washington, D.C.
5-15-43

Men and Women of V.C.A. Corporation
Monticello, Utah

This message from Commander in Chief of Allied Forces in America is relayed by the War Department. Our fighting men standing shoulder to shoulder with our gallant allies, the British and the French, have driven the enemy out of North Africa. In this victory the munitions made by American Industry, labor and management played a very important role. There is glory for us all in this achievement.

Eisenhower
Gen. Com. in Chief of Allied
Forces in Africa

So I got to thinking, I ought to go a little further with this some way or another. There must be a way. I had read where the Germans were saying that the Indians were all against us, that they were fighting us and giving us a terrible time, putting out a lot of rotten, low-down, dirty propaganda. So I wrote a letter to General Eisenhower, and I told him what had happened here.

I got my letter and everything ready, and I went over to the mine and got these different Indians to sign it. Well, they have to sign with a thumbprint, and the fender of my truck, you couldn't see yourself in it like you could a mirror. The letter was handled on the front of that truck, and their hands were not just shining either. By the time I got through, I must have had thirty or thirty-five Indians, I thought, "Gee, I don't know about this." It was such a horrible looking mess, you know; they'd just come out of the mines. But it was there, and it was signed, and all of the fingerprints were just as good as anybody's. But I thought, "I don't know whether a fella ought to send a man like General Eisenhower a thing like this or not." So I slept on it. The next day I says, "No, by gosh, I'm going to send it!" So I mailed it to him.

To Gen. Com. in Chief of Allied Forces in Africa,
General Eisenhower:

We, the undersigned Navajo Indians of Monument Valley on the Northern Navajo Reservation, have heard the telegram from our General. We thank you for what you have said to us in your telegram. We will work harder to get more vanadium from under the rocks on our reservation so the guns and airplanes and munitions you need over there where you are fighting will be strong. We are proud our reservation has vanadium to help win this war.

Among the signatures were: Sheep White, Adakaskie Bodoni, Shini Cly Begay, Hosteen Sour Crout, Hite Chee, Little John, Kelete Black, Discherise Asan, and Luke Yazzie.[7]

And it wasn't too long, here it comes awhizzing, we got the general's answer. It was a wonderful letter. It come in on a Saturday morning. That's when they brought the Indians over in a truck to trade, and I had that letter to interpret to them. Ay gosh, the dust was aflying out of the smoke hole coming out of that mine after that! They really done their stuff!

Do you remember the old newspaper that we got in the First World War, *Stars and Stripes?* They had it again in World War II, and the story was in the *Stars and Stripes.*[8]

So I really got myself in trouble. The FBI wrote me a letter and said there was something they had to see me about. I met them in Monticello at my great friend Donald Adams's house. He was the lawyer for San Juan County. They wanted to know how I knew so much about this vanadium and what it was for, and getting it out in print. We still thought it was vanadium.

Well, I smiled a little bit, I couldn't help it. I says, "It so happens that the vanadium in these mines is the same color as the corn pollen that the Navajos use. There's not a Navajo on the reservation that doesn't have a little pouch of corn pollen." I had one of them too. "Whenever anything goes wrong, they talk to their powers and they get their little pouch out and pinch that corn pollen to the four winds. It's very big medicine with them. I've been telling these Navajos that this vanadium's exactly like their corn pollen." I had some uranium there and I showed them my corn pollen and the uranium; just the same yellow powder.

"Well," they says, "that sounds pretty much like a story!"

So I called Don in, and Don straightened them out right away. "Whatever Goulding told you is just what God loves, it is the truth." So that pleased them. They went back home, and I didn't have to go to jail.

Later, when they changed it so that if a Navajo found some uranium he could get a royalty on it, I got three or four Geiger counters, and I'd take these Indians out and show them how to work it and then let them use it occasionally.[9] I had this fella out one day, and we were way back in, up on a ledge just under the Shinarump. See, there's the Monuments, and there's a clay formation up near the top, and then the Shinarump comes on top of that. The uranium is up on those high rims around, and it's kind of rough going up there. Sometimes, right under the Shinarump there'd be a little bench come out, and you could generally always get around there.

And so we were going along up there, and he was a nephew of old Hosteen Tso. I was following him, and we came to a place where there were these two bushes, was separated. He started through, and there was a snake come out of that other bush, what we call out here a bush snake. The snake came across there, and this Navajo stopped, and he started chanting to this old snake, a long, beautiful snake with stripe-ed colors, and just lightning fast! One of them bush snakes, if he's in that bush, you may just get a glance of him once, and after that you won't see him. He's on the other side of that bush from you, and you can't get around to see him. He's like lightning!

So he started to chant, and he got his *tádídíín* out, his corn pollen. And this old snake come out there, and he stopped, by golly; he was in that chant! He just stopped. And this Navajo got down there and sprinkled some *tádídíín* on that snake's head. Then he put some on himself, and he turned around over to me and put some on my shoulder, and then he put a little pinch out to the four winds. And then the old snake went on. We waited, and as soon as he went on, why we went on, on our prospecting.

What they have is in them so deep! It's a great meaning to me when a man will do a thing like that. It's just so respectful. So many beautiful things!

One of the Navajos that found uranium with one of these Geiger counters was Harvey Blackwater, after he got back from the war. He found a deposit, and he opened it up himself. He did the mining and took the ore out himself, and he made himself some money. And he held onto it. It turned out to be not too big a deposit, but he went clean to the end of it. He did it with wheelbarrows, and wheel it out and then take it in with his truck, and did it the hard way, him and his brother. He had a couple of trucks going out all the time while it lasted.

He got it to where he could borrow a little money off of a bank that I did business with at Cortez. The banker and his wife used to come out home here. Every time he could get his head out of that bank for a day, they'd be down. And he let that boy have a loan, but quick. He got a pickup and he had a truck that he hauled in. We got him to put his money in the bank. The banker helped Harvey out on the money business and watched it for him, and he gave him a lot of advice one way and another too. I don't know how much money Harvey made from his mine, but it was quite a little bit. He lived a good life.

Seth Bigman was another one who made a lot of money from the uranium. He was getting his percent, and boy he was getting money!

SETH BIGMAN: When they start this uranium boom here, then we all start out prospecting. I went out with another fellow I know, named Leonard Young. The first contact I made with him was away back in early days around 1928 or 1929 over at Oljeto. At that time Leonard Young was only a little boy and I was a little boy. And then all the time when I was working for the Soil and Moisture Conservation as a trainee at Kayenta, we came to know each other again. We were like brothers, you know, and we went around together.

So we went out with a big Geiger counter that can go all the way down quite a ways, you know, get the readings out. We borrowed from the Atomic Energy Commission. We used to borrow it Saturday and Sunday and go out prospecting with it. We found this reading of uranium where we have Moonlight Mine. Oljeto means Moonlight Water, Moonlight Spring, and it was south of Oljeto where we found this location.

We got a consultant engineer, and he contact one of the uranium companies, Industrial Uranium Company, to sink a shaft there and mine out the mineral and water. We had the operation going for about two and a half or three years. Then we opened up another mine which was called Starlight.

At that time, we had to split the royalty three ways—the tribe, and the company, and I had to take what was left. It wasn't an equal division. The company had to meet their expense, and of course the tribe will take so much without argument. I got about ten percent, around fifteen, sixteen, seventeen thousand a year for about two and a half to three years. Then the Starlight got a lot of water in it, and the Moonlight, it just sort of ran out of ore, only in pockets. There is still ore down there, but it's not worth going from one pocket to another. You'd have to trench it in between.

Leonard Young wasn't a Navajo, and only Navajos get the royalty benefits, but we built that little Moonlight Trading Post out there by the mine, and as far as the trading post went, we were partners. We thought we would have a little grocery store during the mining operation, and Leonard Young ran it. Then after the mineral petered out, we sold it.

JOSEF MUENCH: When they were searching heavily for uranium in this country, quite a few Indians could be employed. The trouble was that they had to adjust themselves to the white man's way, meaning start at seven o'clock, sort of punch a time clock. But how to get them out of bed? So it was Harry, and I happened to be next to the window. An Indian was over in the trading post buying some supplies, and they were talking about it. He was an older Indian, and they relied on him to wake up the others. Harry suggested to him to have a rooster, because a rooster will crow at a certain time in the morning. And that Navajo thought that a rooster was the best alarm clock to have, to get the fellows out and to work. That idea came out of Harry's mind.

HARRY GOULDING: No, no! No, it was not my idea. It was the old Navvy. He went up there himself. No, Joe's wrong there. The old Navajo, he was the one that went out to get them. He got him four or five roosters and some hens, brought them down there, and they were the ones that woke the folks up. He passed them around to different ones. They had little camps around. And they were the alarm clocks. And then they'd have a few eggs to eat.

25 ▬ POSTWAR CHANGES

MIKE GOULDING: The change didn't come until after the war. I imagine enough of them went out and saw how big the world was, and a lot of them went out and worked, and the uranium mines opened up, so they began to get cars and trucks and things. The pickup came into effect and they could travel anywhere they wanted to. I don't know whether we had welfare in the fifties or not. We must have had some, but not like it is now. The sixties is when that went frantic.

HARRY GOULDING: When the Indians came back after the war, the boys that had been over there had changed altogether. They didn't lose their language, they still had that, but they didn't take the interest in the ceremonies and those sort of things that they did before.

There was one place we always went. Going down into the Valley, there was a place there where an Indian woman had died and been buried. The hogan was right there by the road. I think what happened was, she must have been horseback, and she died, fell off her horse or something, right there, because they wouldn't go across that part of the road at all. They'd made a little loop out around it, and they'd always take the new road. You'd never see a wagon track on top of that spot. But when the boys came back from the war, they just went right across it, paid no attention to it at all.

Every time I'd have an older Indian in the back seat with me, I would watch in the rearview mirror when I was getting close to that place. This Indian, he didn't say anything, or a woman either one, but you could see that they were really thinking about having to go across that place. And when I'd turn out around it and miss it, you could just see their feeling, their gratefulness, the calm that come over them.

▬   The off-reservation experiences of the war years had a varying impact on the Navajos, depending not only on the situation in which they found themselves, whether military or civilian, but also on the degree of their own previous acculturation. Servicemen like Seth Bigman, for example,[1] who had been educated and whose English was good, had seen a great deal of the world. They had found self-respect in their ability to cope with the demands of the white world and in the friendly relationships they had estab-

lished with their buddies, and they returned, often, with a personal understanding of the possibilities and the necessities for change and a strong
motivation for action. On the other hand, some of the migratory farm workers, with no English and little or no education, returned to the reservation
frequently between crops and were left largely unaffected, continuing in the
old traditional ways. In general, however, the war years had a profound and
irreversible effect on the life of the tribe.[2]

Beginning in 1947, President Truman began efforts to establish a program
of improvements for the Navajos and Hopis. It was finally passed into law
as the Navajo-Hopi Long Range Rehabilitation Act in 1950, with funding for
programs in conservation, irrigation, industrial development, off-reservation
employment, health, and many other things, and reserving the largest
amounts for education and the development of roads.[3]

HARRY GOULDING: Even after the war, the highest they could go would
be about the fifth grade. It's only been very recent that they've had even one
high school on the reservation. There was years and years and years through
there! I always tried to get them to go up to Intermountain. And they went
clean out to California and Oklahoma and different places to boarding
schools. After a while it got to where they didn't have room enough to take
them all. They'd pick up some before they got here and they'd have room
for about half a truckload, but we'd have kids in here waiting that would
have filled up two trucks. Them kids would make a run to get into that
truck. They wanted to go!

They finally put a little school in over at Kayenta, and we got to knowing
a fella there who was awful good. Then he went out and took charge of a
school up between Salt Lake and Ogden, Utah, and he seen that our kids
got in there, but it was a long time until they put in the high school at
Kayenta. That's why the kids couldn't go to school; there just wasn't no
place for them to go.

When Mike and I would go out to California, we had children in the
schools there, and we'd stop and look them up and visit with them. We'd
talk Navajo to them, and they said they couldn't talk back Navajo. Wouldn't
permit it. But my goodness they had lovely schools, and those old kids were
full of play. You'd see them playing in the school grounds, and they were
right up in top health and just agoing to it. It would have been a good thing
if they'd have let them keep up with their Navajo, that wouldn't have been
so bad. But to let them come back every year and be with their own folks,
that was a lot better than the old days.

■   Although Harry undoubtedly had grounds for his pleasure in the improved atmosphere of the boarding schools, he was remembering, by com-
parison, the horrors of the 1920s and early 1930s. Many boarding schools

of the postwar period still carried the style of the past to a large extent and left much to be desired.

Tom Tsosie's story, which follows, is the story of a young Navajo who began his schooling with the famous progressive teacher of the Collier era, Mrs. Eubanks of the Navajo Mountain day school. He was raised in the conservative Navajo Mountain area by traditional grandparents, but his father and mother were away most of the time working as sheepherders in Utah, and he therefore lacked some of the strongest elements of the Navajo extended family environment as a child. He was soon moved to boarding school, and his experiences in the boarding schools and border-town schools of the 1950s and 1960s were difficult, perhaps more difficult as a consequence of his background, which combined an unacculturated traditionalism with a small nuclear family group. As Tom says, "You can't stand it, so you have to do something."

TOM TSOSIE:[4]   For our schooling we started out in Navajo Mountain. I started my school when I was about four years old, in kindergarten. I don't know the date when I was born, they just gave me a date at the school. I was born in summer, in July, but the birthday they gave me is December 12. I think I was born about 1948.

Our first teacher, Mrs. Eubanks, in Navajo Mountain, is well known around this area. They started a school up in Navajo Mountain a long time ago. My grandmother didn't want me to go to school, so she kept hiding me, every time. You know, this government car came around and picked us up. The road was very hard to travel on in those days. We lived in Paiute Mesa, we herded sheep there. I guess my father wanted me to go to school. He had a little bit of education, up to about sixth grade.

When I first started my school, I didn't like it at all, I was very homesick at that time. First, I had long hair with a bun on my head, and they cut my bun off. They gave me a shower and gave me some shots. They washed my hair with some sort of material to treat for lice. We had a lot of lice at that time. I didn't like the smell of it at all.

When school-out came around, they gave me back the string to tie my hair in a bun. It had a grain turquoise bead tied to it. Whenever you get any kind of a ceremony in your life, you get a small bead. They tie it to your hair in the string. That means that you are holy. You have to keep that or else you lose the effect of the ceremony. When school-out came around, they gave me that string back because the bead was still on there, but I had no hair to tie it to. [Laughs.] I think my grandmother or my mother still has it. It's the nature that they have to keep it.[5]

I was really raised by my grandmother, I was not with my family. My father and mother were working somewhere up near Moab, herding sheep for quite a few winters. And when I stayed with my grandmother, I got her attitudes. Grandmother was very traditional. Whenever we asked to see if it could rain, she'd give me corn pollen and she'd teach me how to pray and send me out to a pine tree. I would sprinkle the pine tree with water. It's like a small ceremony. She would get up early in the morning and get her corn pollen and pray.

We were living way up on the mesa, and we used to gather different types of grain from the plants. We used to herd sheep, and we had some goats. She would wake me up and we'd milk goats in the morning and drink the milk. We ate horse meat. The fat from a horse is very smelly, and she would call me when she got through eating and put the fat on my hands or face. It's good for your skin. Anyway, I was raised that way.

My grandfather used to sing, so he wanted me to sing with him. Whenever they'd call him to go someplace for a ceremony, I'd go with him, and I learned a little bit of their religion. My grandfather was singing the Spirit Way, so I learned a lot of songs from him.

When I was about second year in Navajo Mountain, Mrs. Eubanks asked my grandmother if she could take me and raise me. I stayed with her for one summer up there. She had two sons. One was Randy, and the other was Shazhi. He was a Navajo, she just raised him, and he was a big boy by that time. Randy was her real son. Mrs. Eubanks didn't have any husband then. I had a real good time when I was up there; she treated me just like a mother. I really respect her now. But my grandmother didn't want me to be raised by Mrs. Eubanks, so she sent me back. I wanted to stay, but I wanted to see my brothers and be at home too.

My father and mother were away all the time. One summer me and my brother were herding sheep up on Paiute Mesa. We knew our father and mother were herding sheep over in the Henry Mountains, so we herded our sheep right up to the canyon, and my brother called from there, "Would you come for us? Would you come for us?"

Then they transferred me to Tuba City. I was about in second grade by that time. Navajo Mountain only went up to first grade, kindergarten and first grade. My father died when I was going to school in Tuba City. He died above Oljeto, in a canyon up there, from tuberculosis, I think. At that time there was a lot of tuberculosis going around. When he died, my mother sent us some piñon nuts in a big sack, my brother and I, one each. They sent us each one dollar bill, and I thought I was rich. It was the first time I saw a dollar bill. My mother remarried to Billy, my father's half-brother. And I came back to my grandmother's place.

The next winter, we were sent to Shiprock boarding school. I stayed there till I was in sixth grade. Then they transferred us up to Richfield, Utah, a border town up there, an Indian school. Two years. I always came back to my grandmother's in the summer time. I was raised by my grandmother and I liked her. They were living all by themselves, my grandmother and grandfather, and I wanted to help them, so I stayed with them all this time.

Then they transferred us to the boarding school at Kayenta. We ran away from Kayenta and got all the way up to Oljeto. I didn't like it at all. You can't stand it, so you have to do something. I guess it's the dormitories. Sometimes they're very strict. In boarding school you get up at the same hour, just like army school. Wash up and sing at the same time. Take a shower at the same time. You get homesick a lot of times. We stayed away for about nine months out of the year and came home for only about three months. I used to count the days. When there was about fifty days to go, then we had to wait those fifty days so school-out would come and we could go back home. I wanted to see how big my dog had grown, and how many more sheep I got, you know, personal sheep, how many more horses we had. I wanted to see my grandmother, because she was alone.

The boarding schools were a bad influence on the Navajos. I guess that's where we get our attitude from, I mean the students that went to boarding school have different attitudes. It seems like the boarding school really was based on favoritism. They had demerits, that if you ran through the hall, or didn't do what you were supposed to, they didn't let you go to the movie. If they caught you about three times speaking Navajo, they made you stay away from the movies, or else during the movie time they made you scrub the walls, or the floors, black marks from the shoes.

One man had a broom stick. He used to knock your head with it if you done things wrong, and they called it the holy stick. It makes you holy, you know. [Laughs.]

And they used to make you march, step by step, from the dormitory to the dining room. They made you learn how to turn around army style and right face and left face. There were no Gomer Pyles in there. [Laughs.] Everybody was stiff in line. One man was just fresh out of the army, in World War II. He really used to walk straight, and I guess there were times when we made mistakes. We used to have names for all of them. One we used to call "Buzzard," he had this nose; and "Camel" too. If he hears you calling him "Camel," he will just really get mad about it, and he'll say, "Scrub the floor!" [Laughs.]

And there's a lot more influence from the boys who come in from different areas. You learned to steal things, and just different bad things. At times it was embarrassing. They used to mistreat other girls, their classmates. They would hit them right out; if something went wrong they would hit them and make them cry. Just bad habits that they had.

The boarding school was there, I think, for a purpose, for disciplining the Indians, but the discipline was sometimes too strict. The stricter you get, and the more laws you get, it makes some people do bad things. They run away, they steal food. The people that are in day schools, if they're going to school from their home, they don't have as bad habits as the boarding school ones. When your parents talk to you in the evening, if you've done something wrong, they can clear things up for you. Or else, the school can call your parents in and they talk to your parents and you get straightened out. But when your parents are not there, you don't have no way to straighten up.

The older guys that go away to school come back home, and their attitudes are, well, contrary to what they used to be. They like their grandparents, naturally you would like your grandparents. It's just that they're kind of like big shots now. When their grandmother cooks something for them or does something for them, they don't seem to appreciate it. It's not misunderstanding, but the fact that you've been away from home so long.

Thinking back about it, when I came back from boarding school, I know that there were some useful things in my life, mathematics and English and everything, the learning areas, but the habits, the character that affected me was not too good.

After Kayenta I went to Flagstaff. Border town and boarding school are different. In a border town you're kind of free. At school you have white students too, and some of them drank, border-town students, so that's another bad influence. One time I got drunk there in Flagstaff and we got caught. We'd go up to this grocery store and steal wine. I don't know why we liked to drink a lot. I guess I got with the wrong bunch. I was about sixteen. I got a real bad attitude at that place. We got caught and put in jail there. They almost sent us home.

Then the uranium mines over here opened up, and I knew my mother was living here with my father, so I came back to my mother in the summer. When I got back with my mother and father, I decided to break away from the bunch there at Flagstaff, so the next fall I went to Holbrook, but the boys at Holbrook had a habit of drinking during the weekends too. All the border towns, all of them. They used to get drunk a lot of times. I graduated from Holbrook in 1965.

26 ■■■ THE NAVAJO TRAIL

■ In 1933, the same year that the Paiute Strip was added to the reservation, a small piece of grazing land in southeastern Utah known as the Aneth Strip was also added. In 1956, large oil resources were discovered in the Aneth Strip and in the surrounding Four Corners area. It is a pleasant irony that this land was finally given to the Navajos in 1933 only after Secretary of the Interior Fall and his oil cronies were satisfied that there was no oil to be found in the area. The income to the Navajos from the Aneth oil field was far greater than their uranium income. In 1957, the year of highest earnings, they received a total of $34.8 million, and corresponding earnings were being developed in neighboring off-reservation wells.[1]

This and the postwar uranium expansion constituted a boom in the Four Corners area, and a clamor for new roads arose in Arizona and New Mexico, the main industrial centers of which were separated from the activity by Navajo country. Harry immediately saw the situation as an opportunity both for himself and for the Navajos, and it was he who was largely responsible for raising the clamor in Arizona.[2] The Navajo Trail, one of the few main arteries across the Navajo reservation, was the result of these efforts.

HARRY GOULDING: I saw a piece in the paper in 1958, where the government had a lot of federal money to be spent on highway projects, but it had to be on a federal highway. What we were lacking was a new Four Corners road from the Ute Reservation up in Colorado, down into New Mexico where the Four Corners are, into Teec Nos Pos in Arizona, and then improved road clean on over to Tuba City and on in to the highway to Flagstaff. That's a long stretch of road through there. The Navajo Trail is what we finally called it. We worked on it for years. In fact, they made me the first president of the Navajo Trail, but I just didn't have the time to put in, to go to the meetings and that sort of thing, so I asked if they wouldn't please overlook me and get someone else. I says, "What I'll do, I'll ride around and kick them out of the bushes. I'll be glad to help anyone that is president, and we'll get something done on it."

When this story came out in the paper about federal money, I remembered when the dam was built at Glen Canyon. Arizona and Utah were making a race to see who could get all the business out of it. Utah was coming in as fast as they could with their road, and old Lew Haas and Hal Jackson, they tied together and started fighting for it for Arizona. Lew was head of the chamber of commerce in Phoenix, and Hal had the same position in Flagstaff. Well, they won that battle. The first one that got in there with a road and pulled the right strings got that business. Everything had to come through Flagstaff and out of Phoenix. Otherwise Utah would have got it. They were quite a ways ahead of the Utah boys.

When I read this paper about the federal money I says, "By golly, the people to get with now is them two old boys." I figured they're the ones to sic onto this Navajo Trail deal. So I took that paper and headed for Flagstaff, and I got in there with Hal and talked to him a little while and showed him the paper. He said, "Just a minute, Harry," and rang a phone number to Lew Haas down at the Phoenix Chamber of Commerce. He told Lew about the money and that I had quite an idea and would he have a meeting with me. So Lew said, yes, he would like to. Hal says, "All right, I'll send him down there, but you've got to guarantee me that you'll leave him in that office for half an hour."

So I went down and visited with him, showed him the paper and everything, and he says, "Well now, let's see. Well, yes," he says, "I can send somebody there and a photographer up with you."

I told him that story about the cowboy. I says, "Mr. Haas, did you ever hear about that old cowboy that got sick? A doggone snake bit him, and he was sick. And he had never prayed, he'd never prayed in his life, but he decided he was going to have to do it. So he prayed to God. 'Oh God,' he said, 'I need you. But please come yourself, God, don't send your boy, Jesus.' " I says, "Mr. Haas, that's just the way this old Indian trader feels, just like that cowboy. I ain't done any praying, but if I've got to, I'll set one out right here in this office."

He looked at me a little while, and he says, "All right, by gosh, I'll go with you! We'll get ready and go up and meet Hal, and we'll take off."

So we came on up to the trading post and stayed there that night. We started out the next morning. Before we left Flagstaff, I didn't tell them, but I phoned ahead to these towns like Blanding and Monticello and Moab and then Telluride and then over the loop and in to Durango and then we came back through Mesa Verde. I phoned them that I was coming and that I had these two fellas by. I said, "Have things set up, because I think these two boys can really do something for us."

We got to Bluff first it was, and those little towns, they have the chamber of commerce in their local homes. There was a fella sitting out front, and I says, "Do you mind, I want to go in and visit with this old boy just a minute."

"Oh no, go ahead, Harry."

I went over, and they were all ready for them, so I says, "Hal, bring Mr. Haas on over here, I want him to meet a friend of mine."

So they came over and my friend invited them in, and here was this gang in there waiting for us, a nice group of fellas.

I have never seen two people work so beautifully as those two fellas together. Just like I figured, they had fought this battle before, so they knew where each other was—just like that! We visited there a while, shot the breeze, and then we got down to business. We were sitting around the table.

Those little local towns, sometimes they weren't too anxious for the other town to get more business, and as we went along with our visit, why they would want to get this Navajo Trail at a different angle so's that it would hit them, see? Some little word would come up, maybe a slight suggestion. Hal and Lew would keep talking. They could feel this coming on, and they always sat across the table from each other. So these two crazy guys would start talking across the table to each other. "Oh say, Hal, do you remember the time we were over at Wickenburg when we were trying to get a little something done on that highway towards Flagstaff, and that other little town below there didn't want to do just what the others did?" They would put that story together so beautifully that it would just tell those folks, "Don't try to hurt your neighbors or you're going to hurt yourselves." I never heard anything like it, oh my gracious! And to be with them! We were together for twelve days.

Every town—Blanding, Monticello, Moab, and Grand Junction, and on up the line clean on up to Ouray, Silverton, Durango, Colorado—all the way along, those two fellas united those people to where they had their sleeves rolled up, not to their elbows, clean to their shoulders! They were ready to fight for this money.

Then I called Window Rock and told them what I was doing. I says, "I want to come over by there, because this is going to mean a lot to the Navajos too." So the Navajos put on a show for them. They kept them there all day, had a lunch for them, a nice meal too, everything, and we got away from there about two-thirty in the afternoon.

Then things started apoppin. All those towns wrote in to the federal people and cooked it up with them, and by gosh, they got the green light on it. There weren't any roads in this country at all. By coming down through there, that was putting Monument Valley, you might say, right between Mesa Verde and the Grand Canyon. That was bound to help the Indians and everybody.

Well, as soon as they got the money, and construction started on that road, New Mexico got busy pouring the coal on their road work. They were trying to get their roads fixed up ahead of Colorado, to link up with this Navajo Trail. The chamber of commerce at Blanding wanted me to make a trip around and see for sure what was going on.

"Well," I says, "I'll be glad to do it." So I did. I went around and covered that loop, and sure enough, they was akickin. I took my four-wheel drive and went over there and inspected the whole works. Then I went on over and seen what they still *had* to do. Pretty near clean across New Mexico. I came back around up to Alamosa and had a visit with the president of the Navajo Trail about it. And all the way back, all the little towns, I called to give them the same report. I told them that New Mexico already had a route that the federal government could accept of, but they didn't have a number for it, and they didn't have their road ready yet. I knew we had to get a federal number for our route. I says, "We already have a federal number, 160, that comes from Walsenburg into Durango and Cortez, and then it heads back north up into Monticello and Moab. We can take 160, and from Cortez we can put that on the Navajo Trail. That can go right out to Highway 66, and it gives a federal number clean through. If we don't do it, why they're going to make it in New Mexico."

They wanted me to make another trip and make another report. I says, "I will, only that's quite a trip, and I was pretty disappointed in the results of the other trip. I just don't have, really, the time to leave my business to be doing these kind of things, but if you fellas mean business, why I'll do it again." So I did. I went around again and came back, and they were getting along with that road, I'll tell you.

Well, they finally decided to let us have it. Now it's 160, comes right down from Walsenburg, past the Four Corners, through Kayenta, on to Flagstaff, and on, clean on. That's the Navajo Trail.

"Now," I says, "we can get more than 160! Utah needs this road up through Moab that used to be 160. Let's get two for one, another federal number from Grand Junction and down to Moab and Monticello, Blanding, Bluff, Mexican Hat, Monument Valley, down to Kayenta. So we did, we got it as far as Kayenta, 163. We got federal numbers and paved highways two ways, into Kayenta from two directions, by prowling a little and seeing what was cooking.

Here we were, sitting out here, all this big, beautiful country, with dirt roads. And I mean, not even dirt roads; hell, they were cow trails! This opportunity came, and by gosh we rode her right out to the end. And it gave the Navajos a main route clean across their reservation. So I blame Lew Haas and Hal Jackson for that highway. They woke this country up. It's too bad that a few more people couldn't have been along to enjoy what I got to enjoy. Them crazy nuts!

■ Meanwhile, in 1956, construction had begun on the power dam at Glen Canyon at the western edge of the reservation, and a resort area was beginning to take shape as Lake Powell filled upstream of the dam into the Colorado and San Juan Rivers. Harry saw the need for another road, opening this area to travelers from the northeast, who would include Monument Valley in their itinerary.

JOSEF MUENCH: The Valley and the Indians were foremost on Harry's mind. It owes much to his pushing that the area was developed, particularly the roads. When you saw the Indian's hogan, you usually saw some dilapidated cars around. That was why he pushed for new roads. He spoke to the influential people over at Window Rock or wherever possible to push the idea that we should have better roads out here. Not so much for himself, but for his Indian friends, or let's say both in conjunction.

For instance, the road that goes east from Page and joins the road from Tuba City to Kayenta. Before that road was built, Harry took me over that country in a jeep. Naturally, he would take the old Indian trails from hogan to hogan. He knew his way, knew his directions. It was in his mind to interest the Bureau of Indian Affairs, the higher-ups, there should be a paved road going through here, a road not only for us palefaces but also for the Indian, so he could use his cars and not ruin them over the roads he had. And all the way, as we traveled from the Valley across, heading for Page on those Indian wagon roads, he kept talking it. He didn't press his idea upon you, it just flowed. He let me know his feeling, and at the same time he let me develop a feeling. I mean after all, while I fell in love the first time I was out here, seeing all this red sandstone country, it took a few years to develop my understanding of the country and the deep love I found eventually. It's in my blood now, and I can't get it out.

HARRY GOULDING: I used to bring guests right over across the Colorado River, just above Page, before they built Page. There wasn't even a trail through there. Horse tracks and things. I had a little trailer, and I boosted the hubs over and got the clearance so's it could clear my jeep trail. A monument sticks up over there a ways, and an old Navajo was in there near the river. So I'd bring them over and I'd stop up there with this old Navajo family. It used to be called Blue Mesa; now they call it White Mesa. And stop there. The old Colorado was a deep, deep canyon. It would just take your old belly and yank it!

Well anyway, there was a road up to the Glen Canyon Dam from Flagstaff, and the Navajo Trail was built from Tuba City up to Kayenta and on to the Four Corners. So what was happening, Lake Powell, up above the dam, was drawing plenty of visitors, but ordinarily people don't like to backtrack on a road. So very few, maybe five percent, might go back to Tuba and across to Monument Valley on the Navajo Trail.

I just made up my mind, now we've got to get a cut-off through here. I made about four or five trips with different ones over there. "We've got to make a loop through here to keep these visitors on the reservation," I told them.

Sammy Day kept after it, and he finally got it started. And I believe it was in a way better that Sammy Day was the one to pick that route. Ordinarily, scenery doesn't appeal to you when you're building roads. Well old Sammy, you'll notice how he picked that route. When you leave Page, you go as far as these ridges, and there's either a nice view on that side or this side and sometimes both sides. He did that till he got over just this side of Kaibito.

There he dove off just where those funny rocks are all shapes, through there for a little ways, and then he went on past Kaibito. The old road was way out away from White Mesa. So he picks a route up in there so's you can see those monuments and things. If you go up into some of them, there's some pictures in there that would just knock you for a loop. It's lovely. And then you go around the point of White Mesa and through those red stones and that big old high butte, Square Butte. Oh it's a lovely trip through there that guy has planned. So by gosh, he kept with it till he got her done.

SAM DAY III: One of the amusing things in the late fifties, the early sixties, was roads. I was always close to the Bureau of Indian Affairs on our recreation program, and the engineers for the bureau once in a while would call me, say, "Sam, where do you need a road?" something like that. So one day they called me.

I said, "By golly, you sure you got some money now?"

"Oh," he said, "we have extra money, do you want a road for your recreation project?"

I said, "We sure do!"

"Where do you want it?"

"Well, let's wait a while. I tell you what. You meet me next Thursday over at Goulding's in Monument Valley and I'll tell you there."

So I called Harry, and I said, "Harry, we've got some hot ones. We're going to meet there at your place. You have reservations for us, two bureau engineers, and we'll go out across country in one of your four-wheel drives and locate that road we've been talking about between Kayenta and Page."

Harold Johnson was the chief engineer and the other fellow was called Thompson. They're both dead now, but they were just wonderful people. So we got to Monument Valley, and they were real surprised that we had things all arranged for them. Harry was just as gracious as could be.

Next morning we got them up and had our usual ranch-style breakfast, Harry had his big bus all set, and away we went. We drove over to Shonto, and after we got to Kaibito, that was where the roughest part of the road was, because we wanted to head right out towards Page. We really had an enjoyable trip, and these fellows were just fascinated by what they had seen and what the potential of this road was.

Well, we got to Page, and that was during the dam construction phase, everything was makeshift shacks. We were all starved, and I said, "By golly, we've got to find someplace to eat."

So Harry says, "Let's go across on the bridge, they have the bridge completed, and I know some old sourdough people over on the other side that I think we can get some meals from."

It was dark when we pulled up to a little store, and there was a cafe, and the booths were all lumber and so on. I said, "This place is closed."

Harry says, "Oh I'll handle it, don't worry." So he went in and came back out and says, "Come on, fellas!"

So we went in, the two engineers, and a writer from a Salt Lake newspaper that Harry had brought along, there were five of us altogether. A lady came in to wait on us, and Harry says, "Where is that so-and-so rattlesnake horse thief, your husband? Tell him I'm out here and I want to see him immediately!" Our eyes were all popping out. [Laughs.]

So pretty soon out comes Harry's cousin that he grew up with, Art Greene. "Why you old son of a gun!" he says. "You old reprobate!"

He had been down in Marble Canyon, and then he saw what was coming at Page with the new dam and Lake Powell, and so he got the land where Wahweap is. They had set up temporarily while they were developing Wahweap, and the marina too along with it, which was way down in the canyon at the time, before the lake filled.

So we located that road, and that road eventually came to pass in about ten years. Harry called it the Sammy Day road and I called it the Harry Goulding road.

27 ■■■ GOULDING'S LODGE

MIKE GOULDING: In 1949, we bought two jeeps. Harry Bennally was the first Navajo to drive tours for us, and he used one of those jeeps. He and Jack Sleeth. We were starting to get quite a few more people in the fifties. It was really getting to be a regular thing. We didn't have to wonder if they were coming, they were there. That's when we went and got the bus, 1956, and Teddy Cly was driving.

■ After the war, Americans rediscovered the road. The motor courts with their bleak little cabins, which had served the travelers of the Depression when they could afford them, gave way to a booming development of motels, scattered everywhere along the highways and frantically competing in luxuries. The Gouldings joined in this movement. In 1953, they tore down their two rock cabins and built a row of motel rooms up on the bench next to their trading post and looking out across the valley to the monuments. In 1956, they doubled the number of rooms. It was a magnificent setting, and one which Time magazine celebrated in a two-page photograph.[1]

John Ford continued to use Goulding's as headquarters for his westerns and always stayed in the last room along the motel row. Gradually during the postwar years, as the fame of Monument Valley spread around the world, the visitors at Goulding's became more and more international, and the long ranch-style dining tables, where everyone sat together and passed platters of food, began to include conversations in German, French, or Japanese.

HARRY GOULDING: Them rock cabins was dandy. When we got to talking about building some nice motel rooms, a lot of people said, "You leave those cabins stay! Whenever you do away with those cabins we're going to quit you!" And after we got the motel rooms done, they'd complain, "Why I thought we told you not to tear those cabins down!"

I says, "They're still here!"

"Well I don't see them."

"That's them right out front there." We took the rocks out of those cabins

Goulding's Lodge, built in 1953 and featured in Time *as one of the first to cater to the country's new fashion in travel—motels.* (Allen C. Reed)

and put them in front there for a retaining wall. I wanted to keep the cabins, so we done the best we could.

If you can get something to eat, is one of the best assets you can have. Frank Douglas was our cook, he stayed with us nineteen or twenty years, I think. Came in 1953. Every year he'd go back to Louisiana, and by God, when it was time to open, here he come. Ansel Hall up at Mesa Verde, we were very close. He'd shoot people down to me that was looking for work, and I'd send people up to him. Never sent anything but just the tops to each other. He got so big that he couldn't get enough colored people to take care of the cooking, and he couldn't work the coloreds and the whites together. It was always a mess, so he couldn't keep them. He thought of me the first thing. We could only use the cook, because we had the Navajo girls, so he sent me the best cook of the lot, Ray Holmes.

Then about a month later, here comes this rig up to the trading post. They were poor people. They drove up wanting gas, and this young colored fella got out. He looked at these big rocks and all, he was giving them the once-over. Well, I come out, and I was going right on down to the gas pump. As

I went past him, he says, "Sir!" and so I stopped and turned around. He says, "Is Mr. Ray Holmes here?"

I says, "You see that door up there, it's open, and there's a screened door there? You just go on up and kick that screen door open, and he'll be glad to see you, I'll betcha."

I started on down.

"Sir!"

I turned around again.

He looked at me and he says, "Sir, Ray Holmes, he's my uncle, and he raise me, and here I is!"

"Well," I says, "go on up there and talk to him." I give the folks their gas, and I knew I couldn't say no. Had to. So the folks went on, and he stayed with us. "Here I is!" He was the dining room boy up at Mesa Verde, Frank Douglas.

So he stayed and waited tables here. Mister, that was the table-waitingest thing you ever saw! When we had the movies in, we had about five or six long tables, and Frank would take care of it himself. He didn't want nobody to help him. He'd slip around like he was on roller skates. He'd just glide. You'd hear a whizz behind him, he was going so fast. Oh my goodness, I'd like to see him right this minute!

A few years later, Ray went up to Denver, so Frank became our cook, and he was just as good a cook as Ray was. No doubt Ray seen to it that he learned to cook so that he would have a break. Frank was a splendid person with the Navajos. He had a lot of fun with those girls; he'd joke them. He was good medicine.

FRANK DOUGLAS: Monument Valley was just amazing to me, because I never had seen the formation of the rock and it was a beautiful setting. It was just something that you couldn't wipe out of your eyes.

I would cook, and help out in the motel, and run back and fix lunch, and everything. There was a group of people there that would just pull together, you know what I mean? If someone needed help, we pitched in and helped. If the well broke down, I made sandwiches and go out and help fix the well and go back and prepare dinner at night. They're a person that you don't mind doing things for because they would certainly appreciate it. You go overboard for them if possible.

A lot of the drivers didn't show up and I had to take trips out into the Valley. The first trip I took out was with Harry, and then I made a second trip, and after that it just look like it fell in place, because I took them out by myself then. I would have enough bread prepared to run me for that one night, and Mike would go up and put my dinner on and start it out, and then I finished after I came back in.

I got where for a while there it was piled on me so regularly, Mike would come up and ask me if I needed any help. I'd say, "Oh no, I don't need any help."

"Well, let me do this little something. I'll peel the potatoes for you." And we set there, and we had the biggest conversation, and I'm carrying my work right along too. She's really a wonderful person.

And the Navajos are a lovable person. First they're kind of shy of you, but after they get used to you, you couldn't meet a better person. I was used to them. I worked with them over at Mesa Verde and they were very nice people to work with.

There were movies there that I had an ordeal into. First off it was quite a chore for me, because I was always the waiter in the dining room. We had six tables and we had to feed in shifts and I was the only waiter. But I met quite a few of the movie actors, and far as I know they all treated me nice, I got along with all of them. One particular day, they had me to come in early that evening. I went into the makeup tent and they put a rave on me which was a Navajo wig and they dressed me up as a chief. And so I had to serve in it that night, a big feather in my head, and my hair was braided up down and so on. Everybody had a good time.

Well, honestly, you want the truth about it? I didn't consider myself Negro either white or Indian, I was just one somebody. I didn't even think about it. No one made me think about it. Didn't anyone give me cause to think what nationality I was, I was just one of the group, and we all got along fine.

28 ◼◻ SEVENTH-DAY ADVENTIST MEDICINE

HARRY GOULDING: Dr. Salsbury's Presbyterian mission hospital at Ganado was an inspiration for us to get a hospital in Monument Valley. We figured that what these Navajos needed the worst was primarily medicine help. We always said, "If we could just get something like Dr. Salsbury has over there, that would be it, wouldn't it?"

I let it be known that we had a piece of land that we would lease free for a hospital. Any of our visitors going into the Valley, I'd tell them. There was a hardware man was bringing things into the Valley. He was tremendously wealthy, and his hired couple were Seventh-day Adventists. They said they would like to talk to their church leaders and maybe they would do it, because they did have hospitals out among people. That's how we got in touch with the Seventh-day Adventists.

I knew Dr. Magan, who was a Seventh-day Adventist there at Loma Linda University in California, and I knew he'd throw a great big long rope in our direction, any time. The head people in the Seventh-day Adventist church were interested, and then Dr. Magan put his shoulder agin the wheel. There was five of them come out to the trading post, and we had a wonderful visit. They said, "You can expect Mr. and Mrs. Walter will be out here to see you." Then they showed up, and things started.

◼ The Seventh-day Adventist church was founded in 1863, in Battle Creek, Michigan, as a part of the awakening of the Adventist belief that the second coming of Chirst was at hand, a movement that swept the country in the middle years of the nineteenth century. The Seventh-day Adventists are vegetarian. They are opposed to the use of alcoholic beverages and tobacco, and the nonmedical use of drugs. They have a strong medical missionary program, with 325 medical units in 185 countries and territories. They also support 450 colleges and secondary schools and nearly 4,000 elementary schools.[1]

The story of Gwen and Marvin Walter is the story of two medical missionaries who in many ways—even in the 1950s, in that part of the reservation—were required to do pioneer work in founding the clinic in Monument Valley. They were replaced by Dr. Lloyd Mason and his wife, Alice, in 1958. With the support of $10,000 from the tribal council, $75,000 from the Indian Affairs Commission, and $75,000 from the church's own fund-raising campaign, a fifteen-bed hospital was completed in 1960, which has since grown to twenty-seven beds, a six-chair dental clinic, and several out-clinics.[2]

HARRY GOULDING: It was in our agreement with the Seventh-day Adventists—after they came in and have been so successful, I'm not too proud of it, but it was in the agreement that seventy-five percent of the funds would have to go towards medicine and care of the Indians, and twenty-five percent on church or religion. I was afraid that if I'd let someone have it, they might have different ideas and it would be the other way around, twenty-five percent for the Navajos and the rest would go to their religion. But everything I asked for, the Seventh-day Adventists were glad to consent to it. They're wonderful people.

GWEN WALTER: Of course, one of the biggest things I think Harry ever did was— I'm prejudiced—was to make it possible for us to come in here.

MARVIN WALTER: At the beginning of World War II the medical work for the Indian in this area was closed out. There had been a government clinic and small hospital at Kayenta, which was to look after the area. So, as Harry said to me the first time I saw him, in 1947, "I'm having to bury too many of my friends! They just don't have anything."

He always said, "I want you to first of all look after these people physically; then you can do something for them mentally." Harry had known P. T. Magan. Dr. Magan and his son were the founders of the Loma Linda University clear back in the early 1900s.[3] Harry said, "Nothing will be grander than the day you have a church up there, but I want the medical first." And I said, "Harry, you know that's just the way we work on our whole world program. We look after a man from every aspect, mentally, physically."

The first thing we got ahold of was a trailer in which to live while we built us something more permanent. It was a twenty-seven-foot trailer, the largest trailer of that kind that had ever been brought over this road on a stock car. I brought it in on back of a Chevrolet. When we got to the foot of Harry's hill down here, for the last little pitch, we had to hook onto it with two jeeps to pull it up the hill and park it up here.

But the *first* thing I had to do was start building a road to even get up here, and the road was built with a pick and shovel and wheelbarrow.

GWEN WALTER: We started having visiting doctors and dentists right away, while we were still down there at the foot of the hill.

MARVIN WALTER: I went down to Holbrook and got a sixteen-foot trailer house that we had used when we first went out to the reservation in 1942, so we wouldn't have to take sick folks into our home. And I had Buster Whitehorse build three hogans where the clinic building sits now, for the Indians to stay overnight when they came in.

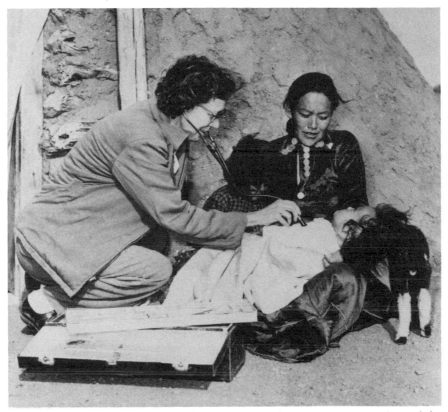

Gwen Walter, nurse and founder with her husband, Pastor Marvin Walter, of the Seventh-day Adventist clinic on Goulding's land. (Herbert Ford)

GWEN WALTER: Maternity ward.

MARVIN WALTER: That was the beginning, just this little trailer while we were building our home and building a clinic building.

We took the old movie set that was out near the Mittens. The movies had put up what they called the fort, to use in filming *She Wore a Yellow Ribbon,* and also down in the flat toward Eagle Mesa they put up a replica of the town of Tombstone, for another film. They had turned these two sets over to the tribe, and the tribe didn't like them cluttering up the landscape. So I made an offer and bought the lumber, and Harry let us use his ton-and-a-half GMC truck to go into Flagstaff for other materials we needed, and we were able to put up our home and the clinic building.

GWEN WALTER: And the three children learned to pull nails.

MARVIN WALTER: Down where the gymnasium is now, there was one outcropping of limestone, and back in that side canyon was another, on Harry's place, so Harry says, "I'll give you permission to use the rock if you'll quarry it out." So Buster Whitehorse and I quarried that rock and cut the rock, and put up a stone exterior.

GWEN WALTER: We used the gates from the old fort.

MARVIN WALTER: Beams, and floor joists. We put up a stone clinic, two rooms. It was a godsend to us.

GWEN WALTER: It was a pretty little clinic, too. We finished it inside with linoleum; it was done up nicely inside. One of the Indians came up one day and looked it over with tears in his eyes. He said, "Do you mean you did this for us?" Because any other work that had been done locally wasn't nicely done.

MARVIN WALTER: Harry was pleased and so were we with the way it turned out. But there was too much to do in those two little rooms, there wasn't room enough. Before we'd cooled off, we had to keep on enlarging. We went right on building a larger clinic building in connection with it. In 1950 we got here, in September; 1951 we built our house; 1952 we completed the clinic; 1953 we were putting up the doctor's cottage; between '53 and '54 we started in on the schoolhouse. Just one right after another. We were here from '50 to '58, and we were continually building the whole eight years, just growing like Topsy.

GWEN WALTER: It was getting too big. I was the only nurse. I had immunization clinics and well-baby clinics and stuff for the government nurse.

MARVIN WALTER: There was one government nurse to cover from Flagstaff, the other side, where the ordnance depot is at Bellemont, clear up to Monument Valley, was all one person's territory.

GWEN WALTER: They had a big uranium mine starting, Number Two Mine, and their water supply was terrible. They were afraid they would get typhoid started, so they had a program of immunization against typhoid— instead of improving their water supply! That's sour grapes, isn't it. But anyhow, I did that. They supplied me with materials and I did the whole area.

MARVIN WALTER: It would take, to get over to the mine with a four-wheel-drive vehicle, two hours between the clinic and the mine. Gwen would take the jeep and go out to the mine early in the morning, two hours to get over there, do clinic all day, and near evening fold up and two hours back again, and maybe there would not have been anyone over her trail during the whole time. There weren't automobiles like there are now; there were about six cars in the whole area then. But that was the type of thing we could do, preventative and emergency work. Many, many times, day and night, we'd take emergency cases clear to Tuba City, to the hospital there.

Monument Valley Hospital was completed in 1961, with twenty-six beds and six dental chairs. The small Adventist church is partially hidden by trees below and to the right of the hospital. The view here is down Rock Door Canyon to the Monuments, in the distance. (Samuel Moon)

Often we'd use the jeep to go back to the hogan and pick up the patient and bring him out where we could transfer him to our car, and you could go faster—*maybe,* depending on the weather and the roads. At any rate, we used both our private car and the four-wheel-drive vehicle. We'd wear our jeep out in a year. Each year we'd have to get a new one, it was that kind of roads.

HARRY GOULDING: We were already started collecting things our guests would send us for the Navajos. We always had a lot of things we'd save for Christmas. When the Walters came, we done it together, and that way they got out among the Navajos. They were giving the Navajo things, and they'd accept quicker of their medicine, is the way I figured it. They worked eighteen hours a day. She was a top hand in medicine and so was Marvin. Marvin was a preacher also. They were a great pair.

They would always permit us to help them any way we could. When they first came in I'd go out with them to interpret; that way I could tell the Navajos who they were and what it was all about.

GWEN WALTER: Harry took me in one time to a fellow that was sick. I had been seeing this boy for some time, but I didn't have an interpreter and they didn't know much English, so our communication was a little bit difficult. Harry said to me, "Why don't we go and see this boy, he's dying."

I said, "Harry, I've been out there doing what I can."

"Well, I'll take you in there and we'll see what we can do."

HARRY GOULDING: We was going out to see Hugh Black. It was his home, but it was his boy that was sick. When we got there they were making medicine over him. He was on a sand painting. I says to Hugh, "This lady is a doctor, and she's my friend, and you're my friend. I want her to check your son as soon as you're through with the painting, and see what she has to say about it."

So she waited, and they let her watch, because Maurice or I or Mike, any of us, were accepted that way, and after it was over she went all over him and checked him.

GWEN WALTER: They told me that the boy saw arrows coming out of the logs and piercing him and this was what was making him sick. We decided that the only thing to do was to take the boy in the jeep to Tuba City. We took the seat out and made a bed there and took his father and mother with us. The boy had developed an abscess in the lung, there's a name for it, and when we got there, the doctor immediately put in a needle and drew out about a quart of pus.

Harry says, "And you know, their eyes rolled right out on their cheeks!" That's Harry! Harry had such a way of expressing it. But it was only because he could interpret for me, and they had confidence in him, because I was fairly new out here then.

HARRY GOULDING: That old kid's been an awful close friend to Gwen and Marvin ever since. I always enjoyed him, he was a nice kid, it tied him a little closer to me too. And his family feel the same way; they was all tickled to death. If they come over, you can see it. With the Navajo, if he finally believes in you, if you get his confidence, why he'll let you know. And they can do it so beautiful!

MARVIN WALTER: This was the basis of the whole thing. Harry had gotten these people to have confidence in him, that they would even allow us to carry on. One of the medicine men said, "You've got strong medicine, and I've got strong medicine. Put them together and you've got very strong medicine."

TED CLY: They still do the ceremonials like old time, some old people and some new ones. Wears down, just like an old record, so they get new ones. They go to school and study on them. Somebody teach them how to do sand painting or how to be doctor.

If the white doctor's medicine doesn't fit into what's wrong with the body, they go to the medicine man. It works pretty good. Then they go back to the doctor. Then they all come together. Xray, or give a bit of pill. And over here there's the herbs from these weeds, or the berry, or the pod, some clear water.

But the Indians who are Christian put the tribe religion down. The missionaries say, "Don't go to the medicine man, don't go to the sing," and the medicine man say, "Don't go to church, the Bible's not for you." So they split up the tribal way.

MARVIN WALTER: They know herb medications and secrets that the medical profession would like very very much to understand. In fact, some are investigating the plants and so on to find out what chemistry there is in them that does what they want, because they do have results from the herb medications they use.

The medicine man learns from somebody that hands it down to him. They don't spread it around or publish it. Each one has his own secrets, and it's only when they have strict confidence in you that they'll show you what they're using. But they have shown my wife things that they use and what they use them for, and they get definite results.

GWEN WALTER: I know what they tell me. One of my very dear medicine men, Katso, was with me one day as I drove along. I'd stop and pick a weed and ask him what he used it for. He'd tell me, and I had a notebook and wrote it all down.

I never saw that notebook again. Somebody else took it, I'm sure, because I'm sure Katso would have let me have it. It was another Indian who was very unhappy about it, but also very happy to get the information for his own use.

Dan Phillips told me, and he was a university graduate, that his wife knew some herbs that could be used to cure gonorrhea, I think it was, or one of the venereal diseases anyhow. They had a young man who had contracted it, had been away in the hospital and it hadn't helped, and they had sent him home in miserable shape. He told me that his wife had cured it.

I know they have a medicine that will render them sterile; a woman that's had enough children may use it. They may have lost it, because these things were handed down only to those who showed respect for the old ways. They have something for rattlesnake bites. I don't know how successful it is, but I know they have it, and I'm inclined to think it is effective. Now for diarrhea and pneumonia and tuberculosis, nothing.

And then I had a child that had a concussion. She was vomiting blood, and the blood would come out of her ears. She'd had a fall. The father was very anxious that I take the child to the hospital, but the mother insisted on having the medicine man. I went down with the father and saw the child, and I had nothing to offer under those circumstances, unconscious child, blood coming out of her ears, possibly internal injuries. My solution was to take her to the hospital, which the mother never allowed. But the medicine man came, and he gave her a mixture of herbs and stuff which stopped her vomiting. She later had some convulsions, but she eventually recovered without white man's medication. *I couldn't stop her vomiting, but he did.*

The psychology definitely has a place. I have seen them relax when the medicine man comes and begins his ceremony. But I also am very convinced that there is satanic power in the thing. One outstanding example in my thinking was a girl living near Oljeto. She and another girl had been having these extreme spells, and they called me out one night. If you have never felt this power I can't explain it to you, but there's a power that you sense in the atmosphere.

As I drove up to the hogan I could sense this power, and I heard the medicine men in there singing. Out of respect to the medicine men, I would always stay in my car or take my time coming in until they knew I was there, and then I would come in quietly and sit down in my place. I would wait until they'd signal me, that I could take over. When I came up they were singing, and the air was charged.

I waited until I heard a pause in the singing, and I went in. The mother and father were sitting on either side of the girl, holding her wrists, because they said that this thing would seize her and just throw her everywhere; she'd roll and thrash around, and they were there to hold her.

When I came in, after prayer, which was my custom, soon the atmosphere was quiet and the medicine men were calm, the girl was calm, everything was calm. We talked it over, and the mother and father indicated that they wanted me to take her to the hospital. There was nothing for me to do there; all her vital signs were okay. So I said, "All right"—this was ten o'clock at night—"I'll take her to the hospital," 103 miles over dirt roads.

And so we got in the car, the three of them in the back seat of the jeep station wagon, which was very tight, so they could control her in case of one of these seizures. We started out from the hogan, and things remained quiet until I got down the road about half a mile, and a coyote went slowly across the road with his tail hanging down. The coyote was a bad omen. A normal coyote will go fast across the road and his tail will be out straight in back. It was a coyote man. This means to them, "No. Don't go any farther." They didn't speak English. I knew what they wanted, but just to test them I kept going, and finally the father got hold of me and said, "Stop!" In English; it scared up his English!

So I said, "We'll go around on the other side where the coyote hasn't been."

"Oh no! No!" This was a bad omen; we must not go to the hospital.

So we went back to the hogan, and I talked to them again. I said, "You know I have babies to take care of, you know I have work too. I've been up all day, I must sleep tonight. If you decide you want her to go to the hospital, you get Patterson." He was a Presbyterian minister that lived not far from them, and he and I worked together nicely. I said, "Tomorrow morning, if she isn't better, you ask Patterson."

As I drove away from there, all hell broke loose! The girl screeching and screaming, those medicine men rattle shaking, and and singing, and the atmosphere came back—fast! It's the kind of thing that makes the hair stand on end. I'm telling you, there was power there!

MARVIN WALTER: They were trying to get rid of this power that was disturbing the girl.

GWEN WALTER: Trying to cast out the devil, that's my evaluation of it. They have witchcraft. The white man who scoffs at it, I don't care who he is; I know. I have seen things and understood things that many, many people have never seen. Harry Goulding was telling me that I'd seen things he'd never seen. Because they accepted me. I came in where they were sick, I came in where they were singing, not for tourists but for their own sake. And I gained their confidence. Some of them explained things to me.

The next day, Patterson took her down to the hospital, and she had a mild convulsion or seizure while he was taking her, within five miles or so of their camp. Then when he got past this certain hogan, everything was quiet the rest of the way down to Tuba. She was fine, normal, when the doctors checked her, nothing wrong. They came back, and as they got close to this one hogan again, she tensed right up, the parents tensed right up, and I think from what he said she had another episode. His conclusion—and he was a man who had seen much of this witchcraft and devil cursing—his conclusion was the same as mine: this was witchcraft, and there's nothing that we can do about it except prayer. In about ten day's time the whole thing cleared up. I never knew exactly, but I do know that old Crosseye was somewhat of a medicine man, and I think he'd put a curse on them. I was too busy to inquire diligently into it, and I didn't have command of the language, and I would not trust an interpreter to tell me those things.

I tried to teach the mothers something of sterilizing bottles and how to feed their babies. One interesting way we had was to provide them with four or five Evenflo bottles and show them how to boil the water. A number ten tin can, a bottle in it, fill it with water, put it on the campfire, and when the water in the can has boiled almost dry, your bottle is sterilized. That's one day's supply of milk. And we showed them how to wash their hands and turn the nipple and feed the baby. Now if the baby doesn't take all of it, you give it to the other little boy and let him finish it. Don't waste it, but don't keep it from one time to the next. And this, I think, helped a lot in checking all the diarrheas.

And of course flies. We tried to teach them to keep things clean around the hogan, but oh! The only time I scolded them was when I came and found a dirty hogan with chickens or lambs inside and they hadn't kept things clean. Of course you can't blame them for keeping the lambs and chickens inside, but you can get after them for not keeping it clean. When you have a dirt floor and the kids contaminate it, you shovel it out, put in some clean sand.

But the hogans are beautiful. Their heat, a little fire keeps it warm, and that big smoke hole, you can have seventeen, twenty-four people in there and you never get stuffy, because you've got this beautiful exchange of air.

They knew how to use sand. I've seen a mother sitting outside the hogan with a baby that spilled over on her skirt, I've seen her reach over and get a handful of clean sand and rub it thoroughly through the dress, sand it right off. I've seen them scrub their kettles with sand. I've seen them put a layer of sand underneath this oozing sore, and change it frequently, carry it way away from the hogan. Here was a nice way to take care of the drainage.

MARVIN WALTER: One of the big problems we had was getting care for the TB patients. The whites were not getting tuberculosis, and the sanatoriums were quite empty, but you couldn't send an Indian into a sanatorium for whites.

GWEN WALTER: Frank Masland, a rug manufacturer from Carlisle, Pennsylvania, came out as a tourist. Very much interested in doing things to benefit the people and the country. He's really the man who helped us get the Indians into the TB hospital.

Harry came by one night and said, "Gwen, Keith Holiday is very sick and probably dying."

I said, "Where is he now?"

"Well I can't really tell you. He's over here on one of the mesas, but just to tell you where to go, I can't really tell you."

"Can you show me?"

"Sure, hop in."

So I went with Harry in the jeep, and I think he really wanted it this way, because he had Frank Masland with him, and he wanted Frank to see things as they were.

We went up the canyon and out over the trails, and we came to this summer shelter which they had built, just juniper poles with a few juniper boughs over it. The family was sitting out there around this dying man, both his wives ministering to him, medicine man there. It was just a very close, touching scene. He had a respiratory infection of some sort. I didn't know that he had TB, I honestly didn't, but I suspicioned it. I mean nobody had confirmed it to me that this was what he was dying of.

Next day I took Keith to the hospital, and I said to Masland, "They won't keep him there, they don't admit advanced tubercular cases in the hospital if they're an Indian."

So he gave me some money and said, "Here, pad his palm."

"I don't think it will work," I said, "I don't work that way myself, and I don't think the doctor will."

We had a wonderful doctor down there at that time. He looked at me and said, "What did you bring Keith here for?"

"I was under pressure to do it," I said, "and I was also told, here," and

I offered him the money, "in case you wouldn't take him."

The doctor said, "You know better than to offer that to me. I wouldn't take a bribe to take anybody in here."

"What can I do with him?"

"I'd like to know that too," he said. "Take him home, make him as comfortable as can be, and that's all I can do." And he said, "You know the outcome."

So I came back and had to tell Frank Masland what had happened. Before he got home, Frank went to Santa Fe, I think, he went different places, and with his influence he was able to get beds for the Indians in these off-the-reservation tuberculosis sanatoriums with downright empty beds. He sent a plane in here one day to get Keith. He'd died, just hours before the plane arrived. Of course it would have been too late to get him in the hospital anyhow.

It was through this incident that the thing broke open. Harry knew the situation, Harry knew Frank, Harry knew how my hands were tied, and Harry knew Frank's influence, so he got Frank to go out to this camp with the best help that we had in the area.

■ Unlike trachoma, whose threat to Navajo health was defeated in the 1930s by the development of sulfanilamide, tuberculosis stubbornly resisted all efforts to eradicate it from the reservation. Malnourishment and unsanitary living conditions contributed greatly to the incidence and spread of the disease, and the lack of pain disguised its danger and led victims to neglect it until too late for effective treatment. In the period following World War II, 10 percent of the Navajo population had some form of tuberculosis. Among school children six to ten years old, an infection rate of 50 to 60 percent was often found, ten to sixty times larger than the national rate.

The war had diverted both funds and personnel from the service of the medical needs of the Navajos, so facilities were actually reduced from the level of the 1930s. In addition to the few hospitals on the reservation, there were ten off-reservation government and private sanatoriums that would accept Navajos. They were overcrowded, with as many as 500 Navajos occupying these beds, and a large waiting list.

It was not until 1952 that help arrived. It is a remarkable story, in which chance provided an opportunity and intelligence seized it, to bring victory at last in the fight against tuberculosis.[4] A group of specialists in infectious diseases had come to Tuba City from Cornell University medical school to help deal with a hepatitis epidemic. They discovered five cases of acute miliary tuberculosis among the 300 children in the hospital with infectious hepatitis. It happened that Cornell had been working on a new drug to combat tuberculosis—isoniazide, I had determined that it was safe to use, but had not yet subjected it to a large-scale trial.

Recognizing the extent of the tuberculosis problem on the reservation, the

Cornell doctors approached the tribal council for permission to treat these children with their new drug. Isoniazide proved successful in combating tuberculosis on the reservation and subsequently in worldwide use. The Cornell project was the beginning of a model program in intercultural cooperation. It is a testimonial to the success of decency in the relations between cultures.

BUSTER WHITEHORSE (translated from Navajo):   Many of our people, young and old, have died because of drinking alcohol. The bottle, with no arms and no head, can destroy a person. It can make you jump off a cliff or it can end you in the fire.

HARRY GOULDING: Gwen and Marvin, and then later the hospital, they stopped quite a lot of them from drinking. Some of the old people would talk to them—we'd all talk to them, but the hospital could have more influence on them than any one. Oh, it was pathetic. Some of those poor things were just absolutely worthless, just winos that you absolutely knew couldn't be helped. But those Seventh-day Adventists would get after them, and we'd pour some coal on with them, and it helped a lot of them in here. They finally got back to be the real old fellas that they was.

They'd go out and get work, that's how it got started. They got to where they were drinking, and then the bootleggers started coming in, and they don't bootleg anything but rotgut. Then they'd go into town and get whiskey, especially on the Arizona side, and it would finally get them.

If they had a bottle when the police found them, they'd arrest them as a bootlegger, and a bootlegger's fine was about a hundred and fifty dollars. If they didn't have a bottle and were caught drunk, it was only ten dollars. So naturally, they'd get ahold of a bottle of whiskey, they'd go back in some alley and just throw it down and get away from that bottle. They wouldn't go very far till they'd go kerplunk. Some of them bootleggers would get them so drunk that they could take their clothes. They'd go in there dressed up with their nice silver concho belts and beads and their old *k'eet'ohs,* their bowguards on their arm, but they'd come back without them, a brutal thing all the way through. We taught the Indians how to drink whiskey, and then we say they don't know how to drink. The very same stinking, rotten things that taught them would say that.

At our place we could have handled beer or whiskey just like Utah does; you have to have a permit and only by the bottle. But when they let the Indians have whiskey, the Navajos voted it off the reservation. They didn't want it. And I would never be the one that put it on.

Willy Cly one time fell off the wagon for a while, but we got on him and he squared himself around a bit. "It's making a bad man out of you," I'd tell him. "Even a medicine man or two around here is doing it. They sing 'mumble-mumble!' That's the way they sing. The powers don't know what they're saying. They can't get to their powers. And you're going to get the

Mike and Harry Goulding, 1960. (Goulding's Monument Valley Museum)

same way." I'd always attach it to their religion. It's their way of thinking, and you can give them a pretty hot fire when you get right on them. And then you get people like the Walters to back you up.

Seth Bigman was a Navajo who made a lot of money on uranium, and he got to drinking when he started making all that money from his mines. He came pretty near killing himself in one of his pickups. He'd wreck them and go get another one. He wouldn't have them fixed.

After Gwen and Marvin came in here, we all got to pouring the coal on old Seth. A wonderful kid he was. He never got mean or nothing. We all got on him, and kept getting on him, and be doggoned if he didn't straighten up, and he's just fine today.

Gwen and Marvin talked to the uranium outfit that Seth was working with and got them to put his money away for him and his family in a trust fund, and they only give him so much. He should have a lot of money left yet, he can only get so much at a time. That was a good turn they did.

The Seventh-day Adventists have one Navajo, Tom Holiday, who finally got to be a minister, the first Navajo minister in the Seventh-day Adventist church. He was a heavy drinker. They took care of him and told him what was going to happen if he didn't straighten up. They talked religion to him. And by gosh, he come with it, he got in the church on account of that. Of course we'd all show that it was making us happy that he was listening to those folks, because they knew what was right.

GWEN WALTER: Harry worked right with us in many cases, and his under-standing of the people was . . . Now, of course, angels would have enemies, and I'm sure Harry had some. I ran into a few situations where, among the Navajos, some didn't favor him particularly, but then they were not the close ones, the ones that he was seeing all the time.

We used to talk to him about letting his tourists take candy down to these kids all the time. So Harry said, "All right, let's take something else." He would have the tourists take oranges, apples, fruit that was in season, and even little toys for the children, rather than giving them candy. He just stocked these things in the store and let the tourists know, "Don't load these kids down with candy."

I was over there one day, and Mike was looking for her leather jacket. It was a nice leather jacket with fringe, and she was looking all over and couldn't find it. She asked Harry where it was. A few days later she saw an Indian come in wearing it, and she said, "Harry!" He just laughed and said, "Yep, somebody was cold."

29 ▄▄ THE ANASAZI

HARRY GOULDING: I remember an archaeologist that was working on the
Aztec Ruin when I was a boy, Earl Morris;[1] I got to talking with him one
time. When I was out on the winter range, one of the herds would go across
the San Juan River, and out in there I would find some old prehistoric ruins.
I knew where this cliff dwelling was, out on the reservation, and he'd never
heard of it, so I took him out there and showed it to him. That was the start
of our relations. After that, if I'd hear of anything like that I'd take out
ahorseback, and if it amounted to anything, I'd come back and tell my friend.
Then we'd go out in a wagon—he'd want to take some equipment with
him—we'd probably be gone for a week, sometimes only two or three days,
it depended on what the description of it was. In a week's time he could just
monkey around in there. He'd size it up and if it justified development, he'd
get a crew and go out there and dig into it and get all the information he
could get out of it.

I'd wait a few days till after he'd opened it up and I'd slip out while they
were working, and then he'd visit with me about it. It helped me out a lot
in later years knowing what to do after I found a place. And where the
burials were. Something up in Colorado I'd find would be altogether different
than maybe something I'd find down in New Mexico. They would have
different ideas of burials.

We'd go out maybe two or three times a year sometimes. He gave me an
awful lot of knowledge about archaeology, a young kid, that helped me a
lot, because I took a great interest in the old Anasazi cliff dwellings after I
got down here. I never forgot this friend that I had as a boy, Earl Morris.

When John Stevens and I first came in and saw Monument Valley, we
found a big three-level ruin. They call it Poncho House now, but we didn't
have a way to do anything about it. If I found anything like that, I would
never say anything about a discovery until I could get ahold of some influential person that I knew could get the proper publicity out of it, so I was
waiting till I found somebody, the right person to talk to about this Poncho
House. Norm Nevills ran boat trips down the San Juan, and he had a writer
that took the boat trip with him, so they took him to Poncho House, and
Poncho House got its reputation that way. I made tracks into Poncho House,

he could have followed those tracks in. But it didn't make any difference, because I was glad that he done it and got the fellow in that early.

■ The Anasazi are the prehistoric people who inhabited the Colorado Plateau of northeastern Arizona and the Four Corners area through several stages of cultural development from the beginning of the Christian era until about A.D. 1300[2] They were preceded by a Desert Culture of hunters and gatherers, dating back to around 5000 B.C. By the beginning of the Christian era they gradually began to cultivate some plants, in particular, maize, which developed in the Anasazi period from a seed head about the size of a finger to the corn still planted by the Navajos and Hopis today.

At first, they lived in pithouses, whose floors were recessed anywhere from a foot or two to six feet underground. Later, they located in small caves, scattered about in the sandstone rock of the region, where they built masonry rooms by fitting the rocks together. They developed finally the complex architecture and society of urban communities at such sites as Mesa Verde, Betatakin, and Kiet Siel, in the last few climactic years of their culture during the thirteenth century. It is remarkable that the complete development from hunters and gatherers to urban communities subsisting on agriculture can be documented in this one location.

This small Anasazi ruin, one of the many jewels scattered in the caves of Monument Valley, is in Rock Door Canyon, not far from Goulding's. (Samuel Moon)

It is not altogether clear why the Anasazi left the region. Perhaps the most plausible expalantion is an extended period of drought years, which first drove them together in cliff cities like Betatakin and Kiet Siel, near the best sources of water, and then, as their increasing numbers exhausted even these sources, drove them away to the Hopi mesas, Zuni, and the Rio Grande pueblos.

MAURICE KNEE: *Anasazi* is a Navajo word. *'Ana'í* is enemy, and *sází* is a bad word meaning dried up, something old. So *Anasazi* means *'ana'í-sází*, "old dried-up enemy." If they didn't like anybody, they'd call him "dried-up hide." But you ask most Navajos what *Anasazi* means, and they say, "the old people," because you can't take the time to translate it.

Corn is *naadą́ą́'*, which is slang for *'ana'í bidą́ą́*, which means "enemy food." Navajos weren't farmers till they finally found out about corn, that it was eatable, and how to plant it. So every cornfield, practically, that the Navajos use today, other than developed stuff by the government that's got water to it, is an old prehistoric cornfield, every one of them. Any time you go and find where a Navajo's planting corn, you can find pottery shards. They're usually up against a cliff where there's a big sand dune, the water comes over the cliff. So *Anasazi* and *naadą́ą́'* are really related.

FRED YAZZIE: My daddy used to have a big flat garden in Mystery Valley, and we had a garden between Bluff City and Mexican Water, right below Mexican Water. We used to have a wash down there, a good soil against the ledge. My mother, she live here in Mystery Valley, and so my father had to go back and forth. And this Mystery Valley, some Navajos used to have a big garden where they cut corn, they used to cut corn right there when I know it.

And they store it, you know, they make a big hole right in the ground and store their corn there. But some of them, they putting it where there used to be a room there, the cliff dweller's house, and they hide their corn in that room. Some of the Navajos, they stay away from those rooms, but we use it, my old people use it, stored the corn in there in Mystery Valley.

My old grandpa used to tell a story about these cliff dwellings over there. He say, "There's nothing that they dead! Nothing dead!" And he cry, he cry about storing the corn there. He worry, you know.

But my daddy, he use the room. Say, "They dead already, there's nothing there."

They all different, these Navajos, their religion. They believe devil, they believe all kinds of spirit, like Navajo wolf, somebody is witching them. They say it's true, you know. Maybe not true. They think it is true, and then they get sick by it because they worried!

Well, my daddy, he used to work with these white men coming through, taking to the cliff dwellers and finding the pottery and all those stuff. John

Sání they call him, John Wetherill, he come through here, hunt those cliff dwellers, about twelve people with him, they had horse and mule, donkey to pack. Taking all the cliff dwellers and clean it out. Find the bone and find what they have, pottery, arrowhead, and everything.

I don't know where they go to now, the cliff dwellers. What happen to them, I like to know. Well, my old old old old grandpa, he say they have a flood. And another old old grandpa, he say they don't have no air, they die, they got no air instead of a flood. I don't know which is true. You can see the skeletons, still sitting up like this when they was killed. Just because they don't have no air, they just die right there.

Well, my daddy, one day he find this corn in the cliff dwellers' room. He think, my old daddy, he think, I just wonder if this corn will grow. And he took it up to his field and plant it. And you know what happen? [Laughs.] It's dry, that corn, it's really dry, you know. It's many many years. Well, he had several corn, this corn he plant in there. He planted that, and he say it grow!

I didn't believe it. I ask him, I say, "Did it really grow?"

He say, "Yeah, it grow!"

Well, it's so many years, that corn just dry out, you know. it don't look like it going grow. He say grow the same thing like our corn. But I like to know if he got it from the pottery. If I see him go and put it in the ground and it grow, then I can believe it. I keep asking and asking. He say, "It grow!"

HARRY GOULDING: There was an archaeologist out of the university up at Salt Lake, and I took him out. He was awful good company in the back country, so we prowled around all over Tsé Bighi'. There's one place that you don't take too many people, but I knew that he would enjoy it, because this old bowl was down there in a big pothole, and you can see it. It's right above one of the cliff dwellings in Tsé Bighi', but you've got to come around from the other side to get up. There was a cedar tree down in there, a big, tall cedar tree. Something blew a seed in and it had grown up in there. It was good and tall, but you had to look down on it. And there was water; that's where the old prehistoric Indians got their water. And evidently the string broke when he was coming up with his load in this bowl and it went back down and settled on the bottom. Nobody had ever taken it out because you can't get down in there and get out alone.

I didn't tell him it was in there, I just took him on up. Now this tree kind of leaned a little bit, not much, but there was a sand dune piled up in back of the tree, and it was deep sand. Well, he seen that bowl in there, and he jerked his packing stuff off of him and jumped! I hollered at him, but he was off before I noticed what he was going to do. He didn't hear me anyway. He was after that pot and that's all there was to it! He landed on that sand dune and had a good landing.

Well, he got his pot, but then he couldn't get back out. I had a little old lariat rope I always carried with me, and I brought his pot out for him, got *it* out. So we talked there. He got scared then.

"Oh," I says, "we'll get you out of there *some* way. I'll go on over to the trading post, and on my way over I'll think the thing over, and by the time I get there if I don't have an answer," I says, "one of the boys there will. So we'll get you out." And I started to get up.

"Oh, no, Harry, don't leave me, don't leave me!"

"Well, I can't get you out of here the way things are." So I started off again, and he was still hollering. I could hear him for quite a ways off. "Please don't leave me!"

I went over and got some ropes and made a rope ladder out of it, and got him out on that rope ladder. He was in there quite a little while; you have to tie a lot of knots to make one that long. I knew what I was going to do before I left him, but there was no use telling him, because he'd probably just be more scared about getting up on a rope ladder, so I didn't say nothing. But he got his pot. He earned it.

The only trouble I've had with archaeologists is the darned markings they put on the walls. One outfit is all that's ever been in Mystery Valley.[3] I won't take an archaeologist around the Valley at all any more, because they went out there and run a doggone row of numbers, oh it was about two feet long, in white on that red sandstone! They have people in the notion that for anybody to put markings on a rock is an improper thing to do, and when I'd take visitors into Mystery Valley, those little ruins that are in there, why I could see the effect on them. So I just went to work and rubbed them numbers off. I would have done it anyway because I don't like them. They tell us we can't do anything, and then they come along and put a thing like that right in one of the nice spots, you know, where it would stand out. So I just got me another old sandstone rock and rubbed her off.

I'd like it all right if they'd come in and study a ruin and dig it, and if they want to improve it some. Just make a code number for each place and put it somewhere so they can say where it's at, and not in a popular place out on the face of the rock. Until they get to doing that, I ain't going to ever take one of them around, myself. Here I am, just a damned sheepherder and an Indian trader, and even I picked that up as an improper thing to do. They've got to have better brains than I've got.

One time I had a group, there was two rigs of us, and we were going up on top of Hoskinini Mesa that day. And just as you got up onto the top of the mesa a little ways there was a canyon come up on the side of us there, about two hundred yards from where we went. There were some piñons and cedars in there, and we got out.

Whenever we went up there I would tell the folks, "When I was in here about a week or ten days ago, there was an awful nice old fella lost his watch here, so let's string out and see if maybe we can't find it." I didn't want them to see what we were coming to. We would look for the watch, and look for the watch, and pretty soon we'd come to this deep canyon. Up in the head of it was this beautiful, beautiful cliff dwelling. It had the tops on all of the rooms—five different rooms in it. It was the most perfect ruin in the whole area and the greatest location that you could imagine.

And so this time we walked up there, we was all together, and I tried to keep their attention off the other way a little. After they'd got over near the canyon I says, "Now look over this way." And my God, somebody had got in there and just blowed those rooms to smithereens! Absolutely ruined! I pretty near got sick. They dynamited them! Everybody in the crowd was just sick about it. It was pretty near the nicest thing in Monument Valley.

Now, Mystery Valley is a beautiful little valley. But without its little jewels here and there and yonder it wouldn't be the same. It's under fence now. Whenever Sammy Day from the tribe at Window Rock would come over, we'd visit about different things, and I told him, "The worst thing they'll do to these monuments is maybe put their name on, and that can be taken off. But Mystery Valley has some beautiful little cliff dwellings, and without them it wouldn't be Mystery Valley. It would just be another ordinary canyon." I said it ought to be fenced in. So he got it fenced across Mystery Valley clean over to Brigham's Tomb there, by Sentinel Mesa.

30 ◼◼ A NAVAJO TRIBAL PARK

HARRY GOULDING: I wanted to see something done with Monument Valley, some control over it. Back home, when the road came across from Gallup over into the San Juan Basin country, Dad was civic minded. He would furnish a couple of cars to take people when they had these meetings, and he let me drive one of the cars, I and Charlie both. I'd drive once and then Charlie, he'd drive. He was trying to get something going before that road came in, and he spoke in some of the meetings. He suggested that there ought to be some planning, that there was going to be an invasion when that road was completed. And there was. The doggone people come in there, they ruined places like the pueblo ruins there out of Aztec. Now it's the Aztec National Monument. And there were other pueblos that were equally as good as that. When visitors came in on that road, they mutilated those ruins. Dad suggested at one meeting when I was with him that there ought to be some thought about that. Of course they weren't so mindful about those things as we are now.

There was one old boy, he bought a ranch, and the Aztec ruins were sitting on his land, right down in the corner of his ranch there. His boy and I were very close friends, we were in the same grade in school. I'd go over there sometimes, and his Dad would let us go all through the ruins. Oh there was quite a number of rooms, and we found a lot of nice things there.

When he fenced his place in, he fenced the cliff dwelling up, and he wouldn't let anybody come in. Everybody felt that they could go into those cliff dwellings and do anything they wanted to do with them—they'd always had that liberty. Well, this old fella put signs up, "No admittance, keep out." The people around there said, "He can't keep us away from digging around in that ruin. We've always done it, and he can't keep us from doing it!" So they got together one Sunday and they were going to go over there and go into that ruin. The old fella was out with his .30-.30, and they didn't go in! If it hadn't been for him, we wouldn't have had enough left up there to have had a national monument.

So I could feel the same thing when they started talking about roads around here. I wanted to see something done with Monument Valley, some control over it. J. Bracken Lee, the governor of the state of Utah, had a black-topped road coming down this way, and he had appropriations that tied the thing up to where after he had served his two terms, why that money had to go to finish the road right to the state line here at our place.

I knew it was coming, so I got with what friends I had in Washington and the tribe and the Park Service to try and get something done to protect this area that had so much interest, the Valley and the cliff dwellings and one thing another in here. I knew it would be tore apart, just like what happened up there in the San Juan Basin. So I gave them five days. We would furnish our cars and everything to go, and I'd take them out. We wouldn't take any reservations for that time or any visitors, and we'd have the whole thing to ourselves and look the whole thing over. That was in the forties, after the war was over.

Years before, Horace Albright had started the possibility of making Monument Valley a national park. I took him down into the Valley there in the thirties. We went on around and spent the day in there. I cooked them a Dutch-oven dinner. And coming back out, we came up to where that last Mitten is, over around there by Castle Butte. A beautiful sight from in there, and just up the side of it a bit Mr. Albright wanted to stop. He looked it all over and he addressed the group, and he says, "Gentlemen, if that monument alone were the only thing setting out there by itself, the National Park Service would have to do something about it." So that proves it is national park quality. They came in here before they went to these other places.

But then Albright retired. The fella that came in after him as park director had been Albright's aide, but his retirement came just before these meetings we were having, and they had to put a pinch hitter in there temporarily, from Washington. He was here with some of the park superintendents. Maurice McCabe was a Navajo and executive secretary for the tribe then, he represented the Indians, and he had about five others with him.

And so that's what we done. We all piled in what rigs we had. There was a big group here. In Monument Valley about fifteen, eighteen people was a lot of people to get together. We went on out and looked it all over, and then we came in and we'd visit out what we had seen at night.

On the last day, we didn't go out only half the day, and we spent the rest of the day in a meeting. And this new man from Washington told us how he would do it.

All he could think about was the way any national park was built. They had to have them all the same. The people living on the land and using it, they could keep it until they passed on, but then the families had to move off and the stock and everything.

Well, when it come to that, why I told him that the Navajo reservation was originally set aside for around twelve thousand Indians. At that time there was fifty-two or -three thousand. Now there's well over a hundred thousand. I says, "These people just can't afford to give away pieces of land like this. They just couldn't possibly, cause they're so heavily overpopulated that it's a big problem for them."

He wasn't satisfied. He says, "If I make a change here with the Navajos, it would make it pretty near impossible to create a park out anywhere else, because they'd say they wanted it just like the Navajos." He said he would be criticized if he did that. He made quite a talk about it.

When he got through, I says, "I just can't agree with that at all." I says, "The American people, in the last few years there's been quite a change coming over the American public. They're starting to see what we have done to these Indians. They're regretting it, and they're starting to think about trying to fix things up with them a little better, and redeem themselves." I says, "The criticism is going to come if you *don't* do it. The fact that you don't give these Indians a break, why you're going to be criticized for that instead of the other.

And then there was Tillotson from over here at the Grand Canyon, and the park superintendent from Bryce and Zion, and another one from Mesa Verde. They got up and told him, "Goulding is absolutely right on that. It's absolutely a fact."

Well, he couldn't accept of it, so the thing blew up.

Right away I got Maurice McCabe. I didn't want to see this thing dropped. It just had to be protected some way. The next thing to do was to try and get the tribe to do it themselves. Maurice McCabe and I were great friends, so I says, "Maurice, I wish you would come over here, and bring your wife over with you, and just get in with my visitors, get in with whoever you want, whatever rig is going anywhere. You come over here and stay with me for ten days and see what a possession you have up on this reservation. I want you just to see of how people feel about this place." I says, "Your oil resources are going to give out one of these days, and I think them tourists will be a pretty good old pony to saddle up and get on, as it goes along.

So he came over, and he would go out, every day he'd go out, and then I'd go out with a group occasionally and he would go along. And after we got through with supper, we had a piano over in the corner of the dining room, and Maurice would go over there. He'd lean his elbow comfortably on that piano, and he would make about a thirty-minute talk, sometimes more than that, as to what the Navajos were thinking about and what they were going to have to do. And he never wrote anything, there was nothing wrote down. It just flowed out of him like water coming out of a spring, and beautifully so! You could have heard a pin drop in there. Nobody hardly breathed while that fella was talking, he was that interesting. And so finally, after he'd stayed the ten days, he went over and put it up to the tribal council. And he sold them on it, of making a tribal park out here. It was the first Navajo tribal park.

So they got things going smooth. Sammy Day was in charge. He was made

the director of parks on the reservation, and he got things agoing. Then the
national parks came to him and offered to put the Navajo Rangers into their
ranger school. They have it once a year, "and if you want to send your boys
over there, we'll be very pleased to take care of them." So it's wound up that
far. Everything is going all right.

In a way, it was just bad luck about the timing in Monument Valley, that
it didn't become a national park. But I don't know whether it was or not,
because these Navajos have got their Navajo tribal parks going. They're
designing their activities a lot after the national parks, where they charge so
much to go into the park, and they have their rangers. They're doing a good
job of it. And you know, those Navajo Rangers, they pick good young men.
They do need training, but the ones that are getting it come out quite
different.

So there's only one thing more. The thing that I think the national parks
should do by all means is to go ahead and give these parks the same publicity
as they give their own. I think that's the best move that they could possibly
make right now. These tribal spots of beauty need the national park publicity.
It would help the Navajos. If they did that, it wouldn't really make any
difference whether it was a Navajo tribal park or a national park.

■ The decade of the 1950s saw a great increase in the mileage of improved
roads on the Navajo reservation. The uranium and oil discoveries brought
good roads to Monument Valley from Mexican Hat and Utah to the north
and from the Four Corners to the east and Flagstaff and beyond to the south
and west. This not only made life easier for the Navajos, but also increased
the number of tourists on the reservation. Thus both the opportunity to
develop and the need to control tourism were at hand.

The tribal council established the Tribal Parks Commission in 1957. The
first commissioner was Sam Day III, who was half Navajo, the son and
grandson of prominent traders, who had been on the reservation and made
significant contributions to the life of the Navajos since the treaty of 1868.
Sam Day III had been on the tribal council for twelve years, during which
time he received his appointment as tribal parks commissioner.

Monument Valley Tribal Park was established in 1960. During its first
year, 22,114 tourists visited the park, paid $4,092 in admission fees, and
bought arts and crafts products valued at $7,855.[1]

SAM DAY III: I was with the tribe first as assistant business manager, and
from there I went into the tribal council for twelve years. On the council I
was chairman of the Parks Commission, where we worked on the parks
program mainly. Then, after a couple of years off the council, Raymond
Nakai wanted me to come back and handle Parks and Recreation, which we
had originally developed. So I came back to the tribe. When the MacDonald

administration came in, he wanted me to direct the business management, so it was just a step across into a higher position.

But I came back really to organize the Parks and Recreation. My interest has always been Navajo. I suppose I could have gone off-reservation and done other things, but I was sort of like my father, I liked to do things for people.

That's where I really got acquainted with Harry Goulding. I knew him before as a little boy. My father knew him, and occasionally we would drive over there to say hello to him. After I became parks commisioner, I had more reason to go to Monument Valley, because I was pushing the parks program, Lake Powell, and all these other things. So we got really acquainted, Harry and I did.

One of the people we had there, a fellow by the name of John C. McPhee, he was with the Bureau of Indian Affairs as a sort of public relations man. He bent over backwards because he knew what the Navajos wanted, and he worked with us too. That's how we got started. He pushed, and of course he relied on me to get the legislation portion started, so I'd say that not individually but working together we got something done. No one does anything alone.

Harry pushed it. He did so much in making Monument Valley notable to the general public. He did a lot towards promotion in magazines, all of the major media, as well as the moving picture people. Naturally, he had a love for the country, all of the people there. I'm sure he made money, but he also made it more sophisticated, put quality into the area.

We withdrew it as a tribal park because I felt that as long as we had a parks program and we had the sovereignty that the tribe had, why couldn't we develop our own park system. The National Park Service already had Canyon de Chelly, which my grandfather, Father Berard,[2] and Don Lorenzo Hubbell had withdrawn, and my grandfather, I think, was the first custodian there, because they could see the damage that could occur to Canyon de Chelly through vandalism and pothunters.

There were some other national monuments that were withdrawn by the Park Service, and I didn't want to see any more done that way. As long as we had a program, we might as well start learning how to take care of things and preserving for the future. This was our basic concept.

Canyon de Chelly is the only national monument or park in existence where people still live in there for perpetuity. That's what they insisted on, and that's how it was withdrawn. That's our big point: we don't want to evacuate people.

MARTIN LINK (formerly archaeologist with the Land Claims Department of the Navajo tribe, later with the Parks and Rangers Department): When I went to work for the Parks and Rangers Department of the tribe, one of my first assignments was to work with the Navajo Tribal Rangers to upgrade their knowledge of both their own history and the areas that they were working on so that they would be able to answer the questions the tourists were asking. I set up a series of classes at Monument Valley for all the rangers in the Western District, and I had similar classes in Window Rock for the rangers in the Eastern District.

I worked very closely with Harry. In fact, Harry was the one that took me on my first trip through Mystery Valley, in 1960 I believe, and got me thoroughly lost. When I go back there, it still takes me a while to get reoriented. I can see why they call it Mystery Valley. But Harry was extremely informative. And the old type. I mean you'd stop at noon and build a fire and heat the coffee up, a couple of handfuls of coffee into the old pot.

His stories about the Anasazi were, shall we say, colorful. They may not have been authentic or accurate, but they were colorful, and my only problem was that I had to combat this in a polite way with the knowledge that I had of the archaeological evidence. I was trying to tell the rangers one thing, and then the visitors would come in and say, "Well, when I went out on Goulding's tour, they told me something else." Harry's academic knowledge of the Anasazi was limited. He was basing a lot of it just on observation.

Things like the fact that the doorways on most Anasazi sites are very low. When you don't have a door, you try to keep the draft out and you try to keep the enemies out. All the time he ran tours up there, he was telling the people that the Anasazi were three- to four-foot high pygmies, and I just could not get him to break that story. He says, "All you have to do is look at the door. We're six feet high, so we build a seven-foot door; they build a four-foot door, so obviously they're three feet, maybe forty-two inches."

I'd say, "Harry, all of the skeletal material we dig up, the men are maybe five-six, five-eight, once in a while even a six-footer; the women are five-two to five-six." I don't think there's any difference in size between the Anasazi then and the Hopi and Zuni today. They just had other reasons for building small doors, it wasn't because they were small people.

The other problem I had with him was in dating. All the sophisticated methods that archaeologists have at hand now in dating—tree-ring dating, carbon-14 dating, pottery analysis correlating the pottery types among known dates from Betatakin and Keet Seel—we can date a ruin down to within twenty-five years of when it was constructed. And you figure that these ruins were occupied at most for one or two generations, so maybe fifty, seventy-five years at the most they were occupied. And we know when the Pueblo II and Pueblo III periods were, which were the predominant Anasazi periods in the Monument Valley area, back anywhere from say 1000 to 1150, 1200 A.D., in that time period. He *still* would tell people that these sites were 10,000 years old, when in actuality they had been there for maybe 800 years.

But I would just say, "Consider the source and the fact that you had a chance to go out with Harry, and forget about all these little inconsistencies." I figured they were so minor compared to the fact that people had the opportunity to spend some time with Harry and listen to him talk and get his feelings. I spent many a night up at Goulding's for a long time. To me it was just the opportunity of rubbing shoulders with Harry.

Many of the rangers would go down to Goulding's, they'd run out of gas or they'd need help with a generator or something like that, and he was always right there to help. Several of the other people who ran tours through the Valley, especially out of Kayenta and out of Mexican Hat, tried to circumvent the ranger station. Monument Valley was theirs, the way they saw it. For years they had run tours up there, they had had a free ride in the sense that they didn't have to account for their conduct, or account for their whereabouts, or pay the entry fee. We really had trouble with some of the others. Harry, one of the first things he did was, by God, every one of his drivers stopped at the visitor's center and paid his fees. Sure, he knew plenty of ways to sneak in the back way and never let the rangers know that he was even down in the Valley. I think some of his drivers may have done that on occasion, but they did it without Harry's knowledge, and definitely without his permission, because he made every effort to cooperate with the ranger station all the time that he was there.

And then he gave his collection of Anasazi pottery to the museum. We accessioned it, we had it on display down at Window Rock for a while, and then we set up the exhibits at Monument Valley. I got a number of those back into exhibits there, since they were from that area. So we had, all the years that I worked with him, an excellent working relationship.

Harry's relationship with the Navajos was the best I've ever seen between an Anglo and a Navajo. I think that was probably his biggest influence on me. It's very easy for an Anglo to be patronizing to the Navajos, because that's just the way it's done. So many of the bureau or the Public Health Service people or government people come in, and they know it all, they're going to show the Navajos how to do it. You're going to teach them, there's nothing they could teach you. Whereas with Harry it was a constant experience of learning from the Navajo, trying to learn their language, meeting them on their ground, and not forcing them to meet you on your ground. His relationship was always one of mutual respect.

I've tried myself to live that kind of life, that same kind of contact with the Navajo people. You don't really see too much of it, I'll tell you. He always acted like he was the intruder, he was the guest, and he never had a domineering attitude. He treated everybody fairly, but he didn't let anybody ride over him. If they had credit at the trading post, when it came time to pay up, they paid up. They knew that he expected them to do that, and at the same time I don't think he exploited or took advantage of any of them.

31 ■■■ Last Thoughts

Harry Goulding: The Navajos brought a lot of their old original philosophy and tradition, and they're holding on to it. They have acquired knowledge that we don't know exists, because it existed then when they had to use it, and they've still got it to hold onto.

Will Rogers, for instance, it wasn't his paleface ancestry, it was that old Indian, the foundation that he brought through with him. When we first came to America, if we'd have kept right with them on a barter and trade business and come through with them in a peaceful way, there's no question in my mind at all that we would have shoveled out a number of people like Will Rogers.

I'm afraid of the welfare they're giving them right now. For the old people, that's fine, but we've got to study what they need, put opportunity in their way. We need to encourage businesses of different kinds to come into this reservation and help them on their way up. There is a possibility that they might lose those great assets they have, but they'll bring them along if we don't spoil it.

The Navajo way is sort of an atmosphere. And memory! They've been so long that they had no way to keep track of anything, they had no writing, so they acquired a wonderful memory. You take those fellas and put them around an automobile, and they'll be watching the mechanic; they'll carry that. Maybe won't have to use it doing something on a car for six months or so, but when they need it, it's there; they remember.

Or you can go out on this reservation to the ceremonials they have. Just any one of the Navajos will get up that you've never heard him make a talk, and they're great orators. It just comes to them because of the way they've been raised. It's your experiences is what you strengthen yourself with. The rougher they are, the more you get out of them. And that's where the Navajo is today.

He needs, right now, in the worst way, he needs attention from us. But not welfare. You can't just give them these different things. If you go too far on that, I think you're going to put a brake on the knowledge they might pick up. You'll welfare 'em off.

Harry Goulding looking at a dessert flower, 1975. (Samuel Moon)

I think the Navajo religion has affected my religious makeup very much. We were with them at a point when they were strong in their religion; and a lot of these young folks still hold to the old Navajo way. They have something, if you get with them and are around them, that you admire about them. You get to feeling it more all the time, you soak up a lot of it. I feel it and I know it, but I'm lost to explain it. I don't have the ability to talk about it. It's in their sings. You go to their sings and you go through quite a bit of it with them. It's a big aid, I think; to me it is, I know. And yet there's a lot to our religion too. I think it makes a pretty good mixture.

Some of the old folks, for all of the things we white folks done to them, and yet they would accept anybody as a friend. And never was there one Navajo hit another one when we came in here, for years. If it came to a point where they did get into a fight, why there was a ceremony to take care of it. In their sings and ceremonies there's an atmosphere carried right through with it that's just digging at you.

And then it teaches you a lot about nature, about what's right around you all the time. There's all these things happen in the sky in the evenings, and nobody pays any attention. That's good medicine, the beautiful things there are in nature, and that's weighed up an awful lot with the old Navajo. It's a big help to a person if you can reach far enough to get ahold of these beautiful things.

Even the old wrecked cars you see scattered around. When you just wanted and wanted an automobile so bad, and all through the years you just couldn't get enough to reach it—like a saddle—and you finally get it, and it's the greatest possession you ever had. Well, you leave it close to your hogan. It's a good old friend that took you a lot of nice places. It's not ugly. It's thankfulness that you have, like a good old horse. I never had a car that I didn't feel that way. If I'd had enough room to pasture them up I'd probably had them in it. No, I've loved every car I've ever had.

The Navajos believe that the earth is their mother and that it's wrong to violate the earth, and yet they're not bothered by the uranium mining. What has given the earth the name of mother is it's fed them and they've lived without anything but what the earth gives them. Where it does you a lot of good, like for instance the uranium, then the mother give it to them. I feel the same way about it as the Navajo does. As far as they know it, that's their mother, and I think it'll never be where a Navajo gets the uranium or silver or whatever, that he won't bless his mother for throwing him a rope.

Yes sir, I like the churches I go to better than the city churches. Down in the Valley, there are so many beautiful places, and you can get in better contact. My clothes, I never liked suits and stuff like that. It don't seem like the highway I drift on. Old blue jeans. If I've got to do something, I put on a brand new pair, just really tog right out, and put my boots on, and do whatever I got to do. Ever since I was a little kid, the only time I was ever out of cowboy boots was when I was in the service. I got in there and shed my boots and got down on low heels, and I thought I'd got hamstrung. The one suit I've got is a nice western suit. Believe when I get my call, I'd like to go in that. If I'm going to be uncomfortable, I'm going to be uncomfortable in something I like. That ought to ease things up a bit.

NOTES

Preface

1. Doris A. Paul, *The Navajo Code Talkers* (Philadelphia: Dorrance, 1973).
2. Robert W. Young and William Morgan, *The Navaho Language: The Elements of Navaho Grammar with a Dictionary in Two Parts Containing Basic Vocabularies of Navaho and English* (Salt Lake City: Desert Book Co., 1972).

Introduction

1. An earlier book on Monument Valley and the Gouldings is Richard E. Klinck, *Land of Room Enough and Time Enough* (Albuquerque: University of New Mexico Press, 1953).

Chapter 1

1. Albert R. Lyman was a local historian who published several books about the settlement of southeastern Utah by the Mormons and their relations with the Paiutes of the region.
2. Paul S. Martin and Fred Plog, *The Archaeology of Arizona: A Study of the Southwest Region* (Garden City, New York: Doubleday/Natural History Press, 1973), 318–33.
3. Ibid., 324–25.
4. J. Lee Correll, "Navajo Frontiers in Utah and Troublous Times in Monument Valley," *Utah Historical Quarterly* 39 (Spring 1971): 146–48.
5. Charles R. Mabey, governor of Utah from 1921 to 1925.
6. *Moab Times-Independent,* June 2 and 23, 1921.
7. *Moab Times-Independent,* September 15, 1921.
8. Harry is remembering what they were actually given (see below), not the land along the river that was at this time proposed by Secretary Fall's representative, Elfego Baca.
9. Frank McNitt, *Navajo Wars: Military Campaigns, Slave Raids, and Reprisals* (Albuquerque: University of New Mexico Press, 1972), 441–46. This book provides a thorough treatment of the Navajo involvement in slavery on both sides of the enterprise.
10. This story is told from the Mormon point of view in Albert R. Lyman, *Indians and Outlaws* (Salt Lake City: Bookcraft Publishers, 1962), and in several interviews in *Southeastern Utah Project,* Utah State Historical Society and California State University, Fullerton, Oral History Program—most fully in the George Hurst interview (O.H. 799b). Another point of view, favoring the Paiutes, is suggested by Carol Lyman's interview from the same collection (O.H. 718) and by Robert S. McPherson, "Paiute Posey and the Last White Uprising," *Utah Historical Quarterly* 53 (1985): 248–67.
11. Carol Lyman interview, p. 49.
12. *Moab Times-Independent,* April 19, 1923, and August 23, 1923.
13. Lawrence C. Kelly, *The Navajo Indians and Federal Indian Policy, 1900–1935* (Tucson: University of Arizona Press, 1968), 17–20, 55–58; and in more detail, *The Assault on Assimila-*

tion: John Collier and the Origins of Indian Policy Reform (Albuquerque: University of New Mexico Press, 1983), 141–61, 181–85, 349–465.

Chapter 2

1. Frank McNitt, *The Indian Traders* (Norman: University of Oklahoma Press, 1962), 271.

2. Ismay, Utah

3. Frances Keegan Heffernan, "Two Pioneer Families" (1945), in Sarah Platt Decker Chapter, D.A.R., *Pioneers of the San Juan Country,* vol. 2 (Colorado Springs: Out West Printing & Stationery Co., 1946), 142. See also McNitt, *Indian Traders,* 309n, 323–24.

4. *Southeastern Utah Project,* Virginia Smith, interview by Elizabeth Scheib, July 20, 1971, interview O.H. 775, p. 19.

5. Ibid., Mildred Hefflin, interview by Dean Sundberg, June 30, 1972, interview O.H. 1168, pp. 2, 13, 15–16.

6. Frances Gillmor and Louisa Wade Wetherill, *Traders to the Navajo* (Albuquerque: University of New Mexico Press, 1934), 71–80.

7. For a treatment of this subject, see Clyde Kluckhohn and Dorothea Leighton, *The Navaho* (Cambridge: Harvard University Press, 1946; revised, Anchor Books, 1962), 184–87; Gladys Reichard, *Navaho Religion: A Study of Symbolism,* 2d ed. (Princeton: Princeton University Press, 1963), 40–49; and Robert W. Young, *The Navajo Yearbook* (Window Rock, Arizona: The Navajo Agency, 1961), 527–32.

8. Elizabeth Compton Hegemann, *Navaho Trading Days* (Albuquerque: University of New Mexico Press, 1963), 230–31.

Chapter 3

1. J. Bracken Lee was born in 1899, entered politics in 1921, was mayor of Price, Utah, from 1935 to 1946, governor of the State, from 1949 to 1957, and mayor of Salt Lake City, from 1960 to 1975. Under his leadership as mayor of Price, the town bought electricity wholesale from Utah Power and Light and sold it retail to consumers at lower rates than previously. With the profit he was able to eliminate property taxes altogether, finance a new civic auditorium and park improvements, modernize the water system and the hospital, and balance the budget. *Current Biography,* 1949 ed., s.v. "J. Bracken Lee."

2. Benjamin Horace Hibbard, *A History of the Public Land Policies* (Madison: University of Wisconsin Press, 1965), 322–23, 342.

3. Donald Adams, interview by author, December 11, 1979, Monticello, Utah.

4. San Juan County, Monticello, Utah, *Minute Book—State Land Office* November 4, 1937, p. 425; January 21, 1938, p. 487.

5. Ibid., H. Warren Taylor, executive secretary, letter to E. R. Fryer dated April 28, 1938.

6. Ibid., May 5, 1938, p. C2.

7. "Ownership," undated map, included in personal correspondence with Karl F. Kappe, Division of State Lands and Forestry, Department of Natural Resources, State of Utah, March 7, 1989.

8. See McNitt, *Indian Traders,* 219.

9. See chapter 9, "The Paiute Strip Returns to Reservation," which tells how Harry was required to move his sheep off the new reservation land.

10. For an anthropologically exact description of this process, see William Y. Adams, *Shonto: A Study of the Role of the Trader in a Modern Navaho Community,* Smithsonian Institution, Bureau of American Ethnology, Bulletin 188 (Washington: U.S. Government Printing Office, 1963), 101.

Chapter 4

1. According to Shonie Holiday, these are songs sung at the Squaw Dance, more properly called the Enemy Way, the most popular of the ceremonials among the Navajos and the most

familiar to white visitors. See Fr. Berard Haile, *The Navaho War Dance: A Brief Narrative of Its Meaning and Practice* (St. Michaels, Arizona: St. Michaels Press, 1946) and *Origin Legend of the Navaho Enemy Way,* Yale University Publications in Anthropology 17 (New Haven: Yale University, Department of Anthropology, 1938).

2. Helen H. Roberts, *Musical Areas in Aboriginal North America,* Yale University Publications in Anthropology 12 (New Haven: Yale University Press, 1936), 33, quoted in Kluckhohn and Leighton, *The Navaho,* 216. See also David P. McAllester, *Enemy Way Music; A Study of Social and Esthetic Values as Seen in Navaho Music,* Papers of the Peabody Museum of American Archaeology and Ethnology 41, no. 3 (Cambridge, 1954).

3. "Who in seriousness or irony named this enclosure, or when, is long forgotten. The term was descriptive, not critical; it seemed to fit, and it was accepted into regional parlance." McNitt, *Indian Traders,* 73.

4. Adams, *Shonto,* 204–10.

5. Pawn practices are described in many sources. See Adams, *Shonto,* 195–99; McNitt, *Indian Traders,* 55–57.

6. Gladwell Richardson, *Navajo Trader* (Tucson: University of Arizona Press, 1986), 74.

7. Ruth Underhill, *The Navajos* (Norman: University of Oklahoma Press, 1956), 194.

8. The classic book on Navajo weaving is Charles Avery Amsden, *Navaho Weaving: Its Technic and History* (Santa Ana, California: Fine Arts Press, 1934). See also Anthony Berlant and Mary Hunt Kahlenberg, *Walk in Beauty: The Navajo and Their Blankets* (Boston: New York Graphic Society, 1977).

9. Adams, *Shonto,* 105–6.

Chapter 5

1. "*Louse* . . . was one of the minor evils threatened by Monster Slayer. He begged off, saying, 'If you kill me, people will be lonesome. They will have no one to keep them company.' Louse was allowed to live." Reichard, *Navaho Religion,* 447.

2. Maurice's version of CCC, the Civilian Conservation Corps.

3. Reichard, *Navajo Religion,* 445.

Chapter 6

1. Robert W. Young, *The Role of the Navajo in the Southwestern Drama* (Gallup, New Mexico: Gallup Independent, 1968), 45.

Chapter 8

1. See Mike Goulding's account of these visitors in Patrick McDonnell, Karen McDonnell, and Georgia Riley de Havenon, *Krazy Kat: The Comic Art of George Herriman* (New York: Harry N. Abrams, Inc., 1986), 72–73.

Chapter 9

1. Lawrence C. Kelly, *The Navajo Indians and Federal Indian Policy, 1900–1935* (Tucson: University of Arizona Press, 1968), 126–27.

Chapter 10

1. The major studies of Collier's work as commissioner of Indian affairs are Donald L. Parman, *The Navajos and the New Deal* (New Haven: Yale University Press, 1976); Kenneth R. Philp, *John Collier's Crusade for Indian Reform, 1920–1954* (Tucson: University of Arizona Press, 1977); Graham D. Taylor, *The New Deal and American Indian Tribalism: The Administration of the Indian Reorganization Act, 1934–45* (Lincoln: University of Nebraska Press,

1980); and Francis Paul Prucha, *The Great Father: The United States Government and the American Indians,* vol. 2 (Lincoln: University of Nebraska Press, 1984), 917–1012. For Collier's work up to the beginning of the New Deal, see Lawrence C. Kelly, *The Assault on Assimilation: John Collier and the Origins of Indian Policy Reform* (Albuquerque: University of New Mexico Press, 1983). Collier's own version of his story can be found in John Collier, *From Every Zenith* (Denver: Sage Books, 1963), and *Indians of the Americas* (New York: W. W. Norton, 1947).

2. My chief source for this account of the stock reduction program is Parman, *Navajos and the New Deal,* 42–49, 62–66, 98–101, 112–15, 280.

3. Young, *Navajo Yearbook* (Navajo Agency: Window Rock, Arizona, 1961), 155–70.

4. E. H. Spicer, "Sheepmen and Technicians: A Program of Soil Conservation on the Navajo Indian Reservation," in *Human Problems in Technological Change,* ed. E. H. Spicer (New York: John Wiley & Sons, 1952), 198–99.

5. *Southeastern Utah Project,* interview by Fern Charley and Dean Sundberg, July 13, 1972, interview O.H.1223.

6. Donald L. Parman was able to document only one incident of a slaughter of goats with certainty and feels that while there may have been others, it did not typify stock reduction procedures. *Navajos and the New Deal,* 64–65.

7. *Southeastern Utah Project,* interview by Fern Charley, June 30, 1972, interview O. H. 1166.

8. The dates are not quite right. Interviewed in 1972, he would have been twenty-two in 1931, too early for stock reduction.

9. See also Elizabeth Ward, *No Dudes, Few Women: Life with a Navajo Range Rider* (Albuquerque: University of New Mexico Press, 1951).

10. *Southeastern Utah Project,* interview by Dean Sundberg, June 27, 1972, interview O.H. 1154.

11. Ibid., June 30, 1972, interview O.H. 1168.

12. Actually, they did succeed in getting an irrigation project for the reservation. See chapter 11, "Shine's Christmas."

13. Collier, *From Every Zenith,* 251–53.

14. See his description of his wartime experiences working in defense plants in chapter 23, "The Navajos Go to War."

Chapter 11

1. Frank Waters, *Masked Gods: Navaho and Pueblo Ceremonialism* (Denver, Swallow Press, 1950), 126–28. See also R. Brownell McGrew, "Excerpts from the Journals of an Artist, R. Brownell McGrew, in the Lands of the Navajos and the Hopis," *Arizona Highways* 45 (July 1969): 4–39.

2. Waters, *Masked Gods,* 128; Parman, *Navajos and the New Deal,* 278–80.

Chapter 12

1. Parman, *Navajos and the New Deal,* 32–35. This book provides a thorough treatment of Collier's soil conservation program, especially chapters 4 and 5.

2. Ibid., 35–36.

3. Anna Wilmarth Ickes was in her third term in the Illinois legislature when her husband became secretary of the interior. Although a Republican, she completed her term but did not run again in 1934. She and her husband both had a long-standing interest in the American Indians. In 1933, she published *Mesa Land* (Boston: Houghton Mifflin), a book about the Navajos. She died in an automobile accident near Santa Fe on August 31, 1935 (*New York Times,* September 1, 1935).

4. Parman, *Navajos and the New Deal,* 125–27.

Chapter 14

1. Dorothea Leighton and Clyde Kluckhohn, *Children of the People* (Cambridge: Harvard University Press, 1948), especially 1–75, 94–114.

2. For the Meriam report description of conditions in the Indian schools, see Lewis Meriam and others, "Education," in *The Problem of Indian Administration* (Baltimore: Johns Hopkins University Press, 1928; reprint with new introduction by Frank C. Miller, New York: Johnson Reprint Corporation, 1971), 346–429; see also 314–40, 573–80.

3. For Collier's contribution to Navajo education, see Parman, "John Dewey among the Navajos," in *Navajos and the New Deal*, 193–216. A thorough treatment of education for American Indians may be found in Margaret Szasz, *Education and the American Indian: Road to Self-Determination, 1928–1973* (Albuquerque: University of New Mexico Press, 1974).

4. See Nedra Tódích'íi'nii's interview in chapter 10, "Stock Reduction."

5. Denis F. Johnston, "Appendix A: Trends in Navaho Population and Education, 1870–1955," in David F. Aberle, *The Peyote Religion among the Navaho* (Chicago: Aldine Publishing, 1966), 362.

Chapter 15

1. The literature on Navajo religion and medicine is enormous. For this summary, I am relying primarily on Kluckhohn and Leighton, *The Navajo*, chapters 5–7.

2. This is David F. Aberle's term in *The Peyote Religion*, 47–48.

3. See chapter 13, "Horse Races."

4. Clyde Kluckhohn, *Navaho Witchcraft*, 2d ed. (Boston: Beacon Press, 1967), 13–42, the definitive study of its subject.

5. Mr. Cly is probably referring to what Gladys Reichard translates as "sunbeam" or "sunray." "*Sunbeam* and *sunray* are partners acting as mentor, protection, and conveyance. Most translations do not differentiate them . . . . The former ["the light ray from a cloud with the sun behind it"] is generally yellow and white in sandpainting; the latter ["the alternating dark rays between the light beams"] is red and blue." Reichard, *Navajo Religion*, 603.

Chapter 17

1. Newton Evans, Percy T. Magan, George Thomason, eds., *The Home Physician and Guide to Health* (Mountain View, California: Pacific Press Publishing Association, 1923).

2. Parman, *Navajos and the New Deal*, 217–20.

3. Ibid., 222–25.

4. Ibid., 226–28.

Chapter 19

1. Karl W. Luckert, *Coyoteway, a Navajo Holyway Ceremonial* (Tucson: University of Arizona Press, and Flagstaff: Museum of Northern Arizona Press, 1979), 8–12.

2. Paiute Farms, on the San Juan River northwest of Goulding's.

3. Karl W. Luckert, letter to the author, June 2, 1989.

4. Rarely seen, even in the 1920s, the Mud Dance is performed at the end of the Enemy Way or Squaw Dance. It is well described in Dane and Mary Roberts Coolidge, *The Navajo Indians* (Boston: Houghton Mifflin, 1930), 183–85.

Chapter 20

1. Walter Wanger, executive producer of *Stagecoach*.

2. See Joseph McBride and Michael Wilmington, *John Ford* (New York: Da Capo Press, 1975), 54.

3. Dan Ford, *Pappy: The Life of John Ford* (Englewood Cliffs, New Jersey: Prentice-Hall, 1979), 125.

4. Maurice Zolotow, *Shooting Star: A Biography of John Wayne* (New York: Simon and Schuster, 1974), 150.

5. Peter Bogdanovich, *John Ford* (Berkeley: University of California Press, 1968), 130–43.

Chapter 23

1. Parman, *Navajos and the New Deal,* 281–87; and Peter Iverson, *The Navajo Nation* (Westport, Connecticut: Greenwood Press, 1981), 49.

2. Utah's "Old Faithful Geyser" is south of Elgin, on the east side of the Green River. The smaller geyser is probably the one at Woodside, twenty-five miles north of Elgin on U.S. 6–191. See Work Projects Administration for the state of Utah, Writers' Program, *Utah: A Guide to the State* (New York: Hastings House, 1941), 397, 400.

3. Parman, *Navajos and the New Deal,* 282.

4. Doris A. Paul, *The Navajo Code Talkers* (Philadelphia: Dorrance, 1973), 4.

5. Underhill, *The Navajos,* 241–42.

6. Paul, *Navajo Code Talkers.*

7. Underhill, *The Navajos,* 243.

8. Paul, *Navajo Code Talkers,* 53–54.

9. Ibid., 73–75.

10. Leland C. Wyman, *Blessingway* (Tucson: University of Arizona Press, 1970), 51.

11. Reichard, *Navaho Religion,* 322–23.

Chapter 24

1. Young, *Role of the Navajo,* 83.

2. Iverson, *Navajo Nation,* 78–79, 160–61, 224; Philip Reno, *Mother Earth, Father Sky, and Economic Development: Navajo Resources and Their Use* (Albuquerque: University of New Mexico Press, 1981), 133–42; *New York Times,* August 31, 1967.

3. See Harry Goulding, "Navajos Hunt Big Game, Uranium," *Popular Mechanics,* June 1950, p. 89.

4. *Navajo Tribal Council Resolutions, 1922–1951* (Washington, D.C.: U.S. Government Printing Office, 1952), 298.

5. J. A. Krug, secretary of the interior, letter to Senator Edwin C. Johnson dated April 7, 1948, National Archives, Record Group 48, Central Classified Files, 1937–1953, 5–1, Navajo Leases.

6. *Navajo Tribal Council Resolutions,* 299–300.

7. *The Stars and Stripes, Algiers Daily* 1, no. 89 (39?), August 17, 1943.

8. Ibid.

9. There is an interesting photo-essay on uranium in Monument Valley in the early 1950s, "Navajos Go into Uranium Business," *Life,* June 4, 1951, 61–65.

Chapter 25

1. See chapter 23, "The Navajos Go to War," and chapter 24, "Uranium."

2. Evon Vogt, *Navaho Veterans: A Study in Changing Values* (Cambridge: Peabody Museum of American Archaeology and Ethnology, 1951), 94–102.

3. Young, *Role of the Navajo,* 74.

4. The young man who gave me this interview wanted the names changed so his identity would remain unknown.

5. According to Gladys Reichard, "The bead token is a permanent symbol in the patient's possession to signify that he has been favored by the gods of a given chant." Reichard, *Navaho Religion,* 524–25.

Chapter 26

1. Young, *Role of the Navajo,* 83–84.
2. See "Boom Opens Four Corners," *Phoenix Action!* 13 (April 1958): 1, a chamber of commerce publication of Phoenix, Arizona.

Chapter 27

1. "The Boom that Travelers Built," *Time* 65 (March 14, 1955), 100–101.

Chapter 28

1. *Encyclopedia Americana,* 1984 ed., s.v. "Seventh-day Adventists."
2. Herbert Ford, *Wind High, Sand Deep: The Story of Monument Valley Mission and Hospital* (Nashville: Southern Publishing Association, 1965), 9. In 1989, the hospital was in the process of adding six beds and planning to build an additional hospital in Kayenta.
3. Percy T. Magan was not the founder, but he was the president of Loma Linda University from 1928 to 1942.
4. See John Adair and Kurt W. Deuschle, *The People's Health: Medicine and Anthropology in a Navajo Community* (New York: Appleton-Century-Crofts, 1970), passim, for the inspiring story of this medical achievement.

Chapter 29

1. Earl Morris was born in Chama, New Mexico, in 1889. He was an archaeologist for the American Museum of Natural History from 1916 to 1924, when he explored the Aztec Ruin for the museum. In addition, he led archaeological expeditions to Guatemala in 1914 and 1934, and to New Mexico and Arizona for the University of Colorado in 1913–16, 1922, and 1924–28. He joined the Carnegie Institution in 1924, for whom he directed excavations in Yucatan from 1924 to 1929, after which he returned to research work in southwestern archaeology. He is the author of *The Temple of the Warriors* (Washington: Carnegie Institution of Washington, 1931) and many archaeological studies in professional journals. He died in 1956. *Who Was Who in America,* vol. 3 (Chicago: A. N. Marquis Company, 1960).
2. My source on the Anasazi is Martin and Plog, *Archaeology of Arizona,* passim.
3. See Andrew L. Christenson, *The Last of the Great Expeditions: The Rainbow Bridge/Monument Valley Expedition, 1933–38* (Flagstaff, Arizona: Museum of Northern Arizona, 1987), a popular account, with bibliography.

Chapter 30

1. Young, *Navajo Yearbook,* 194.
2. Father Berard Haile, 1874–1961, was a Franciscan father at the St. Michaels Mission on the Navajo reservation from 1900 until his death. A well-known linguist, he developed the Navajo alphabet, compiled the first Navajo dictionary, published the first books in the Navajo language, and recorded and translated several Navajo myths.

BIBLIOGRAPHY

Unpublished Documents:

Krug, J. A., secretary of the interior. Letter to Senator Edwin C. Johnson, April 7, 1948, Record Group 48, National Archives, Central Classified Files, 1937–1953, 5-1, Navajo Leases.
San Juan County, Monticello, Utah. *Minute Book—State Land Office.*
"Appraise School Section and Advertise for Sale." November 4, 1937, p. 425.
"Appraisal Accepted & Section to be Offered at Public Sale." January 21, 1938, p. 487.
Taylor, H. Warren, executive secretary. Letter to E. R. Fryer, April 28, 1938. "Public Sale." May 5, 1938, p. C2.

Interviews:

Southeastern Utah Project. Utah State Historical Society and California State University, Fullerton, Oral History Program, California State University, Fullerton, California.
Bedoni, Lamar. Interview by Fern Charley, June 30, 1972. O. H. 1166, transcript.
Heflin, Mildred. Interview by Dean Sundberg, June 30, 1972. O.H. 1168, transcript.
Hurst, George. Interview by Louise Lyne, July 5, 1972. O.H. 799b, transcript.
Lyman, Carol. Interview by Kim Stewart, July 7, 1971. O.H. 718, transcript.
Smith, Edward D. Interview by Dean Sundberg, June 27, 1972. O.H. 1154, transcript.
Smith, Virginia. Interview by Elizabeth Scheib, July 20, 1971. O.H. 775, transcript.
Tódích'íi'nii, Nedra. Interview by Fern Charley and Dean Sundberg, July 13, 1972. O.H. 1223, transcript.

Books and Pamphlets:

Aberle, David F. *The Peyote Religion among the Navaho.* Chicago: Aldine Publishing, 1966.
Adair, John, and Kurt W. Deuschle. *The People's Health: Medicine and Anthropology in a Navajo Community.* New York: Appleton-Century-Crofts, 1970.
Adams, William Y. *Shonto: A Study of the Role of the Trader in a Modern Navaho Community.* Smithsonian Institution, Bureau of American Ethnology, Bulletin 188. Washington: U.S. Government Printing Office, 1963.
Amsden, Charles Avery. *Navaho Weaving: Its Technic and History.* Santa Ana, California: Fine Arts Press, 1934.
Berlant, Anthony, and Mary Hunt Kahlenberg. *Walk in Beauty: The Navajo and Their Blankets.* Boston: New York Graphic Society, 1977.
Bogdanovich, Peter. *John Ford.* Berkeley: University of California Press, 1968.
Collier, John. *From Every Zenith.* Denver: Sage Books, 1963.
———. *Indians of the Americas.* New York: W. W. Norton, 1947.

Coolidge, Dane, and Mary Roberts Coolidge. *The Navajo Indians.* Boston: Houghton Mifflin, 1930.

Christenson, Andrew L. *The Last of the Great Expeditions: The Rainbow Bridge/Monument Valley Expedition, 1933–38.* Flagstaff, Arizona: Museum of Northern Arizona, 1987.

Encyclopedia Americana. 1984 ed. S.v. "Seventh-day Adventists."

Ford, Dan. *Pappy: The Life of John Ford.* Englewood Cliffs, New Jersey: Prentice-Hall, 1979.

Ford, Herbert. *Wind High, Sand Deep: The Story of Monument Valley Mission and Hospital.* Nashville: Southern Publishing Association, 1965.

Gillmor, Frances, and Louisa Wade Wetherill. *Traders to the Navajo.* Albuquerque: University of New Mexico Press, 1934.

Haile, Fr. Berard. *The Navaho War Dance: A Brief Narrative of Its Meaning and Practice.* St. Michaels, Arizona: St. Michaels Press, 1946.

———. *Origin Legend of the Navaho Enemy Way.* Yale University Publications in Anthropology 17. New Haven: Yale University, Department of Anthropology, 1938.

Heffernan, Frances Keegan. "Two Pioneer Families." In *Pioneers of the San Juan Country.* Vol. 2. Comp. Sarah Platt Decker Chapter, D.A.R. Colorado Springs: Out West Printing & Stationery, 1946.

Hegemann, Elizabeth Compton. *Navaho Trading Days.* Albuquerque: University of New Mexico Press, 1963.

Hibbard, Benjamin Horace. *A History of the Public Land Policies.* Madison: University of Wisconsin Press, 1965.

Ickes, Anna Wilmarth. *Mesa Land.* Boston: Houghton Mifflin, 1933.

Iverson, Peter. *The Navajo Nation.* Westport, Connecticut: Greenwood Press, 1981.

Kelly, Lawrence C. *The Navajo Indians and Federal Indian Policy, 1900–1935.* Tucson: University of Arizona Press, 1968.

———. *The Assault on Assimilation: John Collier and the Origins of Indian Policy Reform.* Albuquerque: University of New Mexico Press, 1983.

Klinck, Richard E. *Land of Room Enough and Time Enough.* Albuquerque: University of New Mexico Press, 1953.

Kluckhohn, Clyde, and Dorothea Leighton. *The Navaho.* Cambridge: Harvard University Press, 1946; revised, Anchor Books, 1962.

———. *Navaho Witchcraft.* 2d ed. Boston: Beacon Press, 1967.

Leighton, Dorothea, and Clyde Kluckhohn. *Children of the People.* Cambridge: Harvard University Press, 1948.

Luckert, Karl W. *Coyoteway, a Navajo Holyway Ceremonial.* Tucson: University of Arizona Press, and Flagstaff: Museum of Northern Arizona Press, 1979.

Lyman, Albert R. *Indians and Outlaws.* Salt Lake City: Bookcraft Publishers, 1962.

Martin, Paul S., and Fred Plog. *The Archaeology of Arizona: A Study of the Southwest Region.* Garden City, New York: Doubleday/Natural History Press, 1973.

McAllester, David P. *Enemy Way Music: A Study of Social and Esthetic Values as Seen in Navaho Music.* Papers of the Peabody Museum of American Archaeology and Ethnology 41, no. 3. Cambridge: The Museum, 1954.

McBride, Joseph, and Michael Wilmington. *John Ford.* New York: Da Capo Press, 1975.

McDonnell, Patrick, Karen McDonnell, and Georgia Riley de Havenon. *Krazy Kat: The Comic Art of George Herriman.* New York: Harry N. Abrams, 1986.

McNitt, Frank. *The Indian Traders.* Norman: University of Oklahoma Press, 1962.

———. *Navajo Wars: Military Campaigns, Slave Raids, and Reprisals.* Albuquerque: University of New Mexico Press, 1972.

Meriam, Lewis, and others. *The Problem of Indian Administration.* Baltimore: Johns Hopkins University Press, 1928; reprint with new introduction by Frank C. Miller, New York: Johnson Reprint Corporation, 1971.

Navajo Tribal Council Resolutions, 1922–1951. Washington, D.C.: U.S. Government Printing Office, 1952.

Parman, Donald L. *The Navajos and the New Deal.* New Haven: Yale University Press, 1976.

Paul, Doris A. *The Navajo Code Talkers.* Philadelphia: Dorrance, 1973.

Philp, Kenneth R. *John Collier's Crusade for Indian Reform, 1920–1954.* Tucson: University of Arizona Press, 1977.

Prucha, Francis Paul. *The Great Father: The United States Government and the American Indians.* Vol. 2. Lincoln: University of Nebraska Press, 1984.

Reichard, Gladys. *Navaho Religion: A Study of Symbolism.* 2d ed. Bollingen Series 18. Princeton: Princeton University Press, 1963.

Reno, Philip. *Mother Earth, Father Sky, and Economic Development: Navajo Resources and Their Use.* Albuquerque: University of New Mexico Press, 1981.

Richardson, Gladwell. *Navajo Trader.* Tucson: University of Arizona Press, 1986.

Roberts, Helen H. *Musical Areas in Aboriginal North America.* Yale University Publications in Anthropology 12. New Haven: Yale University Press, 1936.

Spicer, E. H. "Sheepmen and Technicians: A Program of Soil Conservation on the Navajo Indian Reservation." In *Human Problems in Technological Change,* ed. E. H. Spicer. New York: John Wiley & Sons, 1952.

Szasz, Margaret. *Education and the American Indian: Road to Self Determination, 1928–1973.* Albuquerque: University of New Mexico Press, 1974.

Taylor, Graham D. *The New Deal and American Indian Tribalism: The Administration of the Indian Reorganization Act, 1934–45.* Lincoln: University of Nebraska Press, 1980.

Underhill, Ruth. *The Navajos.* Norman: University of Oklahoma Press, 1956.

Vogt, Evon. *Navaho Veterans: A Study in Changing Values.* Cambridge: Peabody Museum of American Archaeology and Ethnology, 1951.

Ward, Elizabeth. *No Dudes, Few Women: Life with a Navajo Range Rider.* Albuquerque: University of New Mexico Press, 1951.

Waters, Frank. *Masked Gods: Navaho and Pueblo Ceremonialism.* Denver: Swallow Press, 1950.

Work Projects Administration for the State of Utah, Writers' Program. *Utah: A Guide to the State.* New York: Hastings House, 1941.

Wyman, Leland C. *Blessingway.* Tucson: University of Arizona Press, 1970.

Young, Robert W. *The Navajo Yearbook.* Window Rock, Arizona: The Navajo Agency, 1961.

———. *The Role of the Navajo in the Southwestern Drama.* Gallup, New Mexico: The Gallup Independent, 1968.

Zolotow, Maurice. *Shooting Star: A Biography of John Wayne.* New York: Simon and Schuster, 1974.

Periodicals:

"The Boom that Travelers Built." *Time* 65 (March 14, 1955), 100–101.

Chamber of Commerce, Phoenix, Arizona. "Boom Opens Four Corners." *Phoenix Action!* 13 (April 1958): 1.

Correll, J. Lee. "Navajo Frontiers in Utah and Troublous Times in Monument Valley." *Utah Historical Quarterly* 39 (Spring 1971): 145–61.

Goulding, Harry. "Navajos Hunt Big Game, Uranium." *Popular Mechanics,* June 1950, 89.

"Navajos Go into Uranium Business." *Life,* June 4, 1951, 61–65.

McGrew, R. Brownell. "Excerpts from the Journals of an Artist, R. Brownell McGrew, in the Lands of the Navajos and the Hopis." *Arizona Highways* 45 (July 1969): 4–39.

McPherson, Robert S. "Paiute Posey and the Last White Uprising." *Utah Historical Quarterly* 53 (1985): 248–67.

Newspapers:

Moab Times-Independent (Utah). June 2 and 23, 1921; September 15, 1921; April 19, 1923; August 23, 1923.

New York Times. September 1, 1935; August 31, 1967.

The Stars and Stripes, Algiers Daily. Vol. 1, no. 89 [39?]. August 17, 1943.

INDEX

Speakers are indicated by boldface type.